Samsung, Media Empire and Family

This book analyses media conglomerates owning multiple media holdings under centralized ownership within and across media markets. It argues that Asian capitalists utilize both a market-oriented ideology and family connections to build their media empires, thereby creating cultural conglomerates that exercise corporate censorship over media markets. It focuses on family-controlled media conglomerates in Korea, specifically the international business giant, Samsung, and its related media companies, Cheil Jedang and JoongAng Ilbo, all of which are controlled by the single Lee family. Utilizing the theoretical approach of political economy of communication, the book examines how and why the Lee family exercise corporate censorship over Korean society.

Offering an essential take on Asia's political economy of communication in order to understand the workings of Asian media empires, this book will appeal to students and scholars of Korean Studies, Korean Business and Mass Communications.

Chunhyo Kim is a lecturer in Foreign Studies at Hankuk University, Seoul, Republic of Korea. She is also involved in media NGOs, including the Free Press Foundation.

Routledge Advances in Korean Studies

Samsung, Media Empire and Family

A power web

Chunhyo Kim

LONDON AND NEW YORK

First published 2016
by Routledge

2 Park Square, Milton Park, Abingdon, Oxfordshire OX14 4RN
711 Third Avenue, New York, NY 10017

Routledge is an imprint of the Taylor & Francis Group, an informa business

First issued in paperback 2017

British Library Cataloguing in Publication Data
A catalogue record for this book is available from the British Library

Library of Congress Cataloging-in-Publication Data
Names: Kim, Chunhyo, author.
Title: Samsung, media empire and family : a power web / Chunhyo Kim.
Description: Abingdon, Oxon ; New York, NY : Routledge, 2016. |
    Series: Routledge advances in Korean studies ; 34 | Includes
    bibliographical references and index.
Identifiers: LCCN 2015040856 | ISBN 9781138949430 (hardback) |
    ISBN 9781315669045 (ebook)
Subjects: LCSH: Mass media—Economic aspects—Korea (South) |
    Mass media—Ownership—Korea (South) | Mass media policy—
    Korea (South) | Monopolies—Korea (South) | Family-owned business
    enterprises—Korea (South) | Samsæong Chæonja.
Classification: LCC P96.E252 K6653 2016 | DDC 338.8095195—dc23
LC record available at http://lccn.loc.gov/2015040856

ISBN: 978-1-138-94943-0 (hbk)
ISBN: 978-0-8153-6878-6 (pbk)

Typeset in Times New Roman
by Apex CoVantage, LLC

I dedicate this work to my mother, Park Hwa-sun, who was always an example of how a human being should manage life's difficulties with dignity. I also devote this book to my two brothers, Kim Yong-hwan and Kim Yong-don, who always gave me the emotional and financial support I needed. Finally, I consecrate this project to the grassroots participators contributing their lives to make a better world, including members of national union of media workers in Korea.

Contents

Figures

Tables

Introduction

Family-controlled conglomerates from the Republic of Korea (hereafter, Korea) expanded their media businesses into the same and different media markets (Kim, 2010). The media expansion of Korean conglomerates has been synchronized with the global trends of media marketization. Consistent with the political and economic liberalization began in the 1980s, each state began to marketize their media systems (Herman & McChesney, 1997; Murdock & Wasko, 2007). This liberalization of political, economic and media systems laid the foundation for the rise of media conglomerates. These media giants are defined as corporations owning multiple media holdings under centralized ownership within and across media markets – that is, in two or more media markets (Kunz, 2007). In consequence, media markets around the world were structured by a few media conglomerates (Winseck, 2008). With high market shares, media giants exercised the determinant power over what was to be produced, distributed and exhibited and, correlatively, over what was not to be produced, distributed and exhibited (Meehan, 2005). Thus, Bagdikian (2000, 2004) named these media giants as the media monopoly. Similarly, Schiffrin (2000, 2006) argued that these media conglomerates played a vital role in exercising market censorship over the decision-making processes to produce media contents.

However, these empirical outcomes regarding the nature of media monopoly were based on the Western context. These phenomena of both the rise of cultural conglomerates and their effects over media markets were not limited to developed Western countries but were also found on other continents (Winseck, 2008). For example in Asia, the Cheil Jedang group (CJ) in Korea runs media businesses in cable television, film, digital convergence media, games and recorded music markets (Lee, 2008, pp. 92–98). In the People's Republic of China (hereafter, China), the Guangzhou Daily group controls multiple newspaper holdings (Lee, He & Huang, 2006). Similarly, Singapore Press Holdings in Singapore, ABS-CBN in Philippines, Media Prima in Malaysia and Bennett & Coleman in India own multiple media nationwide including newspapers, broadcasting and computer-mediated communication markets (Lent, 1987; Anuar, 2008, p. 128; Prasad, 2008, p. 61; Seneviratne, 2008, p. 26). As seen in these examples, media giants have been found in each country in Asia. Despite these facts, research on the nature of media monopoly from non-Western developed countries has been underestimated in critical global media studies. This research matters. As Herman and McChesney (1997) and Schiller (2007) argue, without comprehensive research regarding Asian media giants, one can hardly explain how Asian communication systems have subsisted and thrived in the Asian media markets.

Deficient research regarding Asian media giants has brought about a critical concern raised by Lee (2000): whether the political economy of communication – rooted in Western monopoly capitalism – can be applied to studying media in Asia rooted in state capitalism. In monopoly capitalism, the economy is controlled by large corporations that organize big businesses, dominate markets/industries and are involved in setting national policies. In this way, the gigantic firms are responsible for the conception and execution of economic development (Baran & Sweezy, 1966). In state capitalism, the economy is dominated by the state, which intervenes in markets, controls productive and financial resources and regulates foreign direct investment. In this way, the state decides the direction and pace of economic development (Chang, 1993). Because of the different economic systems between developed Western and Asian countries, Lee's question appears legitimate. Studies by Western critical scholars were based on monopoly capitalism and political stability. In contrast, studies by Asian scholars were founded on both state capitalism and unstable (or stable) political environments. For example, some countries, like China and Malaysia, were under authoritarian regimes with state capitalism (Lee, et al., 2006; Anuar, 2008). Others like Korea, Taiwan and Singapore were under neoliberal authoritarian regimes (Park, Kim & Sohn, 2000; Sim, 2001; Lee, 2008). Nonetheless, the environments of Asian media have gradually or rapidly become neoliberal, producing market-oriented media systems. In this way, they resemble the media systems of the West. Thus, I showcase an Asia-specific research framework based on the approach of political economy of communication.

In fact, critical media scholars have hardly investigated the nature of Asian media giants within the interconnections between media ownership and media markets. Previous literature has focused on analyzing only corporate structures *or* a single market in relation to Asian media conglomerates. Specifically, Asian media conglomerates have been in charge of producing, distributing and exhibiting cultural commodities (Pendakur, 1991). They have also been the global partners of Western cultural conglomerates in local media markets (George, 2008). Moreover, Asian media conglomerates display three patterns of ownership. The most common has been corporate ownership shared between domestic and foreign capital. Most domestic capital has come from industrial conglomerates (e.g., semiconductor, construction and energy) and tends to maintain family media ownership (Lent, 1993). The second pattern of media ownership has been co-ownership between corporations and the state (Lent, 1987). The last pattern of ownership has been state ownership (Lee, et al., 2006). However, scholarship analyzing media conglomerates in multiple media markets in relation to the structural changes associated with neoliberal laws and policies in Asia is sparse. An exception was a study by Lee, et al. (2006) analyzing the relationship between state media ownership and the structure of the press market in China. Lee found that the Chinese Communist Party played a central role in forming both media conglomerates and the conglomerate-oriented market structure in the press industry. But this research was not representative of the media conglomerates in other Asian countries because state media ownership in China is not a typical ownership pattern, but rather family ownership in the era of Asian marketization. Therefore, I conduct a case study to explore the interconnection between media ownership and structures of media markets within the research tradition of political economy in communication.

Political economists in media have explored structural change and continuity in communication systems in relation to political institutions and actors, economic sectors and communication industries (Smythe, 1981; Murdock, 1982). Rather than limiting themselves to a myopic approach, however, political economists have employed an interdisciplinary approach to examine structural changes within the web of social and power relations. Most of their interests have been in 1) media ownership; 2) corporate media structure; 3) connections between media owners and political elites; and 4) the relationship between media policies and media enterprises. But another key question for the political economy of communication is: who benefits from changes in media market structure? Political economists have examined how changes have happened, who has been involved and what interests have been served (Meehan, et al., 1993, p. 114).

There have been some studies showing the interactions between corporate ownership and media markets in the West. As Freiberg (1981) and Curran (2003) found, the rise of press conglomerates facilitated interdependence between press and advertising markets. In selecting news and media content, owners of press conglomerates responded to advertisers' needs to promote their commercial interests because of their own heavy dependence on advertising revenue. In order to make the most of their investment, advertisers preferred the wider influence of the press conglomerates compared to small- and medium-sized companies. The complementary needs of media owners and big advertisers redistributed advertising money in the newspaper market. This led to taming and depoliticizing media content and starving out the popular radical papers. Similarly, Schiller (1991) argued that corporate media systems institutionally allowed advertisers to exercise their influence over the content of the cultural realm through sponsorship. These critical Western scholars showed how owners of conglomerates changed the structure of the advertising market and affected other media companies within the same market. In this project, I will determine the extent to which their conclusions apply to Asian media markets given that Asian media systems are now market driven and financially supported in no small part by advertising capital (George, 2008; Zhao, 2008).

In this project, I argue that Asian media giants can be called family media monopolies, which internally maintain concentrated media ownership and structurally exercise market censorship over the information and entertainment markets to protect family interests rather than public interests.

To examine my argument, I focus specifically on family-controlled media conglomerates in Korea among Asian media giants. I justify why I focus on Korea's four media markets and then explain the importance of the four media markets and family media ownership. Korea was selected as a country of focus for several compelling reasons. Korea is a microcosm of the general conglomeration trends in Asia. Chen (1998) and Lee (2000) argue that the history of media development in Taiwan was similar to that of Korea because of the similar trajectories of political and economic history in modern capitalism. Korea experienced authoritarian regimes (1961–1987), a transitional period from military to neoliberal authoritarian regimes (1988–1997) and neoliberal authoritarian regimes (1998–present) (Kwak, 2012). With these political changes, the Korean economic system had already evolved from state capitalism in the 1990s (Ahn & Lee, 2000), but did not completely transform to monopoly capitalism (Lee, 2010). Within these political and economic changes, Korean media systems were transformed from a state-controlled media structure to a market-driven one (Jin, 2011). Structural changes in Korea's political economy brought about changes in media systems, changes similar to situations in other Asian countries. Since the mid-1990s, as in India and the Philippines, family-controlled conglomerates in Korea expanded their media businesses to cable television, telecommunication and film industries (Shim, 2000). These conglomerates owned multiple media holdings in advertising, cable television, computer-mediated communication, film, game, print, recorded music and telecommunication industries and thereby became powerful media companies in Korea. Thus, Korea offers an opportunity to assess the comprehensive nature of Asian media conglomerates that operate in multiple media markets.

The four market structures of advertising, newspaper, cable television and film are included in this study for three main reasons. First, both the advertising and newspaper markets can be categorized as information markets, which play a vital role in manufacturing public discourse that creates popular culture (Smythe, 1981). In the Korean context, newspaper and advertising markets in Korea are intertwined with each other in terms of creating public discourse in the conglomerated press era (Kim, 2010). Second, cable television is located at the top of the hierarchical structures in paid broadcasting services (Lee, 2008). Third, the Korean film market was liberalized in 1988 by the neoliberal Korean state and through trade threats from the United States. Opening the domestic film market to foreign capital via transnational corporations was a turning point for releasing other media markets to foreign capital (Park, 2005).

Finally, family-owned conglomerates are at the heart of this study for three reasons. First, family media ownership is the popular and pervasive pattern among Asian media conglomerates. Owners of family-controlled conglomerates maintain concentrated media ownership. Second, several family capitalists have expanded their businesses into the media industries because of structural changes initiated by an ideology of market determinism. Third, family capitalists who own major media conglomerates also typically own multiple subsidiaries across economic sectors (e.g., construction, energy, food and/or leisure) (Kim, 2002; Prasad, 2008; Seneviratne, 2008).

In other words, this study is motivated by the following three factors: 1) marginalization of Asian media conglomerates in literature; 2) lack of research examining the multi-faceted relationships between media ownership and market structures across different categories of media, including advertising, cable television, newspaper and film; and 3) the question raised by Lee (2000) of whether the notion of monopoly capitalism relevant to studying media in the West can be applied to studying media in Asia. In consideration of these three factors, I pursue the following three interconnected questions in the Korean context: 1) How have neoliberal laws and policies affected the structures of the four media markets and shaped interactions among them? 2) How have media owners used the informal ties, including family ties, within corporate structures during the process of expanding media businesses? 3) Who have been the major beneficiaries of the rise of media conglomerates from the traditional perspective of the political economy of communication?

Before starting research, I want to provide some information about how to conduct a case study, including research-investigated subjects, applied methods and data. First, the family-controlled conglomerates in Korea are known as "chaebol," a combination of the Chinese characters for "wealth" and "clique." The term is defined as large diversified business groups owned and controlled by families or their close kin (Kim, 2008, p. 64). Owners of these conglomerates and their family members directly control multiple subsidiaries across Korean economic sectors (Kang, 1997). This means that a chaebol's ownership is kept within the family and that a chaebol runs diverse businesses in a wide range of economic sectors under one corporate structure. Let's take the 1990s as an example. The Lee family controlled 80 subsidiaries of the Samsung group. The Chung family dominated the Hyundai group with ownership of over 70 subsidiaries. Similarly, the Koo family commanded the LG group with control and ownership of as many as 70 subsidiaries (Hwang & Seo, 2000). I will discuss chaebol groups in chapter 1.

Among members of chaebol groups, I select Samsung, CJ and JoongAng Ilbo as representative chaebol groups for the study for two reasons. First, CJ became a subsidiary of Samsung in 1997, and JoongAng Ilbo became a subsidiary of Samsung in 1999. Each owner in the three chaebol groups is the Lee family. CJ, JoongAng Ilbo and Samsung were all founded by a single person, Lee Byung-chul.[1] The chairman of CJ is Lee Jae-hyun, Lee Byung-chul's grandson. The chairman of Samsung is Lee Kun-hee, the third son of the founder Lee. The chairman of JoongAng Ilbo is Hong Seok-hyun, whose sister, Hong Ra-hee, is married to Lee Kun-hee, the founder's son and chairman of Samsung. Thus, the survey of the developmental history of Samsung, including the reorganization of the three chaebol groups, offers good insight to the overall chaebol restructuring in the neoliberal mode. Second, Samsung was more interested in media expansions than any other chaebol group in the history of Korean mass communication. I deal with detailed information in chapter 2.

I focus on the period from 1998 to 2014 when the Korean state fundamentally reformed the country's communication system. This media reform enabled chaebol groups, foreign capital, American media conglomerates and existing media companies to expand their media businesses, thereby establishing media empires. To examine the interconnections between media reforms and media expansions by family capitalists, I use both institutional analysis and the corporate profiling techniques. As Murdock (1982) and Schiller (1989) suggested, both methods have enabled researchers to explore the interconnections between media markets and media ownership in a given society. My primary data came from three governmental institutions – the Ministry of Culture, Sports and Tourism (MCST), the Fair Trade Commission (FTC) and the Financial Supervisory Service (FSS). The MCST, in charge of media policies, published 14 White Papers that contained information about 1) media laws and policies, 2) market structures and 3) the identity of major market players. The FTC, in charge of settling conflicts between major market players and independent ones, published 50 special reports on the Samsung, CJ and JoongAng Ilbo groups. These reports showed how the Lee family exercised corporate censorship over the four media markets through its multiple media operations. Finally, the FSS produced 173 annual reports and financial statements – the equivalent of U.S. 10-K reports – on the media operations owned by the three chaebol groups. These data concerned 1) family ties among the owners of three chaebol groups and their families; 2) ownership structures existing between the parent company of each chaebol group and its media subsidiaries; 3) media expansions of the chaebol groups, including mergers and acquisitions; 4) members of boards of directors; and 5) revenues. Additionally, I relied on secondary sources, including scholarly works and news sources.

This project is composed of six chapters. In chapter 1, I survey the nature of chaebol groups in modern Korean capitalism. I also cover chaebol's media businesses with a focus on the four media industries of advertising, broadcasting, newspaper and motion pictures.

In chapter 2, I detail the history of Samsung, including that of the CJ and JoongAng Ilbo groups. This section outlines the family ties among the three chaebol groups, corporate governance and the media businesses of Samsung in the history of Korean mass communications.

In chapter 3, I review the media laws and policies adopted by the Korean government from 1998 to 2014. This chapter highlights four points: 1) re-regulation of the former media laws and policies; 2) the privatization of state-owned media companies; 3) the application of a developmental model for Korean media industries; and 4) market structures in the neoliberal media mode.

In chapter 4, I investigate the processes of how Samsung, CJ and JoongAng Ilbo used informal ties, including family ties, within corporate structures in the process of expanding their media businesses. This chapter focuses on two points: 1) overview of Samsung, CJ and JoongAng Ilbo (e.g., core businesses and ownership structure of each chaebol group) and 2) media expansions and corporate structures of media holdings owned by the three chaebol group (e.g., media ownership structures, directorships and power connections between the Lee family and Korean power elites).

In chapter 5, I analyze the nature of family media monopoly with a focus on the Lee family. This chapter shows how concentrated family media ownership affects structures of media markets and why the Lee family exercises market censorship over the media markets.

In chapter 6, I present my key findings, highlight their theoretical implications, state some of the limitations of this study and make recommendations for future research.

Acknowledgments

Especially, I appreciate Cinzia Padovani, Katherine Frith, Narayanan Iyer, John A. Lent and Wanki Moon – my committee members – for their efforts and supports. My professors have led me to overcome the hardest hurdle I have ever encountered in my life, and I am grateful to arrive at the finish line. While this venture was intellectually challenging, it also tested my ability to survive in the academic world. Being surrounded by these people helped me solve one of the many unanswered puzzles in my life.

I especially appreciate my doctoral advisor, Dr. Padovani, and my academic mentor, Dr. Lent. Without the support of both scholars, my project would not have seen the light of day. They consistently encouraged me to stick to the hidden power embedded in Korean media systems. Dr. Padovani poured several ounces of red ink, spent dozens of weekend afternoons and put life back into an unfinished and dying dissertation. Dr. Lent implanted an academic gene and cultivated me to become a political economist of media with a Korean aspect.

Finally, I want to thank my friends Kathy Fahey, Cheonae Kim, Cindy Park, Mary Sasse, Oliver Witte, Kiran Bharthapudi, Kim H. Song, Sang-ho Lee, Haelim Suh, Hak-lim Shin and Choi Young-Woo. They were my greatest comforts when having to endure my darkest hours. Their contributions in making a better world guided me to dig into the hidden truth in media marketization. There are many more friends and people in Carbondale to whom I offer my thanks.

Note

1 A Korean name consists of a family name first, usually one syllable, followed by a given name, normally of two syllables.

References

Ahn, B.M. & Lee, I.C. (2000). Reforming public enterprises in South Korea. *Policy Review*, 18(1), 181–199. Korean.

Anuar, M.K. (2008). Media commercialization in Malaysia. In C. George (Ed.), *Free markets free media: Reflections on the political economy of the press in Asia* (pp. 137–158). Singapore: Asian Media Information and Communication Center (AMIC).

Bagdikian, H.B. (2000). *The media monopoly* (6th Ed.). Boston, MA: Beacon Press.

Bagdikian, H.B. (2004). *New media monopoly*. Boston, MA: Beacon Press.

Baran, P. & Sweezy, P. (1966). *Monopoly capital: An essay on the American economic and social order*. New York: Monthly Review Press.

Chang, H.J. (1993). The political economy of industrial policy in Korea. *Cambridge Journal of Economics*, 17(2), 131–157.

Chen, S.Y. (1998). State, media and democracy in Taiwan. *Media, Culture & Society*, 20, 11–29.

Curran, J. (2003). Press history. In J. Curran & Seaton, J. (Eds.), *Power without responsibility: The press and broadcasting in Britain* (6th Ed., pp. 1–106). London: Routledge.

Freiberg, J.W. (1981). *The French press: Class, state and ideology*. New York: Praeger.

George, C. (Ed.). (2008). *Free markets free media: Reflections on the political economy of the press in Asia*. Singapore: Asian Media Information and Communication Center (AMIC).

Herman, E. & McChesney, R.W. (1997). *The global media: The new missionaries of corporate capitalism*. London: Cassell.

Hwang, I.H. & Seo, J.H. (2000). Corporate governance and chaebol reform in Korea. *Seoul Journal of Economics*, 13(3), 361–389.

Jin, D.Y. (2011). *Hands on/off: The Korean state and the market liberalization of the communication industry*. New York: Hampton.

Kang, C.K. (1997). Diversification progress and the ownership structure of Samsung chaebol. In T. Shiba & M. Shimotani (Eds.), *Beyond the firm: business groups in international and historical perspective* (pp. 31–58). New York: Oxford University Press.

Kim, S. S. (2002). *A Study of Korea's media ownership*. Seoul, Korea: Press Trade Union. Korean.

Kim, Y.T. (2008). *Bureaucrats and entrepreneurs: The state and the Chaebol in Korea*, Seoul, Korea: Jimoondang.

Kim, S.S. (2010). *Media markets and the public interests in Korea*. Seoul, Korea: Hanul Academy. Korean.

Kwak, K.S. (2012). *Media and democratic transition in South Korea*. New York: Routledge.

Kunz, W. (2007). *Culture conglomerates: Consolidation in the motion picture and television industries*. Lanham, MA: Rowman & Littlefield.

Lee, C.C. (2000). The paradox of political economy: media structure, press freedom and regime change in Hong Kong. In C.C. Lee (Ed.), *Power, money and media: Communication patterns and bureaucratic control in cultural China* (pp. 288–236). Evanston, IL: Northwestern University Press.

Lee, C.C., He, Z. & Huang, Y. (2006). Chinese Party Publicity Inc. Conglomerated: The case of Shenzhen Press Group. *Media, Culture & Society*, 581–601.

Lee, E.J. (2008). *The ownership of media companies in Korea*. Seoul: The Korean Press Foundation. Korean.

Lee, J.B. (2010). *A study on state domination of capital under democratic regime: Based on Samsung group*. Incheon, Korea: SeongKong Hoi University. Korean.

Lent, J.A. (1987). Transnational linkages to Singapore and Malaysian's print culture. *Indian Journal of Communication*, January–March, 1–8.

Lent, J.A. (1993). Four conundrums of third world communications: A generational analysis. In K. Nordenstreng & H. Schiller (Eds.), *Beyond national sovereignty: International communications in the 1990s* (pp. 235–255). New Jersey: Ablex.

Meehan, E. (2005). *Why TV is not our faults*. Lanham, MA: Rowman & Littlefield.

Meehan, E., Mosco, V., & Wasko, J. (1993). Rethinking political economy change and continuity. *The Journal of Communication*, 43(4), 105–116.

Murdock, G. (1982). Large corporation and the control of the communications industries. In M. Gurevitch, J. Curran, & J. Woollacott (Eds.), *Culture, society and the media* (pp. 118–150). Beverly Hills, CA: Sage.

Murdock, G. & Wasko, J. (Eds.). (2007). *Media in the Age of Marketization*, Cressill, NJ: Hampton Press.

Park, E.Y. (2005). *The process of Korean film's corporation.* Seoul, Korea: Korean Film Foundation. Korean.

Park, M.J., Kim, C.N. & Sohn, B.W. (2000). Modernization, globalization and the powerful state: The Korean media. In J. Curran & M.J. Park (Eds.), *De-westernizing media studies* (pp. 111–123). New York: Routledge.

Pendakur, M. (1991). A political economy of television: State, class and corporate confluence in India. In J.A. Lent & G. Sussman (Eds.), *Transnational Communications: Wiring the Third World* (pp. 234–164). Newbury Park, CA: Sage.

Prasad, K. (2008). The false promise of media liberalization in India. In C. George (Ed.), *Free markets free media: Reflections on the political economy of the press in Asia* (pp. 59–71). Singapore: Asian Media Information and Communication Center (AMIC).

Schiffrin, A. (2000). *The business of books: How international conglomerates took over publishing and changed the way we read.* New York: Verso.

Schiffrin, A. (2006). Market censorship. In R. Atkins & S. Mintcheva (Eds.), *Censoring culture: Contemporary threats to free expression* (pp. 67–79). New York: The New Press.

Schiller, D. (2007). *How to think about information.* Urbana and Chicago, IL: University of Illinois.

Schiller, H. (1989). *Culture, Inc: The corporate takeover of public expression.* New York: Oxford University Press.

Schiller, H. (1991). Corporate sponsorship: Institutionalized censorship of the cultural realm. *Art Journal*, 50(3), Censorship I (Autumn), 56–59.

Seneviratne, K. (2008). Journalism by whom, for whom? In C. George (Ed.), *Free markets free media: Reflections on the political economy of the press in Asia* (pp. 20–47). Singapore: Asian Media Information and Communication Centre (AMIC).

Shim, D.B. (2000). *Korean big business awakens to media industry.* Wisconsin-Madison, WI: University of Wisconsin-Madison. Dissertation.

Sim, S.F. (2001). Asian values, authoritarianism and capitalism in Singapore. *Javnost/The Public*, 8(2), 45–66.

Smythe, D. (1981). *Dependency road: Communications, capitalism, consciousness and Canada.* Norwood, NJ: Ablex.

Winseck, D. (2008). The state of media ownership and media markets: Competition or concentration and why should we care. *Sociology Compass*, 2(1), 34–47.

Zhao, Y. (2008). Neoliberal strategies, social legacies: Communication and state transformation in China. In C. Paula & Y. Zhao (Eds.), *Global communications: Toward a transcultural political economy* (pp. 23–50). Lanham, MA: Rowman & Littlefield.

1 Chaebol groups in modern Korean history

Chaebol groups, Korea's family-controlled conglomerates, have a long and complex history rooted in interactions among the Korean state, Korean power elites and the sacrifices of Korean workers (Oh, 1975; Woo, 1991). To encourage the rapid development of the Korean economy, the Korean state created and nurtured chaebol groups by tightening controls over labor (Cumings, 1984). Chaebol groups typically involve multiple businesses across economic sectors ranging from food, fabrics, heavy chemicals, construction and semiconductors to leisure industries (Kim, 1997). They also run media businesses that include the advertising, broadcasting, recorded music, gaming, print and film industries (Seo, 2003).

Chapter 1 focuses on the nature of these chaebol groups and their component media businesses in relation to historical developments in the Korean political economy. The early part of this chapter discusses the nature of chaebol groups, their corporate governance and power networking with Korean power elites and the development of chaebol groups in modern Korea. The latter part of this chapter focuses specifically on chaebol media businesses in relation to changes in media law and policy from the 1960s to the mid-1990s when the Korean political system was transitioning from authoritarian to democratic governance.

1.1. Chaebol groups and family capitalism

A chaebol is a gathering of formally independent firms under the common administrative and financial control of one family (Kim, 2006, p. 186). A chaebol's economic activities are wide ranging and can include everything from agriculture, light industry, heavy chemicals and information technology to mass media. In addition to its diversified business operations and family ownership/management, a chaebol is also characterized by the enormity and complexity of its economic structures. Thus, a chaebol is really a *chaebol group* or network of related companies (Choi, 2014). The number of Korean chaebol groups has varied from 30 in the 1980s to 60 conglomerates in the early 2000s.

Since the early 1980s, the Korean state has set standards of membership in chaebol groups based on each chaebol's industrial assets rather than its financial assets. From 1987 to 1992, the standard of chaebol entry amounted to 400 billion Korean won.[1] This standard was based on the industrial assets of chaebol groups rather than both financial and industrial assets. During those periods, the number of chaebol groups reached 30. However, in 2002, the Korean government increased the standard of chaebol entry to 5 trillion won (U.S. $5 billion) in industrial assets. Since then, the number of chaebol has ranged from 43 to 63, including the 30 largest business groups and some privatized corporations (e.g., Korean Electronics and Korea Telecommunication) (Secretariat of National Assembly, 2010).

In addition, chaebol groups are divided into two tiers. The first-tier chaebol are the top 10 conglomerates controlling the highest percentages of the Korean economy (see Table 1.1).

First-tier chaebol include Samsung, Hyundai, Lucky and Gold Star (renamed LG) and sometimes Daewoo, SK, Hanjin and Lotte. The other conglomerates make up the second tier of chaebols. These Korean conglomerates share some common developmental characteristics. Among them are: 1) rapid business expansion in both related and unrelated industries, 2) a oligopolistic position in a market, 3) close relations with political regimes, 4) a highly centralized structure with a top-down decision-making process and 5) paternalistic leadership practices (Hattori, 1997). The characteristics of Korean conglomerates are similar to those of the pre-war Japanese *zaibatsu*,[2] which relates to the shared history of Japan, Korea and the U.S. I will detail the relationship between chaebol groups and modern Korean history later in this chapter.

Chaebol groups can also be categorized as family firms since a family of owners exercises power over the chaebol's corporate structures (Chang, 1988; Fox, 1995). Family-controlled firms are enterprises in which the founders and their heirs continue to be influential shareholders, hold executive managerial positions and exercise decisive influence on a company's control (Church, 1993). Since most of the original chaebol founders have died, their children and heirs now own and operate the holdings. For this reason, informal and family ties such as birth, marriage and adoption exert a great deal of control over the corporate structures of chaebol groups (Ryu, 1991). For instance, Samsung is owned and controlled by the Lee family, Hyundai by the Chung family, LG by the Koo family and SK by the Choi family. As the major stockholders, these family members influence the corporate structures of each chaebol's multiple holdings (Choi, 2014). Looking at ownership statistics from the 1990s, the Lee family controlled 80 subsidiaries of the Samsung group. The Chung family dominated the Hyundai group, owning over 70 of its subsidiaries. Similarly, the Koo family commanded the LG group with control of as many as 70 subsidiaries (Hwang & Seo, 2000).

Family control of major business and corporate enterprises is not unique to Korea (Colli, 2003; Sjogren, 2006). At the turn of the twentieth century, family firms represented 17 percent of the top 100 corporations in both the U.S. and Germany, accounting for 8 percent and 12 percent of GNP respectively. In 1993, 46 percent of the major Dutch corporations were family companies, while about one-third of the top 100 Swiss corporations were family corporations. In Italy, the proportion of family firms among the 100 largest companies has been estimated at 50 percent for the same period (Colli, 2003, p. 27). Further, in the early 1990s,

Table 1.1 Top 10 chaebol groups in 1998 and 2007

Rank	1998				2007			
	Chaebol Name	Owner	Number of Affiliates	% of Korean Economy	Chaebol Name	Owner	Number of Affiliates	% of Korean Economy
1	Hyundai	Chung Joo-yong	62	8.08	Samsung	Lee Kun-hee	59	8.33
2	Samsung	Lee Kun-hee	61	7.09	Hyundai Car	Chung Mong-goo	36	4.27
3	Daewoo	Kim Woo-jung	37	5.82	SK	Choi Tae-won	57	3.90
4	LG	Goo Bon-moo	52	5.80	LG	Goo Bon-moo	31	3.38
5	SK	Choi Tae-won	45	3.22	Lotte	Shin Kyuk-ho	44	2.59
Percentage of Korean Economy Held by Top 5 Chaebol Groups				30.01				22.47
6	Hanjin	Cho Chung-hoon	25	2.14	Posco	Posco	23	2.11
7	Ssang-yong	Kim Seok-won	22	1.72	KT	KT	19	1.77
8	Hanhwa	Kim Seun-yeon	31	1.37	GS	Hur Chang-soo	48	1.62
9	Keum-ho	Park Seong-won	32	1.14	Keum-ho Asiana	Park Sam-goo	38	1.43
10	Dong A	Choi Won-seok	22	.99	Hanjin	Cho Yang-ho	25	1.48
Percentage of Korean Economy Held by Top 10 Chaebol Groups				37.37				30.88

Source: Choi, 2014, p. 33.

one-third of Fortune 500 companies in the U.S. were family-controlled companies (Shanker & Astrachan, 1996). About one in eight of the British companies listed among the FTSE's largest companies possessed strong family connections in 1989 (Sjogren, 2006, p. 162). Similar patterns can be seen in East and Southeast Asia, including Japan, Singapore and Taiwan (Hamilton, et al., 1990; Jones & Rose, 1993; Chung, 2008).

Because of the family firms' high visibility, critical scholars have explored the nature of both ownership and directorship patterns in family-controlled conglomerates. For instance, Scott (1986) analyzed the ownership patterns and corporate structures of family-owned conglomerates in the U.S., the U.K. and Japan. Lincoln, Gerlach and Takahashi (1992) investigated the ownership and organization of the Japanese Keiretsu networks. Soref and Zeitlin (1987) and Silva, Majluf and Paredes (2006) examined the impacts of Chile's family-controlled conglomerates on its market structures. Zang (1999) and Brookfield (2010) investigated inter-corporate directorships among family members in big business groups located in Taiwan and Singapore. Casson (1999) and Sjogren (2006) explored corporate governance of Sweden's family-owned conglomerates. Kadusin (1995) researched the nature of corporate governance in French family conglomerates.

These scholars commonly found that 1) family companies played central roles in sustaining and expanding the economic structures of family capitalism and 2) the families used informal ties (e.g., family ties, regional ties or social circles) to create corporate alliances with other family capitalists. Family capitalists across the globe have created class cohesion and inter-directorship within their corporate structures through shared ownership, irrespective of differences in the socio-economic settings of different countries (Ungson, et al., 1997; Zang, 1999; Chung, 2008). Having said this, the corporate cultures of family enterprises around the world are also affected and shaped by their national contexts and historical conditions (Colli, 2003). This is certainly the case with the Korean chaebol groups, which are recognized as family conglomerates both across Korean economic sectors and in the world economy.

1.2. The power origins of chaebol groups

Corporate culture refers to the values, behaviors and norms shared by an organization's members across organizational levels (Cho & Yoon, 2002, p. 71). Corporate culture lacks a uniform character because individual business enterprises are rooted in different cultures and stages of the historical development of capitalism. For example, family companies rooted in Protestant values (mainly developed Western countries) display a more individualistic corporate culture than do family enterprises based on Confucianism from the East and Southeast Asia (Hofstede, 1980; Ungson, et al., 1997). East Asian patterns of corporate culture pay more attention to social relationships both inside and outside their groups, while Anglo-American corporations emphasize individual liberties (Hofstede & Bond, 1988).

The collective corporate culture of family-controlled conglomerates from Japan, China and Korea is strongly rooted in Confucianism (Chang, 1988). This ideology emphasizes the values of patriarchal authority, filial piety, loyalty and the need for social relations among the extended family. The major moral principles of Confucianism that have profoundly influenced chaebols' development include loyalty to the state, filial piety for elders (especially male elders) and allegiance to the family with a focus on the father's side. This male-oriented moral system established a familial hierarchy with its accompanying web of duties and obligations. Inequality within the family extended into the social, economic and political orders (Chen & Chung, 1994). Although Confucianism focuses on hierarchical order, it also gives weight to social relations, emphasizing both individual and collective harmony. Confucian values have served to encourage emotional harmony within families, organizations and the social order (Kim, 2009). This interplay between hierarchy and harmony, in turn, has affected the patterns of interpersonal communications within chaebol groups as well as organizational communications in East Asia (Yum, 1987).

In spite of shared Confucian social norms and values, Asian cultures understand and focus on different nuances of meaning in the word "harmony." For example, social relations and activities in Korea have been associated with *inhwa*, or harmony, on the basis of respect for hierarchical relationships, including submission to authority. In Japan, society has operated in the context of *wa*, stressing group harmony and social cohesion (Alston, 1989). In both Japan and Korea, employees often consider their workplace a family environment with the company director as the family head. They have been taught to identify themselves as members of a big family, typically organized along the order of a Confucian family hierarchy (Kim, 2009).

While the Japanese *wa* emphasizes harmony in the group itself, the Chinese notion of harmony stresses relationships (networking) beyond the group. In China, social relations and organizational practices reflect the concept of *guanxi*, or personal connections, which works at the individual level. The Korean *inhwa* is similar to the Chinese *guanxi*. But while *inhwa* pays more attention to the emotional aspect of relationships, *guanxi* focuses on the exchange of favors (Alston, 1989; Cho & Yoon, 2002, p. 73). *Guanxi* operates between two persons of unequal rank. The weaker partner might ask for special favors for which he is rarely called to reciprocate (Alston, 1989). This individualistic aspect of *guanxi*, apart from its primary stress on family ties, has played a central role in connecting communities in both mainland China and Greater China, including Hong Kong, Taiwan and Singapore (Zang, 1999; Kim, 2009).

In Korea, owners of chaebol groups exploit collective social norms and values both internally to control the corporate structures of their affiliates and externally to connect to the Korean power elites. First, these collective norms are embedded into the corporate structure of chaebol groups. Owners of chaebol groups exercise absolute power over the corporate structures of their multiple affiliates (Ryu, et al., 2005). The owner, or chairman, and his kin are the largest stockholders of the holding company at the top of the chaebol corporate structure. This holding company controls a few core subsidiaries. These core subsidiaries are, in turn, major stockholders of sub-subsidiaries across Korean economic sectors. Ownership links exist both horizontally among individual sub-subsidiaries and vertically with the chaebol holding company itself (Kim, 2007). This web of cross-ownership between the holding company of a chaebol group and its holdings is known as "circular ownership." Circular ownership enables the owner of a chaebol group to maintain tight managerial control over multiple subsidiaries (Choi, 2014). Within the circular ownership structure, affiliates of a chaebol group seem to have technical autonomy. However, they are actually directed by the chaebol group through the structural planning office (Kim, 2005).

The structural planning office (i.e., the secretarial office of the chairman) is the control tower of a chaebol group located at the apex of its corporate structure (Kim, 2005). Its director is both appointed by and an agent of the chairman. The director also controls a few elite employees selected from multiple subsidiaries within a chaebol group. Members of the structural planning office are in charge of these tasks: 1) establishing group-related policy (e.g., long-term goals, strategic financing and investment planning); 2) directing the individual affiliates' daily businesses; 3) managing the owner's assets including succession of properties; and 4) administering human resources for all the subsidiaries (Chang, 2003; pp. 99–103; Hwang & Seo, 2003).

Of equal importance, chaebol groups use the collective social ideology of *uye-ri* ("justice" or "just cause" in English) to create a power complex with the Korean elites. The term *uye-ri* is not new, but springs from the Confucian values of communal life. *Uye-ri* connotes both obligatory reciprocity and interdependence among group members where, in a sense, a person is forever indebted to others (Yum, 1987; Chen & Chung, 1994). For example, if you had a close friend or were in a position to incur *uye-ri* from another person, you would be able to ask for a very big favor from that person knowing you would be able to reciprocate someday. Those who are asked cannot easily refuse a favor because ignoring the obligations of *uye-ri* could mean being ostracized by the group (Yum, 1987, pp. 90–91).

Similarly, *uye-ri* plays a central role in binding the rules of social interaction among members, Korean power elites and owners of chaebol groups. Through the cohesive power of *uye-ri*, owners of chaebol groups find and cement their social, economic and political connections. These connections include informal, social ties to other power groups in Korean society (Chen & Chung, 1994; Park, Kim & Sohn, 2000). Owners of large corporations tend to utilize social ties (e.g., schools or clubs) to connect to the power elites, creating a power network within their own corporate structures (Mills, 1967; Domhoff, 1990, 2006).

In Korean history, the power elites were junior partners of chaebol groups responsible for allocating natural and financial resources and monopolistic rights to chaebol groups. Under the post-colonial and authoritarian regimes (1945–1987), owners of chaebol groups established a power network with high-ranking military officers, bureaucrats and politicians. Since the fall of those regimes, journalists and professors have replaced military officials in that role (Kim, 2005). Consequently, informal connections like regionalism, school ties and marriage ties began to play crucial roles in linking owners of chaebol groups to Korean power elites (Kim, 2007). Regionalism, connection based on shared hometowns and/or early educational locations, was openly promoted during the presidential campaign of 1971 and has since been a major factor in defining political practices. Ruling groups have often been formed by people from the president's home region (Park, et al., 2000, p. 115). The example of the "TK mafia" illustrates how chaebol groups have also used these regional ties to exercise political power.

The TK mafia was made up of politicians, military generals and owners of chaebol groups from Taegu in the Kyongsang Province. The letters *T* and *K* in the title refer to *T*aegu and *K*yongsang. The TK mafia has been the strongest of the power elites since the early 1960s. Seeking to enhance its own political clout, Samsung established its businesses at Taegu and recruited members of the TK mafia to fill its high positions. For instance, Samsung employed Shin Hyun-hawk, a former prime minister and the so-called "godfather of the TK mafia," as honorary chairman of Samsung. In 1992, in return, Samsung won government approval to enter the securities business and produce commercial vehicles (Kim, 2008, p. 178).

Regional ties have played an especially vital role in connecting media owners of the mainstream newspapers with those in political power, including the president. Media companies have filled their top posts with people from the regional base of the ruling camp (Park, et al., 2000). Media owners have tended to replace their senior staff with figures from the president's hometown. For example, after the government of Kim Dae-jung was inaugurated in February 1998, major newspaper and broadcasting organizations rushed to appoint figures from Jella Province, Kim's political bastion, to their top posts. This move illustrated a feudalistic feature of the relationship between the government and the Korean media (Park, et al., 2000, p. 115). Moreover, media owners themselves were involved in the presidential elections in order to extend their power in the next administration. They rarely publicized their preferred candidate in the presidential election, but instead put forth a concerted effort to ensure that the presidential candidate who maintained a close relationship with them was elected. They sent staff and journalists to the election camps to analyze public opinion and set up presidential election strategies (Park, et al., 2000, p. 115).

Importantly, regionalism was supported in this case by both school and marriage ties between the owners of chaebol groups and Korean power elites. School ties promoted personal interactions among the Korean capitalists and the Korean political and economic elites (Kim, 2008, 2007). Marriage ties were also a key mechanism for creating corporate alliances (Kong, 1989; Cho, 2004). The maintenance of marriage and kinship networks played an integral role in protecting the interests of Korea's business and power elites (Kong, 1989; Kim, 2007).

In sum, chaebol groups of family-controlled conglomerates exploit Confucian social norms and values to control corporate structures. This enables owners and their family members to maintain centralized decision-making mechanisms and exercise paternalistic and authoritarian leadership. Family-controlled Korean giants also employ informal ties to connect to the Korean power elites and consolidate their power according to the Confucian-derived concept of *uye-ri*.

1.3. Chaebol groups' history in the Korean political economy

The historical trajectory of chaebol groups was synchronized with historical developments in Korea. These include: the Japanese occupation (1910–1945); the formation of the post-colonial state (1945–1960); the military regimes (1961–1987); the transitional period from authoritarian to neoliberal authoritarian regimes (1988–1997); and the neoliberal authoritarian governments (1998–present). The periods of Japanese occupation and post-colonialism corresponded with the birth of chaebol groups. Military regimes nurtured chaebol groups as big business groups. However, the collapse of authoritarian regimes ironically enabled chaebol groups to become Korean monopoly capital. Further, the introduction of a market-oriented ideology in Korea institutionally allowed chaebol groups to increase their influence over Korean society.

In 1910, Japan forcibly annexed the Korean Peninsula and began turning it into an East Asian colony. Japanese colonization marked the collapse of the Chosun Dynasty, the last of its kind in Korean history. Colonial Japan intervened in the Korean economy, creating a market for Japanese manufacturing products and spawning new industries for the Japanese economy. Japan also installed an authoritarian colonial state under the control of the Government-General in Seoul (Cumings, 1997). Several economic institutions were also installed as vanguards of Japan. They included 1) the Bank of Korea, which was the central bank; 2) the Industrial Bank of Chosen, which was responsible for the deposits of commercial banks and small loans to local financial cooperatives; 3) the Oriental Developmental Company, which arbitrated for the reorganization and purchase of land and agricultural settlement; and 4) the Railway and Communications Bureau, which controlled transportation and communications in the Korean Peninsula (Woo, 1991, pp. 21–41).

These institutions allowed Japan to exploit Korean economic resources. By 1930, the economic structure of Korea was geared to provide a food base for Japanese markets. Japan did not permit Koreans to own factories without its permission, thus eliminating the possibility of competition from Korean industries. As a mercantilist nation, Japan maximized resource extraction from its colonies and captured markets for Japanese goods. From 1930 to 1945, Japan shifted from treating its colonies as market resources to using them as sources for war suppliers. During this time, Japan had invaded Manchuria, the northern part of the Chinese mainland. Korea was considered a natural supplier of mineral resources, cheap labor and hydroelectricity. On the Korean Peninsula, the colonial state promoted *zaibatsu*, the economic partners of the Japanese state on the Korean Peninsula. However, the *zaibatsu* were forced to retreat after the defeat of Japan in 1945 (McNamara, 1990; Hart-Landsberg, 1993; Young, 2006).

The second phase of modern Korean history, marked by the formation of a post-colonial state, lasted from 1946 to 1960. This period can further be divided into two parts. The period from 1945–1948 was that of American Military Government in Korea (AMG).[3] The post-AMG period between 1948 and 1960 was the second phase of post-colonialism when Rhee Seung-man ruled as the first president of South Korea. During the period from 1945 to 1948, the U.S. established AMG and built the anti-communism system in order to block the expansion of the Soviet Union and China across East Asia and institutionalize liberal democracy in the peninsula (Jeon, 2002). The AMG built a Korean army to defend the line of control (the 38th parallel), which became a confrontation zone between South and North Korea. The AMG also rebuilt coercive apparatuses such as the police, the bureaucracy and the judiciary. The Americans used the existing governing agencies without any reforms to counter a leftist threat. The AMG formed an alliance with South Korean security agencies who had maintained a pro-Japan stance. Thus, the groups that were sympathetic to the earlier Japanese occupation retained their high positions within the AMG (Park, 2002).

Further, the American officials oppressed Korean leaders who opposed the separation of the Korean Peninsula and demanded the liquidation of the vestiges of Japanese imperialism. They labeled Korean nationalists as communists or leftists and eventually purged them from all government agencies including broadcasting, telecommunications, agriculture, treasury, police and schools. As a result, the AMG transplanted American liberal democracy and its institutions to South Korea's political and judicial systems (Park, 2002). Specifically, the AMG supported the formation of the Korean Democratic Party (KDP), which formed the political base of Rhee Seung-man, whom the American military authorities chose as a local partner. Rhee Seung-man, who had earned a doctoral degree from Princeton and lived in the U.S. for more than 40 years, publicly expressed strong anti-communist and pro-American sentiments (Kim, 2003).

Rhee Seung-man took office as the first president of Korea in 1948 after the U.S. transferred state power to him. President Rhee shuffled the Korean economic structure, nationalizing all the formerly Japanese-owned state enterprises and controlling public monopoly offices in transportation, communications and electricity. The Rhee regime reassigned confiscated properties left by the Japanese to a few private firms that were politically well-connected to the Rhee regime (Lee, 2007). It also set the assessed value of the vested industrial properties at 25–30 percent of the market value. The new owners of these properties provided kickbacks to Rhee's regime in return for the windfall (Hart-Landsberg, 1993).

Samsung, Hyundai and LG were notable beneficiaries and exchange partners of the Rhee regime (Kim, 1976). Further, the regime discretionarily allocated aid, goods and dollars (mainly from the U.S.), import licenses and government contracts to a few chosen firms as a means of consolidating this power base. At the time, the U.S. provision of staples such as sugar, cotton yarn, white flour and dollars was a life vest that allowed the survival of the Korean state. In essence, with support from the U.S., the Rhee regime established a type of crony capitalism in Korea favoring a few chosen firms (Ryu, 1991; Lee, 2007).

As it turned out, the Korean War (1950–1953) contributed to Japan's economic reconstruction in a way comparable to the Marshall Plan in Western Europe. The Japanese lobbied intensely to get the U.S. to spend its Korean aid in a way that was beneficial for Japan. In addition to Japan's economic recovery, the Korean War played a fundamental role in reshaping conservative and anti-communist

Korea. After the Korean War, Rhee Seung-Man, during the second term of his presidency, strictly prohibited any kind of trade unions and progressive social movements. Anti-communism became the most important national policy to gain political legitimacy during the Rhee regime. Later, military dictators including Park Jung-hee (1961–1979) and Chun Doo-whan (1980–1987) deployed anti-communism as a catalyst for economic development (Cumings, 1984; Kim, 1999).

In May 1961, General Park Jung-hee carried out a military coup against the civilian government, took political power and became the third president of South Korea. Park grafted the Japanese developmental model onto the Korean economy (Kim, 1997). The state became responsible for economic planning and providing huge amounts of capital to support and discipline big business. As examined earlier, the Japanese state used finance as a tool to implement industrial policy and create an entrepreneurial class that relied heavily on political leaders (Chandler, et al., 1997). Unlike Japan, the Park regime nationalized all commercial banks under the supervision of the Ministry of Finance. This department made major monetary decisions such as setting interest rates and discount rates and conducting open market operations (Chang, 1993 p. 133). By controlling a credit-based system of industrial finance and owning the monopolized rights to allocate policy funds to chaebol groups, the Park regime cultivated chaebol groups into big business groups in the 1960s (Kim, 2005).

The Park regime acted as entrepreneur, banker and architect of the industrial structure and provided a vision for a new society (Chang, 1993). This regime was the only agency that represented the interests of the whole society from the 1960s to the 1970s (Chang & Rowthorn, 1995). This allowed chaebol groups to gain momentum and accumulate capital due to financial and industrial monopolistic support from the Park regime. As a result, Korean economic structures transformed from light industry (e.g., textiles, apparels and wigs) in the 1960s to heavy-chemical industry (e.g., steel, petrochemicals and shipbuilding) in the 1970s. In maintaining this cooperative relationship, the Korean state and chaebol groups established a large corporation-oriented economy structure (Amsden, 1989; Kim, 1997).

Park was assassinated by his junior staff, Kim Jae-kyu, a chief of the Agency for National Security Planning (equivalent to the America Central Intelligence Agency) on October 26, 1979. Two months later, military general Chun Doo-hwan mounted a coup and became president of Korea. In opposition to the coup in the early 1980s, college students and the middle class built and expanded massive protest movements all across the Korean Peninsula. College students at Chunnam National University of Kwangju in southern Korea were part of the largest national protests against the military takeover by General Chun (Jin, 2011). When the students were viciously attacked by soldiers, outraged citizens joined the protest. Paratroopers killed them indiscriminately. Angered, people across the Kwangju area seized arms from police stations and army stockpiles, drove the army out of the city and controlled the city for six days beginning on May 21, 1980. On May 27, the Chun regime sent the 20th Army Division into Kwangju and staged a massacre there. While it quelled the uprising, this brutal slaughter led to the Chun regime losing its political legitimacy. At the same time, the Chun regime was under external pressure from the U.S. to open its economic markets to international organizations and institute more comprehensive and rapid financial liberalization (Sa, 1993).

Because of both political and economic reasons, Chun sought to offset his political illegitimacy through fostering economic growth. Instead of adopting the developmental model used by the previous regime, the Chun regime selected a neoliberal model as the new strategy for the Korean economy (Lee, 1990; Ryu, 1991). Chun appointed neoliberal economists as high officers in economic and financial departments and vitalized economic marketization and privatization. This resulted in the spread of neoliberal thinking across all national policies. These neoliberal officers pursued a market-oriented ideology in the financial sector to bring the Korean economy into compliance with the changing global economic environment (Kim, 1999).

Further, the Chun regime attempted to control chaebol groups by introducing the Monopoly Regulation and Fair Trade Act (MRFTA), the Korean anti-trust law. Chaebol groups misused their market-dominant position to the detriment of small- to medium-sized Korean companies. In response the Chun regime enacted MRFTA in 1986 in order to prevent excessive concentration of economic power among members of chaebol groups (Lee, 1990). This Korean anti-trust law prohibited chaebol groups' unfair business practices, including abuse of a market-dominant position, anticompetitive mergers and acquisitions and resale price maintenance (Seong, 2007).

On June 10, 1987, however, the Chun regime collapsed as a result of mass democratic movements in the Korean middle class. Although the Chun government had succeeded in economic re-growth through neoliberal policies with chaebol groups, it had failed to obtain popular support. The military regime had coercively oppressed the democratic movements and illegally arrested, tortured and even killed ordinary Koreans, including college students and activists. In February 1987, the Chun regime had killed Park Jong-chul, a student at Seoul National University, by using water torture. The death of Park Jong-chul had sparked continuous protests over four months in 1987 and served as the tipping point for the fall of the Chun Doo-hwan regime (Choi, 2006).

The fourth phase of modern Korean history was the transitional period from authoritarian to neoliberal authoritarian regimes (1988–1997). Neoliberal authoritarian regimes during this period focused on financial liberalization and privatization of state-owned companies, allowing chaebol groups to expand into the financial and telecommunication industries. Although political power came from free elections and economic power drew from the market, Korea was an incomplete democracy due to the formidable legacy of cultural norms from previous authoritarian regimes (Choi, 2006).

In 1988, Rho Tae-woo (1988–1992), ex-military general and a close friend of Chun Doo-hwan, was elected president. Because of its close relationship with the marred Chun regime, the Rho government also suffered from a lack of political legitimacy. Much like the earlier regime, it experienced pressure from the U.S. to further liberalize the Korean economy. The Rho regime was forced to liberalize the Korean economy, including the partial liberalization of the financial and media sectors (Sa, 1993). Subsequently, Kim Yong-sam (1993–1997) accelerated the move toward neoliberalism. The Kim regime launched active responses in the name of *segyehwa* (Korean for globalization) by joining the Organization for Economic Cooperation and Development (OECD) (Kim, 1997). In 1996, the U.S. presented deregulation and economic privatization as pre-requisite conditions for becoming a member of OECD (Kristof, 1999). To join the OECD, Korea lifted all financial barriers to direct and financial investment in Korea (Hart-Landsberg, et al., 2007).

In this deregulated environment, chaebol groups expanded their financial markets, freely issuing bonds and stocks in overseas markets without the Korean state's permission and borrowing short-term money from international capital markets. Most of the influx of foreign capital to Korea was in the form of short-term speculative funds rather than direct foreign investment (Lee & Crotty, 2001). The rapid increase of short-term speculative funds made the economic structures of Korea respond sensitively to external economic environments. In the mid-1990s, the financial crisis of Thailand and Indonesia spread into Southeast Asia. Consequently, foreign financial institutions that had provided financial loans to chaebol groups pushed the family-owned conglomerates and the Korean government to redeem the loans in late 1997. Foreign institutions demanded that the Korean government guarantee short-term loans. They also refused to roll over loans borrowed or issued by chaebol groups. These pressures from foreign financial institutions drove chaebol groups to the brink of bankruptcy and the Korean economy close to default (Woo-Cumings, 2001). This led to a grave financial crisis in Korea.

In the final phase of modern Korean capitalism (1998–2012), the Korean civil government institutionalized neoliberalism more than the previous regimes in order to escape the financial crisis (Lee, 2010). In December 1997, Kim Dae-jung was elected president. He made an agreement with the International Monetary Fund (IMF) in return for receiving emergency funds of U.S. $57 billion from the IMF and the World Bank. Both international institutions required the Kim regime to implement structural reforms, including corporate reforms of chaebol groups, labor relations, privatization of state-run corporations and financial restructuring (Lee & Crotty, 2001).

The financial reform included 1) restructuring through the closure, sale or merger of insolvent financial institutions; 2) the settlement of bad debts through injection of public funds; and 3) the expansion of the assets of financial institutions. The Kim regime also revised regulation for mergers and acquisitions (M&As) to activate the financial markets for the first time. The ceiling on foreign equity ownership in a Korean company increased from 55 percent to 100 percent of total stocks. The ownership limit by a single foreign nation increased to 33 percent of total stock in a company. This provision applied to Korean companies as well. Moreover, the Kim regime simplified regulations on small-scale M&As in the Korean economy and carried out industrial reforms related to restructuring of both a chaebol's businesses and its corporate structures, called the "Big Deal Plan" (Chang, 2003, p. 209). The term refers to business swaps among chaebol groups. This plan included restructuring the core of chaebol groups' businesses, increasing the accountability of owners of chaebol groups and enhancing management transparency in chaebol groups (Ahn & Lee, 2000).

Under this restructuring, chaebol groups were forced to streamline their business focuses along the lines of eight industries: aerospace, automobiles, electronics, engines, oil refining, petrochemicals, power-generation machinery, and semiconductors. In the process of swapping subsidiaries in accordance with the core business lines of each conglomerate, 20 affiliate members of chaebol groups were shut down (Jung, 2007). For example, Hyundai Electronics acquired LG Semiconductor. In the oil refinery industry, Hyundai took over Hanhwa. In the automobile industry, Hyundai acquired Kia. Samsung sold 80 percent of its total stocks to Renault of France. In railroad vehicles, Hyundai, Daewoo and Hanjin established a new joint company. Similarly, Hyundai, Daewoo and Samsung established a joint business entity in the aerospace industry (Chang, 2003, pp. 204–207).

The Kim government carried out these structural reforms relative to chaebol groups. The first reform was to revise MRFTA, the Korean anti-trust law, in order to disclose internal information about chaebol groups (e.g., their assets, their decision-making processes, the activities of their boards of directors and their businesses) (Song, 2008). The second reform required chaebol groups to appoint outside directors and independent auditors as members of their boards of directors (Jung, 2007). The final action was to require chaebol groups to abolish the structural planning office (Ahn & Lee, 2000).

Chaebol groups, however, used the structural reforms initiated by the Kim government to transfer some businesses to their family members (Kim, 2007). For example, the first-tier chaebol groups (e.g., Samsung, Hyundai, LG and SK) had more interest in corporations' separation than the second-tier ones did. The first-tier chaebol groups felt more compelled to evade the government's control than the second-tier ones because they owned more assets than the second-tier ones (Seoul Shinmun, 2005). Owners of first-tier chaebol groups also wanted to resolve the chronic issue of inheritance among their family members (Kim, 2005). For instance, Samsung reorganized into six conglomerates in the 1990s: CJ, Hansol, Samsung, JoongAng Ilbo, Shinsaegae and Saehan. These conglomerates are called pan-Samsung (or New Samsung) (Kim, 2007). In the early 2000s, the Hyundai group likewise reorganized into pan-Hyundai (or New Hyundai), which included Hyundai, Hyundai-Kia Automobiles, Hyundai Department and Hyundai Heavy groups. LG group, owned by the Goo and Hur families, split into a New LG group, including LG, GS and LS-LG groups. Most of the spilt corporations from the first-tier chaebol groups currently belong to the second-tier ones in the Korean economy (Seoul Shinmun, 2005).

In sum, chaebol groups are the family-controlled conglomerates across Korean economic sectors that maintain hierarchical corporate structures and concentrated ownership. These Korean giants were nurtured by Korean authoritarian regimes related to the changes in foreign policy in Japan and the U.S. The Korean state applied the Japanese economic model of a strong state and big business to the

Korean economy, which in turn allowed chaebol groups to become the big business conglomerates of monopoly capital.

1.4. Chaebol groups in the history of Korean mass communication

Media plays a vital role in forming consciousness, which binds the system of modern society and the everyday life of ordinary people (Smythe, 1981; Jansen, 1988). Because of this mediated role of media, political and economic institutions exercise influence over media systems. Political institutions regulate media laws and policies, while economic institutions establish media companies within and across media industries.

In modern Korean history, chaebol groups ran media companies in the print, broadcasting, film and advertising industries from the 1960s to the 1990s. However, chaebol groups' attitudes toward the media changed in accordance with the characteristics of the political regimes. In the early years, authoritarian regimes considered the mass media an educational tool to cultivate the demand (or need) for economic development, drum up public support for military regimes and promote anti-communism throughout Korea (Hahn, 1978). Under these circumstances, chaebol groups used their media holdings as channels to maintain a benefit-exchange relationship with the state. They also deployed their media operations as a means to resist political pressures (Seo, 2003). However, chaebol groups gradually altered their attitudes toward the media, from seeing them as shields to protect private interests to considering them as means to earn profit. In 1990, the Korea state applied the neoliberal model to Korean media industries. At that time, Korea faced limited economic growth. Labor costs were rising at home, and the manufacturing sector was faltering. Uruguay Round (UR) agreements and the World Trade Organization (WTO) pushed Korea to further open its long-closed service markets including finance, tourism, retailing and media. These internal and external pressures made the Korean government turn to alternative industries to advance the Korean economy (Chang, 2003). In this process, the Korean state recognized the economic potential of the information technology and communications industries, which were deeply related to Korea's manufacturing industries. They then started to explore cable television and film as experiments in the communications industry. Adapting to these changes in national policies, chaebol groups gradually increased their investments in the cable television and film industries. They looked to the media as new profit businesses (Shim, 2000).

Simply put, chaebol groups adjusted and evolved their media business outlooks and interests in accordance with the policies of the political regimes, especially after the dawn of the neoliberal era.

1.4.1. Newspapers and chaebol groups

The Korean state revised media laws and policies four times during the period from 1960 to 1997, which included abolishment of Ordinance No. 88 in 1960, the

Law Concerning Registration of Periodicals in 1961, the Basic Press Act of 1980 and the Act on Registration Periodicals of 1987. The revisions of media laws and policies corresponded to political changes in Korean society. In 1960, 1961 and 1980, authoritarian regimes controlled Korean newspaper companies – directly or indirectly – with political power rather than via economic ownership. Since 1988, Korean newspapers have been under a market-oriented structure (Yoo, 1989).

In April 1960, the Korean state abolished Ordinance No. 88, a media law that had been established by the U.S. military regime. Temporarily, Korea enjoyed almost unlimited press freedom in the second republic of Korea (July 1960– May 1961). The number of newspapers increased to 112 in 1960 from 41 in 1959, while the number of news agencies was 274 in 1960 compared to a mere 14 in 1959 (Jin, 2005, p. 78). General Park Jung-hee, however, led a military coup in May 1961 and ended the unlimited freedom of the press. The Park regime enacted the Law Concerning Registration of Periodicals, which specified minimum stand-ards and required newspapers and news agencies to register with the government. This junta also canceled about 1,170 periodicals in the name of purification of the media industry. Following the regime's media cleansing, only 23 newspapers and 6 news agencies remained (Kim & Shin, 1994).

Chaebol groups under the Park regime owned and operated newspapers to pro-tect their interests from political pressures, as well as to create an audience favora-ble to their other business interests (Hahn, 1978). As such, the Samsung group ran the *JoongAng Ilbo*, a nationally circulated daily newspaper. The LG group published the *Kukje Shinmun* and the *Kyung Nam Ilbo*, a local daily newspaper with a focus on the southeastern region of the Korean Peninsula. The Samyang and Kyung Band groups published the *DongA Ilbo*, a nationally circulated daily newspaper. The Il Shin group controlled the *Chungchong Ilbo* covering the mid-dle west of the Korean Peninsula. The Donhae group owned and ran the *Kangwon Ilbo*. The Ssangyong group owned Dongyang News Agency. Finally, the Doosan group controlled Hapdong News Agency (Jin, 2005, pp. 94–95). As seen with the military regimes, a few members of the chaebol groups entered the press system in order to protect their interests from political pressures, support the interests of their subsidiary companies and publicize their new businesses (Yoizi, 1988, p. 81; Seo, 2003).

In 1980, however, the Chun Doo-whan regime enacted the Basic Press Law integrating media laws regarding newspaper, broadcasting and advertising. The Basic Press Law banned the cross-media ownership of newspaper and broadcast-ing stations and forbade individual business from advertising in the broadcasting sector. This act also limited the number of papers and even the number of pages via heavy censorship. Through the Basic Press Law, the Chun regime forced the press to fire 933 journalists, enforced mergers of press corporations by chaebol groups and closed 172 periodicals, 15 daily newspapers and two news agencies in the name of the "Plan for the Purification of the Press" (Kim & Shin, 1994). These forceful steps taken by the Chun regime led to further strangulation of the Korean press. As such, the "Daily Guidelines for Reporting" issued by the Public Coordi-nation Office under the Ministry of Culture and Information were an effective tool to control the press in the 1980s. The daily guidelines set the boundary for how or whether to report certain events. Staff from the Agency for the National Security Plan regularly visited newsrooms around deadline times (Jin, 2005, p. 102).

Because of the policy of no cross-media ownership between newspaper and broadcasting under the Chun regime, most chaebol groups were forced to choose between a newspaper identity and a broadcasting identity. The LG group deserted the *Kuk Je Shinmun* and the *Kyung Nam Ilbo*. The Samyang and Kyung Band groups selected the *DongA Ilbo*. The Il Shin group and the Donhae group gave up *Chung Cheong Ilbo* and the *Kangwon Ilbo* respectively. Additionally, the Ssangyong (*Dongyang News Agency*) and the Doosan (*Hapdong News Agency*) groups gave up their news agencies, as the Chun regime had forcefully nationalized them. Unlike other members of chaebol groups, however, Samsung kept *JoongAng Ilbo*.

In addition, Chun exercised conciliatory methods to placate media owners and journalists. For example, his regime allowed media owners to receive bank loans with low interest, borrow foreign capital and diversify their businesses into magazine publications. This regime also reduced taxes on imported machines for newspaper companies and the income tax on journalists and provided public funds for training journalists (e.g., overseas training and overseas observation trips). The regime promoted the welfare of journalists (e.g., loans for housing and the education of children), regularly bribed journalists with cash or gifts and recruited journalists as politicians and bureaucrats (e.g., minister and vice minister at the Ministry of Culture and Information). These favors quieted the frustrations of media owners and journalists and created a patron-client relationship between the Chun regime and the media owners, with journalists largely cooperating with the dictatorial regime (Yoo, 1989; Park, et al., 2000, pp. 113–114).

These institutional and personal favors for media owners and journalists led to the creation of a press cartel or a "political power-press" complex among the military regime, media owners and journalists. Through the press cartel, the military regimes easily controlled the media and disseminated the ideology of dictatorship-for-development including anti-communism, a growth-at-any-cost policy, a middle-class bias and a consumption-is-virtue orientation (Kim & Shin, 1994, p. 45). Through political cooperation, media owners were allowed to access high-quality information (e.g., the developmental policies of real estates and the future policies of economic developments) and to exercise their influence on presidential elections by sending journalists to election campaigns as key staff for setting up election strategies (Park, et al., 2000, p. 115).

In early 1987, however, Korea was under pressure from mass democratic movements that had cropped up across the country. The Korean middle classes and young college students held protest rallies following the killing of a college student who had died due to water torture by the state. They demanded that the Chun regime step down and revise the constitution to make direct presidential elections possible. Although the Chun regime cracked down on the mass protests and averted immediate threat, it had to concede to the demands of the Korean people on June 29, 1987, when Rho Tae-woo, Chun's close friend, announced that the Korean president would be directly elected by ordinary people for a single five-year term. Rho Tae-woo was elected as the new president in 1987. Although Rho's political foundation was that of a military regime, he had to follow the pervasive market rationale in the Korean economy, including the media (Kim, 1999). The Korean newspapers finally put an end to the paper cartel that privileged a few selected companies. With the shift to political liberalization in 1987, the Korean newspapers were forced to enter into a more competitive market.

Rho Tae-woo, newly elected president in 1987, announced that "the government cannot control the media, nor should it attempt to do so" (Yoo, 1994, p. 207). He abolished the Basic Press Act, established by the Chun regime, and enacted a new press law – the Act on Registration of Periodical Publication – in November 1987. This law contained the notion of Korean freedom of press. While the Basic Press Act emphasized the function of forming public opinion via the press, the Registration of Periodical Publication primarily focused on the sound development of the press. This meant that the Rho regime at least tried to "deauthoritarianize its restrictive legal mechanism" (Youm, 1994, p. 67). For example, the Registration of Periodical Publication abolished the licensing system regarding newspaper companies, allowed chaebol groups and religious organizations to establish new companies without strict conditions and empowered media owners to control corporate structures. This meant that the Korean state officially gave up controlling the newspaper companies, accepted demands for freedom of the press and loosened regulation on the printing businesses. New press laws guaranteed freedom to publish and led to expansion of the advertising market as necessitated by economic growth and an explosion in demands for information (Kim & Shin, 1994). As a result, the total number of paper companies rapidly increased from 2,412, including 30 daily papers, in 1987 to 7,867, including 112 daily papers, in 1993 (Kwak, 2012, p. 33).

In the period from 1988–1989, four news dailies – the *Hankyoreh*, the *Pyung-Hwa*, the *Kukmin* and the *Segye* – were established in Seoul alone. Except for the *Hankyoreh*, all three papers were owned and operated by religious organizations. *Hankyoreh*, established by citizen funds, was owned by about 3,000 Koreans. In addition, chaebol groups established new dailies, including economic newspapers, and acquired existing newspaper companies. The Hyundai group launched the *Munhwa*, an evening paper. The Lotte group established the *International*. The Daewoo and Duksan groups founded local dailies the *Pusan Maeil* and the *Moodeung Ilbo* respectively. The Daenong group launched an English paper, the *Korea Herald*. The Hanhwa group acquired the *Kyunghyang* (Kim, et al., 2000; Kwak, 2012, pp. 32–33). This meant that political liberalization empowered chaebol groups and monied religious organizations to exercise their power over newspaper markets (Yoo, 1989).

During the transitional period from authoritarian to neoliberal authoritarian regimes (1988–1997), the Korean press moved from being under direct state control to being under market control. Among the changes this shift produced was a 50 percent annual growth in advertising income among the major dailies from 1989 to1992 (Cho, 2003, as cited in Kwak, 2012, p. 33). This prompted an increase in the number of pages allocated to advertising space to meet the growing demands of advertisers. Increased competition among daily papers made commercial revenue all the more important. They also allocated greater coverage for feature pages or special sections on topics like money/finance or women's issues. This provided readers with more versatile and in-depth information. Moreover, the proliferation of papers brought about pluralism in news reporting, as journalists were able to write more freely and critically and access more diversified news sources than in previous times (Kwak, 2012, pp. 30–50).

1.4.2. Broadcasting and chaebol groups

Like the newspaper industry, the development of Korean broadcasting was related to Korean political liberalization from authoritarian to neoliberal authoritarian regimes. During the periods of military regimes (1961–1987), dictators used both television and radio as tools to acquire political legitimacy and social integration (Kang & Kim, 1994). Since the transition between authoritarian and neoliberal authoritarian regimes (1988–1997), political leaders dealt with broadcasting as a national industry for economic growth (Nam, 2008).

From the late 1950s to the early 1960s, the Korean television broadcasting system remained in its infancy compared to print media because Korea was still recovering from its civil war (Hahn, 1978). Television broadcasting in Korea started in 1956 with the opening of HLKZ-TV, established by the RCA Distribution Company (KORCAD) in Seoul. However, HLKZ found it difficult to secure financial backing because the Korean economy had not yet reached the level of mass production and mass consumption required for broadcast advertising. One year later, HLKZ was sold to Chang Ki-yong, the owner of the *Hankook Ilbo*, and renamed DBC-TV. Yet change in ownership did not resolve the financial issue, and the company had to close after a mysterious fire. The second television station in Korea was the American Forces Korean Network (AFKN) established by the U.S. in 1957. The AFKN began broadcasting to a target audience of 60,000 U.S. military personnel, civilian employees and their dependents (Yoo, 1994, pp. 198–200).

In 1961, the Park Jung-hee regime introduced the state broadcasting system in order to promote its political legitimacy and advance its political economic ideology. It started the Korea Broadcasting System (KBS)-TV, a state-owned company. Although KBS-TV was branded as a state broadcasting system, its money initially came from both advertising and a monthly subscription fee from ordinary Koreans. The Park regime established a fundamental foundation of co-existence between the commercial media system and the public broadcasting system in order to buy the broadcasting devices and expand the broadcasting zones nationally (Hahn, 1978).

Additionally, this military regime allowed chaebol groups to own commercial television stations in the 1960s. The Park regime provided preferential treatment to the oligopoly of established media companies that supported the authoritarian rule in return for their loyalty (Yoo, 1994). Two commercial television networks were Tongyang Broadcasting Company (TBC), established by Samsung in 1963, and Munhwa Broadcasting Company (MBC), founded by Kim Ji-tae, owner of the *KyungHang Shinmun* as well as a businessman, in 1969. Both of them were financially supported by advertisers. They focused on commercial media content to acquire more advertisers. This led to a fierce ratings competition between KBS (the state-owned station) and both TBC and MBC (chaebol-owned stations) (Kang & Kim, 1994). Although these three television stations competed with each other to earn advertising money, they were all under direct control of the military regime. On a monthly basis, stations reported summaries of broadcast programming to the state (Yoo, 1994, p. 203). In the early 1970s, Park issued new television licenses to chaebol groups. The LG group owned Pusan MBC and Jinju MBC. The Donga group controlled Taejeon MBC. The Ssangyong group operated Taegu MBC. The Il Shin group ran Chungju MBC. The Miwon group controlled Chungju MBC. The Donhea group owned and operated Chunchun MBC and Samchuk MBC. Chaebol's broadcasting stations disseminated their corporate ideology to the public (Jin, 2005, pp. 94–96). However, the Park military regime forcefully took over these chaebol broadcasting companies and established an additional state-owned broadcasting station, MBC. Since then, MBC has been re-categorized as a public broadcasting company.

Following the military regimes, the Chun Doo-whan regime changed the Korean broadcasting landscape in 1980 from a co-existence of public broadcasting and commercial broadcasting systems to only public broadcasting system. Based on the Basic Press Law in 1980, Chun confiscated what had been a private broadcasting system and brought it under government control. He forcibly reshuffled 29 broadcasters into an oligopoly of two public broadcasters, Korea Broadcasting System (KBS) and Munhwa Broadcasting Company (MBC) (Jin & Shim, 2007, p. 23). All television stations were integrated into KBS and MBC-TV. KBS absorbed TBC, which became the KBS-2 broadcasting station. KBS also bought 65 percent of the shares of MBC that later became the second public broadcasting network.

Unlike the Park regime, Chun banned cross-media ownership of newspaper and broadcasting interests (Kang & Kim, 1994). Based on this media policy, chaebol groups that had owned both newspaper and broadcasting companies had to give up their broadcasting stations. The Samsung group gave up TBS because it owned the *JoongAng Ilbo*. The Samyang and Kyung Band groups had to abandon DBS due to *DongA Ilbo*. The Il Shin group selected Chungju MBC instead of *Chung Cheong Ilbo*. Finally, the Donhae group gave up the *Kangwon Ilbo*. Additionally, the Ssangyong (*Dongyang News Agency*) and Doosan (*Hapdong News Agency*) groups gave up their news agencies because the Chun regime forcefully nationalized them. The *Yonhap News Agency* was the only news agency by 2002. Most chaebol groups selected broadcasting stations in spite of the local affiliates of MBC, while the Samsung, Samyang and Kyung Band groups chose their national daily newspapers over broadcasting stations (Jin, 2005, pp. 99–119).

Subsequently, the Rho Tae-woo regime (1988–1992) revised the Broadcasting Act to reorganize the public broadcasting system once again allowing for both public and commercial systems. In 1990, the National Assembly enacted the new Broadcasting Law, by which the government granted a license to a new commercial broadcasting company, Seoul Broadcasting System (SBS), in 1991. SBS was the first commercial television station to be established since 1980 (Shim, 2008, p. 23). This revised broadcasting regulation also split into KBS and the education broadcasting system (renamed EBS) in 1991 (Jin, 2005, pp. 205–211). Chaebol groups were not allowed to own a national broadcasting system, but they were indirectly involved in the Korean broadcasting system as program producers. At that time, the Rho regime started to enforce the "outsourcing system" on territorial broadcasting channels. This policy required 3 percent of all broadcasting programs to be supplied by independent media companies. Under this policy, chaebol groups started to establish media production holdings in the audio-visual industries (Choi, 1998).

Following the start of the neoliberal authoritarian regime, Kim Yong-sam (1993–1997), introduced cable television at the national level in 1993. The Korean cable TV industry was divided into three subcomponents, which included the program provider (PP), the system operator (SO) and the network operator (NO). The PP was in charge of media content for cable television. The SO was responsible for distributing media content as the cable networker. The NO took charge of establishing the infrastructure of cable television and Internet broadband. The government's rationale for designing the industrial structure of cable in this tripartite way was to ensure the rapid growth of the broadcasting industry and promote structural diversity in this industry (Nam, 2008). Under this cable television plan, the Kim government allowed chaebol groups to become the PP in 1993.

In order to induce balanced development among PP, SO and NO by 1997, chaebols were rarely permitted to take control of an SO or NO. Chaebol groups thus focused on acquiring 14 channels categorized as gold channels. The most potentially profitable were taken by the first-tier chaebol groups. The Samsung group took the only pay film channel, while Daewoo had the movie channel. The Hyundai group acquired the entertainment channel (Kim, 1996; Jin, 2005). The first-tier chaebol groups owned the cable channels and audio-visual corporations, including film importations and video film production. Instead of establishing media subsidiaries, some chaebol groups' subsidiaries ran the audio-visual businesses. Chaebol groups were reluctant to invest capital in the early stage of the Korean audio-visual media industries. Familiar with the favors of the Korean government, chaebol groups were seemingly waiting for preferential treatment from the government in order to minimize losses from the cable business.

At the same time, chaebol groups also made alliances with transnational corporations (TNCs) to broadcast over the new cable channels because they had not prepared sufficient content for their new media businesses. Instead of importing media products from TNCs, chaebol groups exercised two strategies: exclusive licensing agreements through partnership and direct investment in Hollywood. For example, Samsung's pay channel "Catch One" made exclusive licensing agreements with Disney, Warner Brothers, Paramount, Twentieth Century Fox and Universal Studios. Samsung's basic cable channel, "Channel Q," the Korean equivalent of the Discovery Channel, made program supply contracts with Japan's NHK, the BBC and Discovery. The Daewoo group also made an agreement with New Line Cinema to bear a percentage of the studio's production costs (6 percent for the first two years) in return for distribution rights in Asian markets. The Hyundai group, running the entertainment cable channels HBS, made an output deal with the French studio Canal Plus. Finally, the SK group made a production contract with Cinergy Motion Picture and Mandalay Entertainment guaranteeing 5 percent of each studio's budget (Shim, 2000, pp. 232–243). In 1995, the Kim regime continued the licensing of regional private broadcasters for the chaebol groups in four large cities: Pusan, Taegu, Kwangju and Taejon. The continuous introduction of new media in the audio-visual sector resulted in "a full scale return to commercial broadcasting" after a decade of state-controlled duopoly in the 1980s (Kim, 1996, p. 91).

In sum, the authoritarian regimes tightly controlled both public and private broadcasting companies in Korea to propagate political legitimacy over the Korean Peninsula. As media partners, chaebol groups cooperated with the military regimes. However, political liberalization allowed chaebol groups to be out of the control of the state and expand their media businesses into network television, cable television and local broadcasting stations.

1.4.3. Advertising and chaebol groups

Since advertising had been considered as a profit-seeking business, the Korean state did not develop advertising policy (Kim, 1994, p. 143). Chaebol groups established the Korean advertising industry to sell their manufacturing products effectively in the 1970s. As chaebol groups diversified their businesses across Korean economic sectors, they established in-house advertising agencies that were under the supervision of the chaebol groups. They covered full services including marketing strategies, advertising production, media planning and consumer research (Yun, 2008). For example, Cheil Communication was responsible for all the advertising of the Samsung group and its subsidiaries. The LG group controlled LG Ad. The Taepyungyang group controlled Dongbang Ad. Chaebol groups developed in-house advertising agencies to save money and exert control over campaign development. The advantages of in-house agencies include the acquisition of expected clients without external factors such as economic recession and the obtaining of detailed information on marketing strategies from their inside clients (Kim, 1994, p. 135). By 1980, the chaebol groups' advertising agencies directly transacted with Korean press corporations and broadcasting corporations without mediated brokers. This trading practice between chaebol groups and their advertising holdings, however, was changed in the Chun Doo-hwan regime.

In 1980, Chun Doo-hwan enacted the Korean Broadcasting Advertising Corporation Law (KBACOL), which stipulated the Korea Broadcasting Advertising Corporation (KOBACO) as the only sales agent for all broadcast time. The main functions of KOBACO were to accredit advertising agencies and sell advertising time on the broadcast media companies. KOBACO also collected a certain percentage commission on advertising revenues from the broadcast media to provide a collective public fund for small- to medium-sized media corporations. KOBACO returned approximately 9 percent of the commission to the advertising agencies and kept about 1 to 1.5 percent for operational expenses (Kim, 1996, p. 144). In 1981, only four advertising agencies received a certification from KOBACO. In 1989, KOBACO certified 35 advertising agencies, which were in charge of using the advertising monies for both print and broadcasting companies (Lee, 2008).

The number of advertising agencies gradually increased as the Korean government liberalized the advertising market. In 1988, the Rho government was under pressure, mainly from the U.S., to open the advertising market. The U.S. pushed this government to 1) have daytime broadcasting; 2) raise prices for advertising time/space in media; 3) establish new private television stations; and 4) increase the amount of advertising time from 8 percent of total broadcasting airtime to 10 percent. As a result, in 1991, the Korean government launched a new commercial broadcasting network – the Seoul Broadcasting System (SBS) – and increased the airtime of broadcasting advertising (Kim, 1996, p. 142). It also gradually opened Korean advertising markets to foreign advertising agencies in the late 1980s and completely liberalized the Korean advertising market in the late 1990s.

In short, chaebol groups owned in-house advertising agencies that provided financial support for Korean papers and broadcasting stations. This meant that chaebol groups were owners of advertising agencies as well as big advertisers. In addition, since the 1980s, the Korean state has established a state-controlled advertising agency, the KOBACO, to control the broadcasting advertising market. The Korean advertising market was liberalized in the late 1980s, allowing transnational advertising agencies to enter the Korean advertising market.

1.4.4. Motion pictures and chaebol groups

Because it considered films as mechanisms to perpetuate the Cold War ideology, militarism and political centralism, the Korean state tightly controlled the local film market and provided monopolized rights for a few privileged persons instead of chaebol groups. For example, in 1962, the Park regime enacted the Motion Picture Law, which introduced a registration system for film producers, importers and exporters. Only registered film producers were allowed to produce motion pictures or import foreign films. This law also stipulated that motion picture producers should have 35-millimeter movie cameras and over 661 square meters of studio to register as film producers. They also had to produce more than 15 motion pictures every year to maintain their status as film producers (Jin, 2005, pp. 227–236).

Further, in 1966, the Park regime introduced a system of screen quotas that required local theaters to play Korean films 146 days per year. Based on the Motion Picture Promotion Ordinance, the Park junta transferred the supervising rights of screen quota to local governments, which had 40 days of discretion. This meant that local governments could allow theaters to play Korean films for 126 days in large cities and for 106 days in small cities. Through the strict market controls over Korean motion pictures, the Park regime allowed the two dozen registered producers to monopolize the Korean film market rather than chaebol groups. They determined what to produce, what to distribute and what to exhibit at Korean film markets (Shim, 2000, p. 107).

In the early 1980s, however, Korea was under consistent pressure from the U.S. Trade Representatives (USTR). They used Section 301 of the Trade Act of 1974 to open the Korean markets to insurance, tobacco, wine and film (Sa, 1993, pp. 130–131). To delay U.S. pressure on the Korean manufacturing sector, the neoliberal authoritarian regime of Rho Tae-woo allowed Hollywood to distribute films directly to Korea in 1988. As a result, Western TNCs set up branches in the Korean film market. As such, United International Pictures (UIP), Twentieth Century Fox, Warner Brothers, Columbia and Walt Disney established branches for the video trade. CIC, Buena Vista, Col/Tri-Star, Warner Brothers and Fox Video earned licenses to import foreign videos in 1988 (Park, 2005).

These steps were met with criticism from the public, which accused the Korean government of abandoning the domestic film industry. To suppress the criticism, the Korean government took steps to re-establish the screen quotas. This played a central role in supporting the domestic film market, deregulating the licensing system and removing the import quota for foreign films (Jin, 2005, p. 117). As a result, foreign films' share of all Korean box office receipts increased. As of 1989, foreign films held 79.8 percent (U.S. $44.2 million) of the box office total in Korea. That was to say that the Korean film industry had been eclipsed by Hollywood and struggled to survive in the 1980s (Shim, 2000, pp. 110–111).

Against these film market situations, chaebol groups made inroads through the video industry. Family-controlled conglomerates established media holdings to create a manufacturing demand for video cassette recorders (VCRs) with a focus on the importation of American films and the production of film video. The Samsung group established Starmax, a video-circulation company. The SK group founded SKC, another major video-circulation company. In the 1990s, these video holdings began to produce and distribute Korean and Hollywood motion pictures (Jin, 2005, pp. 118–121). In 1995, as the Kim Yong-sam regime enacted the Promotion Law of the Korean Motion Picture (KMP) in order to promote the Korean film industry, chaebol groups (e.g., Samsung, SK and Daewoo) expanded their media businesses to include film production. This new law loosened the legal barriers regarding ownership, financing and market strategies and reclassified film production from a service industry to a manufacturing industry to provide tax breaks for production companies. In this environment, chaebol groups funded capital ranging from 20 percent to 50 percent of production costs for several domestic films (Jin, 2011, p. 133). They also shared their advanced business know-how (e.g., systematic planning, marketing and accounting) with Korean film producers (Shim, 2008, p. 19). Further, family-owned conglomerates held independent film festivals and film scenario contests with considerable cash prizes, recruited fresh talent to infuse new sensibilities into Korean cinema and financially supported young directors with degrees from prestigious film schools all over the world.

In brief, chaebol groups rarely ran film holdings by the 1970s, when the military junta excluded them. However, they entered the video industry in the 1980s and developed the Korean film industry in this area in the 1990s.

Conclusion

Chaebol groups of family-controlled conglomerates have grown in accordance with the growth of the Korean economy. The Korean state has nurtured chaebol groups and allowed them to become monopoly capital to avoid the rapid development of the Korean economy. In the process, chaebol groups connected to the Korean power elites through formal and informal ties. They have also tightly controlled multiple subsidiaries through concentrated family ownership. In addition to the power connection to Korean power elites, chaebol groups expanded their media businesses from newspaper and broadcasting in the 1960s to advertising in the 1970s. By 1997, their holdings included the cable television and film industries. Simply put, chaebol groups are Korean monopoly capital entities with multiple media operations.

Notes

1 The monetary unit in Korea is the won. The official exchange rate between the Korean won and the U.S. dollar has been flexible since the mid-1990s. During this project, the rate was 1,000 won to the dollar.
2 *Zaibatsu* were Japanese big business groups before World War II. These Japanese conglomerates were owned and managed by a family or kinship group. Mitsubishi, Mitsui, Nissan, and Sumitomo were typical *zaibatsu*. They played a vital role in rapid economic growth in Japan (Young, 2006).
3 Agreements reached at the Yalta Conference in February of 1945 divided Korea at the 38th parallel. After this, the Korean Peninsula became a frontline between communism and capitalism in East Asia (Kim, 1994, p. 48).

References

Ahn, B.M. & Lee, I.C. (2000). Reforming public enterprises in South Korea. *Policy Review*, 18(1), 181–199. Korean.

Alston, J. (1989). Wa, guanxi, and inhwa: Managerial principles in Japan, China and Korea. *Business Horizons*, 32(2), 26–31.

Amsden, H.A. (1989). *Asia's next giant: South Korean and late industrialization*. New York: Oxford University Press.

Brookfield, J. (2010). The network structure of big business in Taiwan. *Asia Pacific Journal of Management*, 27, 257–279.

Casson, M. (1999). The economics of family firms. *Scandinavian Economic History Review*, 47(1), 10–23.

Chang, C.S. (1988). Chaebol: The South Korean conglomerates. *Businesses Horizon*, March–April, 51–57.

Chang, H.J. (1993). The political economy of industrial policy in Korea. *Cambridge Journal of Economics*, 17(2), 131–157.

Chang, H.J. & Rowthorn, R. (1995). *Role of the state in economic change*. Oxford, UK: Oxford University Press.

Chang, S.J. (2003). *Financial crisis and transformation of Korean businesses groups*. Cambridge, UK: Cambridge University Press.

Chandler, D.A., Amatori, F., & Hikino, T. (Eds.). (1997). Historical and comparative contours of big business, In A.D. Chandler, F. Amatori, Jr.,& T. Hikino (Eds.), *Big business and the wealth of nations* (pp. 3–23), Cambridge, UK: Cambridge University Press.

Chen, G. & Chung, N.J. (1994). The impact of Confucianism on organizational communication, *Communication Quarterly*, 42, 93–105.

Cho, K.M. (2004). *A research about marriage ties among the owners of Korean newspaper companies*. Seoul, Korea: Korean University. Unpublished thesis. Korean.

Cho, Y.H. & Yoon, J.K. (2002). The origin and function of dynamic collectivism: An analysis of Korean corporate culture. In C. Rowley, T.W. Sohn, & J.S. Bae (Eds.), *Managing Korean business: Organization, culture, human resources and change* (pp. 70–87). Portland: Oregon, Frank Cass.

Choi, J.J. (2006). *The Democratization after democracy in Korea*, Seoul, Korea: Humanitas. Korean.

Choi, J.P. (2014). *History of Korean Chaebols*. Seoul, Korea: Hanam. Korean.

Choi, Y.S. (1998). The history of development of the Korean video industry. In *Korea music and video yearbook 98* (pp. 101–102). Seoul: Recording Industry Association of Korea. Korean.

Chung, H. (2008). Ownership structure, expatriate policy, and regionalization: Evidence from Taiwan's family business groups, 2000–2002. *Multinational Business Review*, 16(2), 43–63.

Church, R. (1993). The family firm in industrial capitalism: International perspectives on hypotheses and history. *Business History*, 35(4), 17–43.

Colli, A. (2003). *The history of family business 1850–2000*. New York: Cambridge University Press.

Cumings, B. (1984). The origins and development of the northeast Asian political economy: industrial sectors, product cycles, and political consequences. *International Organization*, 38, 1–41.

Cumings, B. (1997). *Korea's place in the sun: A modern history*. New York: W.W. Norton & Company.

Domhoff, W. (1990). *The power elite and the state: How policy in made in America*. New York: Aldine De Gruyter.

Domhoff, W. (2006). *Who rules America: Power, politics, and social change* (5th Ed.). New York: McGraw-Hill companies.

Fox, J.D. (1995). Finance capita and the State: An analysis of ownership and control of large corporations in an East Asian newly industrializing country. *Sociological Inquiry*, 65(3/4), 339–364.

Hahn, B.H. (1978). *Communication policies in the Republic of Korea*. Paris: United Nations Educational, Scientific and Cultural Organization.

Hamilton, G., Zeile, W., & Kim, W. (1990). The network structures of East Asian Economies. In S.R. Clegg and G. Redding (eds.), *Capitalism in contrasting culture* (pp. 105–129). Berlin: de Gruyter.

Hart-Landsberg, M. (1993). *The rush to development: Economic change and political struggle in South Korea*. New York: Monthly Review Press.

Hart-Landsberg, M., Jeong, S. & Westra, R. (2007). *Marxist perspectives on South Korea in the global economy*. Burlington, VT: Ashgate.

Hattori, T. (1997). Chaebol-style enterprise development in Korea. *The Developing Economics*, 35(4), 458–477.

Hofstede, G. (1980). *Culture's consequences: International differences in work-related values*. Beverly Hills, CA: Sage.

Hofstede, G. & Bond, M.H. (1988). The Confucius connection: From cultural roots to economic growth. *Organizational Dynamics*, 16(4), 5–21.

Jansen, C. (1988). *Censorship: The knot that binds power and knowledge*. New York: Oxford University Press.

Jeon, S.S. (Ed.). (2002). U.S.-Korean policy and the moderates during the U.S. military government era. In B.B.C. Oh *Korea under the American military government, 1945–1948*. (pp. 79–101). Westport, CT: Praeger.

Jin, D.Y. (2005). *Political economy of communication industry reorganization: Republic of Korea 1987–2003*. Urbana, IL: University of Illinois Press. Dissertation.

Jin, D.Y. (2011). *Hands on/off: The Korean state and the market liberalization of the communication industry*. New York: Hampton.

Jin, D. Y. & Shim, D.B. (2007). Transformation and development of the Korean broadcasting media. In M. Patrick and I. A. Blankson (eds.), *Globalization and media transformation in new and emerging democracies* (pp. 161–176). New York, NY: SUNY Press.

Jung, K.H. (2007). The transformation of the Korean economy after the financial crisis. *Trends and Perspective*, 69, 235–256. Korean.

Kadusin, C. (1995). Friendship among the French financial elite. *American Sociological Review*, 60(2), 202–221.

Kang, J.G. & Kim, W.Y. (1994). A survey of radio and television: History, system and programming. In J.W. Kim & J.W. Lee (Eds.), *Elite media amidst mass culture: A critical look at mass communication in Korea* (pp. 109–136). Seoul, Korea: Nanam.

Kim, B.J. (2003). Paramilitary politics under the USAMGIK and the establishment of the Republic of Korea. *Korea Journal*, Summer, 289–322.Kim, J.B. (2005). *The corporate structure of Korea's chaebol groups*. Seoul, Korea: Nanam. Korea.

Kim, E.M. (1997). *Big business, strong state*. New York: State University of New York Press.

Kim, J.B. (2007). The circular ownership structure of 30 chaebol groups, *The Research of Economic Development*, 13(2), 171–201. Korean.

Kim, J.H. (2006). Family businesses and consultation to them in various countries: Korea. In F.W. Kaslow (Ed.), *Handbook of family business and family business consultation: A global perspective* (pp. 179–202). New York: International Business Press.

Kim, J.W. & Shin, T.S. (1994). The Korean press: A half century of controls, suppression and intermittent resistance. In J.W. Kim & J.W. Lee (Eds.), *Elite media amidst mass culture: A critical look at mass communication in Korea* (pp. 65–108). Seoul, Korea: Nanam.

Kim, K.D. (1976). Political factors in the formation of the entrepreneurial elite in South Korea, *Asian Survey*, 16(5), 465–477.

Kim, K.K. (1994). *The globalization of the Korean advertising industry: History of early penetration of TNAAs and their effects on Korean society*. College State, PA: Pennsylvania State University. Unpublished dissertation.

Kim, K.K. (1996). Advertising in Korea: International challenges and politics. In K.T. Frith (Ed.), *Advertising in Asia: Communication, culture and consumption* (pp. 125–154). Ames, IO: Iowa State University Press.

Kim, T. (2009). Confucianism, Maternities and Knowledge: China, South Korea and Japan, *Springer International Handbooks of Education*, 22(6), 857–872.

Kim, Y.T. (1999). Neoliberalism and the decline of the developmental state. *Journal of Contemporary Asia*, 29(4), 144–161.

Kim, Y.T. (2007). Korean elites: Social networks and power. *Journal of Contemporary Asia*, 37(1), 19–37.

Kim, Y.T. (2008). *Bureaucrats and entrepreneurs: The state and the Chaebol in Korea*. Seoul, Korea: Jimoondang.

Kong, J.J. (1989). *A study on marriage ties among chaebol groups*. Seoul: Ewha Women's University. Unpublished dissertation. Korean.

Kristof, N. & Sanger, D. (1999). How U.S. wooed Asia to let cash flow in, *New York Times*, 16 February.

Kwak, K.S. (2012). *Media and democratic transition in South Korea*. New York: Routledge.

Lee, H.K. (2007). Influence of the vested companies on Chaebol's accumulation in Korea. *The Journal of Historical Management*, 22(1), 187–218.

Lee, J.B. (2010). *A study on state domination of capital under democratic regime: Based on Samsung group*. Incheon, Korea: SeongKong Hoi University. Korean.

Lee, J.H. (1990). *A study with respect to forming monopoly capital in Korea*. Seoul: Seoul National University. Unpublished dissertation. Korean.

Lee, K.K. & Crotty, J. (2001). *Economic performance in post-crisis Korea: A critical perspective on neoliberal restructuring*. Working Paper of Political Economy Research Institute, 23, Amherst: University of Massachusetts.

Lee, M.H. (2008). Transformation of the Korean advertising markets. In S.K. Yun (Ed.), *Korea's advertising* (pp. 69–98). Seoul, Korea: Nanam. Korean.

Lincoln, J.R., Gerlach, M. & Takahashi, P. (1992). Keiretsu networks in the Japanese economy: A dyad analysis of inter-corporate ties. *American Sociological Review*, 57, 561–585.

McNamara, L.D. (1990). *The colonial origins of Korean enterprise, 1910–1945*. New York: Cambridge University Press.

Mills, C.W. (1967). *The power elite* (6th Ed.). New York: Oxford University Press.

Nam, S. (2008). The politics of compressed development in new media: A history of Korean cable television, 1992–2005, *Media, Culture & Society*, 30(5), 641–661.Oh, K.H. (1975). The Origin of chaebol groups in Korea: The social background and stratum of economic elite. *Inmunsaeikwahak*, 20, 207–232. Korean.

Park, C.P. (2002). The American military government and the framework for democracy in South Korea. In B.B.C. Oh (Ed.), *Korea under the American military government, 1945–1948*. (pp. 123–149). Westport, CT: Praeger.

Park, E.Y. (2005). *The process of Korean film's corporation*. Seoul, Korea: Korean Film Foundation. Korean.

Park, M.J., Kim, C.N. & Sohn, B.W. (2000). Modernization, globalization and the powerful state: The Korean media. In J. Curran & M.J. Park (Eds.), *De-westernizing media studies* (pp. 111–123). New York: Routledge.

Ryu, J.K. (1991). The historical change between Korean state and chaebol groups. *The Korean Academy of Business Historian*, 6, 109–125. Korean.

Ryu, T.H., Kim, D.W. & Kim, D.M. & Jung, J.H. (2005). *The corporate governance, informal tie and marriage of chaebol groups*. Seoul, Korea: Nanam. Korean.

Sa, K.I. (1993). *Korea in the world economy*. Washington, DC: Institute for International Economics.

Scott, J. (1986). *Capitalist property and financial power: A comparative study of Britain, the United States and Japan*. Sussex, UK: Wheatsheaf Books.

Secretariat of National Assembly. (2010). *A study about policies about chaebol groups from 1980s to 2000s*. Seoul, Korea: National Assembly. Korean.

Seo, H.J. (2003). *A study about media management of chaebol groups including its reporting in the 1960s*. Seoul, Korea: Yonsei University. Unpublished Thesis. Korean.

Seong, S. (2007). *Institutional and policy reforms to enhance corporate efficiency in Korea*. Seoul, Korea: Korea Development Institute. Korean.

Shanker, M., & Astrachan, J. (1996). Myths and realities: Family business' contribution to the U.S. economy-A framework for assessing family business statistics. *Family Business Review*, 9(2), 107–124.

Silva, F., Majluf, N. & Paredes, R. (2006). Family ties, interlocking directors and performance of business groups in emerging countries: The case of Chile. *Journal of Business Research*, 59, 314–321.

Shim, D.B. (2000). *Korean big business awakens to media industry*. Wisconsin-Madison, WI: University of Wisconsin-Madison. Dissertation.

Shim, D.B. (2008). *Preparing for the post-Korean Wave age*. Paper presented in Korea-Asian academic conference on pop culture formations across East Asia in the 21st century: hybridization or Asianization, February 1–4, Burapha University, Thailand. Chonburi: Burapha University, pp. 14–32.

Seoul Shinmun (2005). *The pulse of chaebol*. Seoul, Korea: Moohan. Korean.

Sjogen H. (2006). Family capitalism within big business. *Scandinavian Economic History Review*, 54(2), 161–186.

Soref, M. & Zeitlin, M. (1987). Finance capital and the internal structure of the capitalist class in the United States. In M.S. Mizurichi & M. Schwartz (Eds.), *Intercorporate relations: The structural analysis of business* (pp. 56–84). New York: Cambridge University Press.

Smythe, D. (1981). *Dependency road: Communications, capitalism, consciousness and Canada*. Norwood, NJ: Ablex.

Song, S.H. (2008). Where is the succession of Samsung for Lee Jae-Yong? *The Wolgan Chosun*, pp. 96–113. Korean.

Ungson, R.G., Steers, R. & Park, S.H. (1997). *Korean enterprise: The quest for globalization*. Boston, MA: Harvard Business Press.

Woo, J.E. (1991). *Race to the swift*. New York: Columbia University Press.

Woo-Cumings, M. (2001). Miracle as prologue: The state and the reform of the corporate sector in Korea. In J.E. Stiglitz & S. Yusuf (Eds.), *Rethinking the East Asia miracle* (pp. 343–377). New York: A Co Publication of the World Bank and Oxford University Press.

Yoizi, I. (1988). *Lee Byung- chul and the empire of Samsung*. Seoul, Korea: The Editorial Room of Dolsam. Korean.

Yoo, Y.C. (1989). *Political transition and press ideology in South Korea*. University Minnesota. Unpublished dissertation.

Yoo, Y.C. (1994). Political economy of television broadcasting in South Korea. In J.W. Kim & J.W. Lee (Eds.), *Elite media amidst mass culture: A critical look at mass communication in Korea* (pp. 191–213). Seoul, Korea: Nanam.

Young, N. (2006). Impact of the zaibatsu on Japan's political economy: Pre and post war period. *International Area Review*, 9(2), 211–236.

Youm, K. H. (1994). Freedom of the press: A legal and ethical perspective. In J.W. Kim & J.W. Lee (Eds.), *Elite media amidst mass culture: A critical look at mass communication in Korea* (pp. 65–108). Seoul, Korea: Nanam.

Yum, J.O. (1987). The practice of Uye-Ri in interpersonal relationships. In D.L. Kincaid (Ed.), *Communication theory: Eastern and Western perspective* (pp. 87–100). San Diego, CA: Academic Press.

Yun, S.K. (Ed.). (2008). The environmental changes in the Korean advertising industry. In S.K. Yun (Ed.), *Korea's advertising* (pp. 11–39). Seoul, Korea: Nanam. Korean.

Zang, X. (1999). Research note: Personalism and corporate networks in Singapore. *Organization Studies*, 20(5), 861–877.

2   The history of Samsung

Given the meteoric rise of Samsung, it's odd that no scholarly work has yet fully covered its complete history from the mid-1930s to the 1990s. The following chapter will do just that. I have drawn much information from documents published by Samsung and its family members. Specifically, I have collected information from books authored by Samsung's founder and his first son,[1] as well as Samsung's web sites,[2] yearbooks[3] and the conglomerate's annual historical books. In addition, I have drawn from academic articles and books in the fields of economics,[4] sociology[5] and mass communications.[6]

I have consulted literature from a wide variety of sources in an effort to document a more informed history of Samsung. My historical review is arranged in the following four sections: 1) Samsung in the Korean economy; 2) corporate governance of the Samsung group; 3) the Lee family's Samsung power complex; and 4) Samsung in the Korean media system.

2.1. Samsung in the Korean economy

Samsung developed its businesses in conjunction with changes in the Korean political economy. As discussed in chapter 1, the Korean political economy shifted from Japanese-sanctioned colonialism to U.S.-imposed post-colonialism and, thereafter, from authoritarian military regimes to neoliberal authoritarian civil governments. Throughout these changes, Samsung diversified from food businesses and low-tech exports to heavy-chemical production and high-tech industries (Kim, 1993). I will discuss the developmental history of Samsung in terms of three periods: establishment (1936–1960), diversification (1960–1987) and reorganization of the New Samsung groups (after 1988–present).

2.1.1. The establishment of the Samsung group

Samsung started its business during the period of Japanese occupation. In 1936, Lee Byung-chul, the founder of Samsung, opened a rice mill and a small transportation company at Masan on the southeastern coast of the Korean Peninsula. At that time, Masan was the largest port city used by imperialist Japan as an exit station to transport exploited Korean resources to battlefields across Asia (Lee, 1986,

p. 25). In 1937, when war broke out between China and Japan, Lee was forced to move his business to Taegu in northeastern Korea, hometown of the political leaders in the military regimes. He established the Samsung General Store exporting dried fruits, dried seafood and general merchandise to Manchuria in northeast mainland China, which at that time was also a Japanese colony. Lee also launched a small flour mill and cotton-processing business. See Table 2.1.

Samsung was financed by the Lee family and the Japanese Bank (Yoizi, 1988, p. 78). The ability to borrow money from the Japanese Bank demonstrated Lee's business competency, as the general public did not have access to such funds. In 1943, Lee acquired liquor companies that manufactured raw and refined rice wine (Yoizi, 1988, p. 78). His business expanded rapidly during World War II when he mobilized workers living in barracks on the grounds of his factories (Cumings, 1997, p. 327). Although Lee did not make huge profits at that time, he learned how to run firms and turn a profit. He also learned how to read the market and when to pursue a business opportunity (Lee, 1986). Lee carefully observed how *zaibatsu*, the pre-war Japanese conglomerates, ran and organized their corporations in Korea. He then applied *zaibatsu* business practices to Samsung's diversification (Cumings, 1997, pp. 306–308).

During the U.S. military administration (1945–1948), Lee Byung-chul moved his business headquarters to Seoul. In 1948, he established the Samsung Trading Corporation, which later became one of the top 10 trading firms[7] (Yoizi, 1988, p. 79). At that time, trading was a high-profit business because it did not require outside capital. It was similar to legal smuggling in that the Rhee regime issued trading licenses to only a few businesses, including Samsung Trading Corporation. Most commodities came from Japanese military storage in Korea and the inventory of Japanese trading firms in Manchuria. After Japan was defeated in World War II, it simply abandoned the military goods it had stored in Manchuria and Korea. This allowed Lee to make huge profits in the trading business. By 1950, Samsung had established trading companies in Masan, Taegu and Seoul. However, the company went bankrupt as a result of the Korean War on June 25, 1950. Lee fled empty-handed to Busan since, except for Busan, the Korean Peninsula was under North Korea's control (Lee, 1989, pp. 12–19).

In spite of the war, Samsung kept growing. After United Nations Forces entered the Korean War in September 1950, relief supplies and capital poured into Korea.

Table 2.1 Businesses in the early years of Samsung

Name	Year Established	Business	Additional Information
Hapdong	1936	Rice milling	Joint company
Inchul	1937 (acquisition)	Transportation	Borrowed money from Japanese
Kyung-nam	–	Real estate	
Samsung Corporation	1938	Trade	Capitals from bank loans
Chosun Alcohols	1943 (acquisition)	Brewery	Korean wine; sake

Source: Author's elaboration from Yoizi, 1988; Lee, 1989.

The U.S. provided the financial resources and materials necessary to reconstruct Korea for the Rhee regime as the U.S. considered Korea an anti-communism bulwark in East Asia (Cumings, 1997). Along with these external conditions, Samsung grew rapidly between 1946 and 1960 because of political favors from the Rhee regime. The Korean War through postwar recovery was a period of extensive state-supported diversification for Samsung. President Rhee provided foreign aid and capital for Samsung to diversify its businesses in the areas of food, trading, sugar refining, liquor, textiles and clothing. Rhee also guaranteed monopolized rights in the manufacturing markets and selected Samsung as a priority firm for contracts on national projects (Cumings, 1997). Samsung further expanded its business to include banks, security, insurance, fertilizer and cement in the late 1950s (Samsung, 1998, pp. 42–61).

During this time, Samsung founded three important firms that marked its emergence as an empire: Samsung Corporation (a trading company); Cheil Foods and Chemicals (a food firm); and Cheil Wool and Textile Corporation (a clothing firm). The Samsung Corporation, established in 1951, was in charge of exporting and importing military materials (e.g., scrap iron), sugar and fertilizers during the Korean War. While imposing strict limits on other firms, the Rhee regime set Samsung's export quota at approximately 50,000 tons of scrap iron. With Rhee's assistance, Samsung Corporation became a central node responsible for importing the raw materials needed by Samsung and for exporting industrial products produced by Samsung.

Cheil Foods and Chemicals, established in 1953, was in charge of processing sugar, flour and canned food. Because of deficient production in domestic markets and heavy dependence on importation, items produced by Cheil Foods and Chemicals were considered the golden geese. Enormous profits were possible for firms that succeeded in localizing these goods. However, the food business required huge amounts of money and large factory sites. This meant that no firm could start a food business without favors from the Korean state. The Rhee regime, via the Chosun Bank, loaned Samsung approximately U.S. $180,000, the cost of the equipment needed to fund Cheil Foods and Chemicals. They also provided factory sites to Samsung at cheap prices (Lee, 1989). It is thus not surprising that from 1954 to 1956, the average annual rate of growth of Cheil Foods and Chemicals was 93 percent (Kim, 1993, p. 28).

In 1954, Samsung founded the Cheil Wool and Textile Corporation, which was responsible for its clothing business. Like Cheil Foods and Chemicals, the clothing firm also received favors from the Rhee regime in terms of the cost of equipment and factory sites. The Rhee regime equipped Cheil Wool and Textile with spinning machines from West Germany. Although the spinning machines were technically a national asset, Samsung retained exclusive use of them (Yoizi, 1988, p. 78; Lee, 1989, pp. 20–28). The Cheil Wool and Textile Corporation grew rapidly at an average annual rate of 91 percent between 1956 and 1960 (Kim, 1993, p. 28). Such successful ventures enabled Samsung to become the largest company in Korea during the 1950s (Yoizi, 1988, p. 79). In addition to its manufacturing businesses, Samsung also took over three of the five commercial banks controlled by the Rhee regime: the Hanil Bank in 1957; the Commercial Bank of Korea in 1958; and the Chohung Bank of Korea in 1959. Samsung acquired Chunil Security in 1957 and Ahn Kun Fire Insurance in 1958. As for heavy chemicals, Samsung acquired Samchuk Cement in 1957 and Honam Fertilizer and Hankuk Tier in 1958 (Kim, 1993). That is to say, Samsung had already established the foundation to become a chaebol conglomerate by the late 1950s, nearly a decade ahead of other chaebol contenders (Choi, 2014).

In the 1960s, Samsung diversified further into heavy chemicals and made inroads in the insurance and service industries. Samsung established the Ulsan Fertilizer company in 1961. It acquired the Hanil Nylon Company and the Daehan Oil Refining Company in 1963. Hankuk Fertilizer was added in 1964, and the Jeonju paper-manufacturing company was acquired in 1965. Samsung also aggressively pursued financial subsidiaries. After purchasing Dong-Yang Fire Insurance in 1962, Samsung acquired three more insurance firms the following year: Ahn-Kuk Fire and Marine Insurance, Dongbang Fire and Marine Insurance and Tong-Yang Fire and Marine.[8] In addition to these acquisitions and mergers, Samsung poached several service subsidiaries including the Dongbang Department Store,[9] Dong-Nam Security and Dong-Hwa Real East.[10] In 1964, after Samsung sold Taegu University, SungKunkwan University became one of its properties. In 1965, Samsung established the Korea Hospital[11] and the Samsung Cultural Foundation.[12] In the same year, Samsung acquired a seasoning corporation and a paper-processing firm (Yoizi, 1988).

In 1963, Samsung began building the Hankuk Fertilizer Corporation, the largest fertilizer factory in Asia. Lee Byung-chul borrowed construction funds from foreign companies, in large part from the Japanese firm Mitzi. He imported raw materials as well as machines to manufacture fertilizer (Lee, 1993, p. 124). In the process, Samsung illegally imported raw materials such as saccharine, whole wheat, cement and the machinery needed to process raw food. As a result, Lee Byung-chul announced in 1967 that he would give up the fertilizer business, donate 51 percent of the Hankuk Fertilizer[13] stock to the Park regime and resign as chairman of Samsung (Kim, 1988, p. 110; Lee, 1993, pp. 130–180). Lee's actions show that Samsung was not above illegal activities if they served the cause of diversification.

In 1969, Lee Byung-chul returned to the position of Samsung chairman and established the Samsung Electronics Company (SEC). Chairman Lee forged connections with transnational corporations in order to acquire the technological and financial resources needed for further expansion. Park Jung-hee, the ruler during that period, accommodated the growth of Samsung in electronics by enforcing favorable regulations such as the Basic Plan for Electronics Industry Promotion and the Electronics Industry Promotion Law. These regulations reduced corporate taxes by up to 50 percent for export incomes, exempted tariffs for imported raw materials, provided low-interest loans for export industries/firms and established the Korean Trade Promotion Corporation and the Korean Foreign Trade Association to provide information about overseas markets (Kim, 1993).

In the 1970s, Samsung particularly strengthened its electronics and semiconductor business. Lee Byung-chul actively set up joint ventures with TNCs to acquire investment and technology (Kim, 1997, pp. 131–163). Samsung received technology transfers from TNCs, mainly from electrical and electronics corporations, but also in the areas of shipbuilding, textiles and petrochemicals. In these areas, Lee preferred joint ventures and formed Samsung subsidiaries of Japanese TNCs like Sanyo and the Nippon Electric Corporation. Samsung-Sanyo Electric produced its first TV sets in 1970. At first, most TVs were exported because local demand was small. Production of television sets for the domestic market began in 1972, followed by refrigerators and washing machines. In the latter half of the 1970s, Lee Byung-chul decided to expand Samsung's modest electronics business into semiconductor chips since he considered this field to be the future of the electronics business (Lee, 1993, pp. 194–230).

Along with the electronic businesses, Samsung kept expanding into heavy chemicals, hotels, machinery, construction and even a theme park in the 1970s. Between 1972 and 1974, Samsung's operations in heavy chemicals included agricultural chemicals, petrochemical manufacturing, paints, coatings and other finishing product manufacturing, as well as plastic and fiber manufacturing. In 1973, Samsung established the Hotel Shillar. Samsung's machinery businesses included shipbuilding, automobiles, aerospace products, trains and helicopters. From 1975 to 1978, Samsung established a variety of construction companies in the fields of heavy and civil engineering, nonresidential and residential construction and highway and street construction (Samsung, 1998).

In the 1980s, Samsung expanded its holdings in knowledge-based industries. Specifically, since 1982, Samsung has owned and operated commercial building maintenance and securities services. The same year the Korean government encouraged chaebol groups to establish professional baseball teams, Samsung launched a professional sports business. In 1984, Samsung established a medical system with a focus on pharmacies, hospitals and nursing. The following year, Samsung entered into the computer-mediated communication business by founding Samsung SDS. This company produced technology and systems for computer-based communication such as Internet chatting, e-commerce and Internet content (Lee, 1997). Further, in 1986, Samsung established the Samsung Economic Research Institute (SERI) based on Lee Kun-hee's suggestion. SERI has conducted research for both Samsung internal projects and Korea's long-term vision relative to economic, political and social issues. SERI focuses on promoting neoliberal thinking on the news by providing special information for journalists (SERI, 2006; Kim, 2007).

In brief, since Lee Byung-chul established Samsung in 1936, Samsung has diversified its economic activities, moving into food, textiles, petrochemicals, heavy industry, electronics, service businesses and finance. The 1960s saw the first stage of Samsung's diversification into chemicals, insurance, real estate, department stores, hotels, universities, cultural foundations and media. In the 1970s, Samsung focused on heavy industry and electronics. By the mid-1980s, Samsung covered almost all Korean economic sectors. Samsung's entrance into petrochemicals, heavy industry and electronics was bolstered by the shift in national economic policies from light industry (e.g., textiles, wigs and toys) to heavy and chemical industries (petrochemicals, fertilizer and electronics). With the encouragement of the Korean state, Samsung evolved from a low-technology operation into heavy chemicals and electronics (Kim, 1993; Kang, 1997). In 1987, Samsung's founder Lee passed away. The new Samsung chairman, Lee Kun-hee, oversaw the rise of the new Samsung groups.

2.1.2. New Samsung groups

In November 1987 upon the death of Lee Byung-chul, Samsung entered a new phase. Lee Kun-hee, his third son, took charge of the conglomerate. Unlike his father, Lee Kun-hee upgraded Samsung's position from an original equipment manufacturer (OEM) of developed Western TNCs to a transnational corporation in the global market. After founding the Samsung Winners Card in 1988, Lee Kun-hee expanded its financial businesses to include investments, savings and loans, securities and insurance (life, fire, marine and casualty). However, he did not own any commercial banks because the Korean state did not allow chaebol groups to control them (Samsung, 1998, pp. 172–173). In 1993, Chairman Lee announced "Samsung's New Management." Its goal was to restructure Samsung from a focus on cheap, quantity-oriented production to high-quality production and distribution. Under the leadership of the new Chairman Lee, Samsung's management style changed from a cautious, conservative business approach to one that saw risk as opportunity (Rowley & Bae, 2003, p. 197). Samsung reformed and aggressively took businesses risks, discarding the old management styles (Samsung, 1998, pp. 212–289). This reform also included radical changes in working hours and practices, as well as the decentralization of operations and authority. Samsung introduced new working practices in order to facilitate the company's internationalization and technological advance. The firm hired more professional managers than before and focused on electronics as a core field. Samsung also empowered the majority of its top executives and engineers who were familiar with technological challenges (Dodgson & Kim, 1997, pp. 57–58).

In addition to management reform, Chairman Lee employed both horizontal integration and spin-off[14] in the Samsung Electronics Company. Samsung added 28 firms in this period, 24 of which were built and 4 of which were acquired. Among the firms' industries were included 9 firms in the electronics and electric industry, 3 companies in heavy machinery and 3 in petrochemicals. Samsung consciously focused many of its business resources on the booming electronics industry. The Samsung Electronics Company was the core firm controlling other subsidiaries that produced the parts, components and materials for electronics. Together with its vertical expansion in electronics, Samsung diversified horizontally into the service areas important for people with high incomes or advanced age (Kang, 1997, p. 43). As a result, Samsung became a transnational corporation with a focus on digital devices in the 1990s. SEC played a central role in transnationalizing Samsung. It became the largest producer of dynamic random access memory (DRAM) and memory chips, owning 62 overseas offices in 50 countries. Samsung also owned 8 domestic and 13 international research and development

(R&D) centers established alongside regions or institutions that specialized in scientific and technological expertise. Under the control of Samsung, domestic and global R&D centers maintained cooperative relationships (Dodgson & Kim, 1997, 57–64).

Transforming Samsung from a domestic conglomerate to a transnational corporation, Lee Kun-hee regrouped Samsung's businesses into six corporations in the 1990s: Samsung (electronics, finance, heavy chemicals, information technology, advertising and trading); CJ (food, bio-chemical and audio-visual media businesses); Saehan (textiles and components of digital devices); Shinsaegae (department stores and retail); Hansol (a paper-manufacturing company and telecommunication); and JoongAng Ilbo (telecommunication devices, convenience stores and media). More specifically, Lee Kun-hee divided the shares of Samsung among five people: a brother, two sisters, a nephew and a brother in-law. Lee In-hee, the eldest sister of Lee Kun-hee, inherited Hansol in 1993. Lee Chang-hee, the second brother of Lee Kun-Hee, became responsible for running Saehan in 1995. Lee Myung-hee, the youngest sister of Lee Kun-hee, was in charge of distribution businesses with a focus on retail and department stores in 1997. Lee Kun-hee transferred the shares of CJ to his nephew Lee Jae-hyun in 1997. Finally, Samsung transferred shares of both the JoongAng Ilbo and some parts of its manufacturing businesses to Lee's brother-in-law, Hong Seok-hyun, in 1999 (Seoul Shinmun, 2005, pp. 12–150).

In short, after starting as a small rice mill in 1936, Lee Byung-chul expanded Samsung from a low-tech manufacturer to a heavy-chemical producer and, finally, to a high-tech conglomerate (see Table 2.2). Founder Lee also maintained a close relationship with the Korean state in order to receive favors.

Table 2.2 Samsung's diversification from the 1930s to the 1990s

Period	Industry	Businesses
1936–1945		Trading, rice milling, baking bricks
1945–1948	Food	Rice wine, yeast
1950s	Finance	Five commercial banks, security, insurance
	Food	Sugar, flour, food processing
	Clothing	Textiles, wool
1960s	Petro-Petrochemicals	Fertilizer, nylon, paper processing
	Electronics	Electronics
	Medicine	Hospitals and pharmaceuticals
	Finance	Insurance (life, fire and marine) and securities
	Distribution	Department stores
	Education	Universities
	Mass media	Newspaper and television and radio stations
	Other	Real estate, cultural foundations
1970s	Petro-Petrochemical	Agricultural chemicals, paints, plastic and fiber manufacturing
	Machinery	Shipbuilding, automobile, aerospace and trains

Period	Industry	Businesses
	Construction	Heavy and civil engineering, nonresidential and residential construction and highway and street construction
	Electronics	Semiconductors, household appliance and consumer products
	eisure	Theme park and hotel
	Mass media	Advertising
1980s	Security	System security
	Medicine	Pharmacies, hospitals and nursing
	Sports	Professional baseball team
	Mass media	Recorded music, computer-mediated communication
1990s	Mass media	Cable television, online newspaper and film

Source: Author's elaboration on Kim, 1993, pp. 169–172; Kang, 1997; Seoul Shinmun, 2005.

After Lee Byung-chul died in 1987, Lee Kun-hee, the third son of the founder Lee, transformed Samsung into a multinational corporation. He broke Samsung into six corporations: Samsung, Hansol, Saehan, Shinsaegae, CJ and JoongAng Ilbo. Each new corporation was controlled by a Lee family member. Except for Saehan, the new corporations are members of chaebol groups. Samsung is a first-tier chaebol. Hansol, Shinsaegae, CJ and JoongAng Ilbo are second-tier chaebol groups. Saehan was assigned to the commercial banks (Seoul Shinmun, 2005).

2.2. Corporate governance of the Samsung group

Samsung's corporate governance, or Samsungism, is rooted in the founding philosophy of Samsung established by Lee Byung-chul to legitimate his family's control over what would become the Samsung Empire. Samsungism is based on three major principles: business for national interests (*saupbokuk*); support for talented people first (*injaejeil*); and the pursuit of rationalism (*haprichuku*) (Lee, 1986, pp. 40–247).

The principle of business for national interests indicates that Samsung regards its development in the same light as that of the Korean economy. Founder Lee Byung-chul emphasized the organic relationship between national development and Samsung businesses. As each Korean maintains a Korean identity without Korean nationality, so should the businesses in Samsung (Lee, 1986, P. 46). Although Samsung's development was based on political favors from authoritarian regimes, Lee offers a slightly skewed perspective on this relationship. In his view, Korean economic development was attributed to the contributions of Samsung. In essence, Lee based the first Samsung principle on the economic nationalism of Korea.

The second Samsung principle is support for talented people first. This ideology illustrates Samsung's management style with respect to employees (Hoam Foundation, 1997; pp. 64–125). Samsung implants elitism among staff using the mantra, "Samsung treats you best. Thus, you are the best." This suggests that Samsung respects the discretionary power of its employees. However, Samsung tightly controls new staff, training them to become Samsung men who will show loyalty to the Lee family and produce outstanding results for the company (Kim, 2010). Since the 1950s, Samsung has regularly educated new employees and existing ones to become Samsung men, evaluating them at the end of every year. Staff members receive various rewards or punishments based on their performance evaluation by the Lee family. Those receiving high marks are promoted, while others are left behind. Thus, Samsung's control and management of personnel is a meritocracy centered on the delivery of capitalistic results.

The final Samsung principle is the pursuit of rationalism to maximize profits. The management style of Samsung is fundamentally based on long-term profits. The Lee family has the final decision on whether to enter new businesses (Lee, 1986). For example, Lee Byung-chul decided that Samsung would strengthen its semiconductor businesses in the early 1980s. Since the semiconductor businesses required huge amounts of money and high technology at that time, the think tanks within the conglomerate and its business allies held strongly opposing viewpoints about Samsung's expansion into the semiconductor business. Lee Byung-chul, contrary to conventional wisdom, decided to make semiconductors the core business of Samsung. Despite early setbacks and challenges, Samsung had become one of the top three semiconductor firms in the world within a decade (Samsung, 1998, pp. 111–121).

As to the ownership structures of Samsung, the Lee family is the largest stockholder, which holds at most 10 percent of the value of the Samsung group (Kim, 2007). Instead of direct control with stocks over all its multiple subsidiaries, the Lee family controls the Samsung group through a circular corporate structure, a complex web of ownership within the Samsung group. Under a pyramid ownership structure, Chairman Lee Kun-hee and his family members became the largest stockholders of a de facto holding company located at the top of the Samsung ownership structure. This holding company maintains an interlocked ownership and uses a few leading subsidiaries within the entire Samsung group to dominate over the sub-groups. For example, the Lee family is the largest stockholder of Samsung Everland, a de facto holding company of Samsung and the largest theme park in Korea. Other major stockholders of Samsung Everland include Samsung Electronics Company, Samsung Corporation and Cheil Wool and Textile Corporation. These leading companies share ownership and control multiple sub-subsidiaries in multiple economic sectors. This interlocked ownership structure between a de facto holding company and a few core holdings allows the Lee family to institutionally control the Samsung Empire either directly or through layered structures (Song, 2014).

This hierarchical order exists within the Lee family as well. At the top of the hierarchy is Chairman Lee Kun-hee, who exercises his power over all members of the Lee family. The relationship between the chairman and his family is based on filial piety and an authoritarian hierarchy reflecting the influence of Confucianism and patriarchy. Top executive positions are also occupied by prominent Lee family members. While a key executive position in the subsidiaries may be rationed to nonmembers, Lee's family holds the right to appoint or dismiss any executives who are responsible for managing subsidiaries under the Samsung flagship (Kim, 1997, pp. 55–58).

Equally important is the structural planning office, which plays a vital role in maintaining the hierarchical corporate structure of Samsung (Kim, 2005). The structural planning office belongs to the chairman's office at the apex of the hierarchical structure. Chairman Lee rarely involves himself in the workings of the structural planning office, but regularly meets with its director and a few of its sub-directors. The director of the structural planning office, appointed by Chairman Lee, is Samsung's second-in-command. He accounts for all affairs of the structural planning office. This office is in charge of 1) personnel management; 2) financial affairs and the Lee family's assets; 3) account auditing as a supervisory tool for internal deals related to Samsung; 4) promotion and public relations for enhancing Samsung's image; 5) information gathering about the power elites, including political leaders and high officers in the National Tax Service and public prosecutors; and 6) legal issues related to Samsung's internal and external affairs (Kang, 1997; Song, 2006). Members of the structural planning office come from Samsung's subsidiaries. Without permission of the chairman, however, it is impossible to become a member of this control tower (Kim, 2010).

To recap, the Lee family is the Samsung Empire, controlling its corporate structures and wielding influence from the structural planning office, which in turn controls the CEOs of its affiliates. Although the CEOs in Samsung's subsidiaries exercise power over their organizations, they are ultimately under the control of the structural planning office, which represents Chairman Lee and his family. Because of the pyramid-like structure through which power flows, the management style of Samsung is known as "emperor-like management" (Kim & Kim, 2008).

2.3. The Lee family's Samsung power complex

Samsung founder Lee has further strengthened Samsung's position by marriages of his children to Korean power elites. This has allowed him to receive favors from the military regimes and establish a power complex between the Lee family and the Korean power elites.

Lee Byung-chul (1910–1987) was born in Uiryeong-gun in the southeastern part of the Korean Peninsula. His father was a landlord, enabling Lee Byung-chul to study at Waseda University in Japan. Although he did not graduate, he started working at a small general store in the mid-1930s (Lee, 1986, pp. 10–20). Lee rarely made big money during the time of the Japanese occupation. However, his experience during the Japanese occupation period taught him how to forge connections with the power elites. For example, Lee Byung-chul conducted his businesses in Taegu, the southern center of Kyongsang Province, during the American military occupation (1945–1948). During this time, he organized a friendly society called "Ulyuhoi" and invited most of the managers appointed by the U.S. military to become members. Members of Ulyuhoi were Korean power elites who had a close relationship with the American military government. Through his experience with Ulyuhoi, Lee realized the power of informal ties, which later played important roles in the expansion of Samsung's businesses (Lee, 1989; Kim, 2007). He was granted a special license, one not available to ordinary people, to manage the largest factory of rice wine in Korea and produce refined rice wine (Yoizi, 1988, p. 78). Possession of this liquor license was a result of Lee's adeptness at forging informal ties.

During the post-colonial period (1948–1960) and the authoritarian regimes (1961–1987), Lee Byung-chul used regional ties to connect with power elites. These ties involved connections based on hometown geography and early educational locations (e.g., high schools) (Kim, 2007). Most Korean power elites came from the Kyongsang Province, the most powerful region of Korea. Lee Byung-chul contacted retired high officials from political and military realms whose hometowns were in the Kyongsang Province and recruited them to high positions within Samsung subsidiaries. Through these connections, Lee formed a network with the Korean power elites (Yoizi, 1988, pp. 84–87).

Lee also extended his family's connection to the Korean power elites through the marriages of his three sons and five daughters (Kong, 1989). As seen in Table 2.3, marriage was a key mechanism for creating social ties between the Lee family and Korean power elites. His children married children of political leaders, an ex-cabinet member, chaebol group leaders, a Japanese businessman, a hospital owner and a professor. The new family members, added by marriage, were involved in Samsung's management as executives or top managers. Lee and his relatives by marriage cooperated to expand Samsung's businesses and form a power group among their companies (Yoizi, 1988, pp. 81–86; Ryu, et al., 2005, pp. 338–339).

Specifically, Lee's first son, Lee Mang-hee, married Sohn Bok-nam, a daughter of the Kyonggi governor as well as the owner of the Ahn-Kuk insurance company. Since the early 1970s, however, Lee Mang-hee has not been involved in

Table 2.3 Children of Lee Byung-chul and their spouses

Child	Spouse	New Samsung
1st daughter	A son of the owner of the Korean Hospital (renamed the Kangbuk Samsung Hospital)	Hansol
1st son	A daughter of the governor in Kyonggi Province and owner of the Ahn-Kuk insurance company	CJ
2nd son	A daughter of the owner of MMKA, a Japanese company	Saehan
2nd daughter	The third son of the LG group	
3rd daughter	A professor at SeoKang University	
4th daughter	A son of a middle-class person	
3rd son	A daughter of an ex-cabinet member	Samsung JoongAng Ilbo
5th daughter	A son of the owner of Dongbang Department	Shinsaegae

Source: Author's elaboration from Yoizi, 1988, p. 83; Seoul Shinmun, 2005, pp. 15–38.

Samsung's businesses because Lee Byung-chul designated Lee Kun-hee, his third son, as his heir in the mid-1970s (Yoizi, 1988, p. 81). Instead of Lee Mang-hee, his children and his wife's family members became involved in Samsung's food business, CJ (see Table 2.4). Lee Jae-hyun, the first son of Lee Mang-hee, was the owner of CJ (Kong, 1989; Seoul Shinmun, 2005, pp. 100–116). Lee Myung-hee also had one more son and a daughter, both of whom have been involved in CJ's businesses as high managers.

The second son, Lee Chang-hee, married a Japanese woman, the daughter of the owner of MMKA. Although he was one of his father's closest assistants, he was not appointed as Samsung's successor. After being jailed for smuggling saccharin in the case of the Hankuk Fertilizer Corporation in 1967, he was relegated to manage a paper company, a videocassette and audiocassette company and textile firms (Yoizi, 1988, p. 83; Seoul Shinmun, 2005, pp. 58–70). Lee Chang-hee had three sons and a daughter, all of whom married other members of chaebol groups, including the DongA, the Dongbang and the Life group.

The third son, Lee Kun-hee, married Hong Ra-hee, a daughter of Hong Jin-gi (1917–1986), who had been a judge during the period of Japanese occupation and an ex-cabinet member in the Rhee regime (see Table 2.5). Hong Jin-gi played the role of mediator in connecting the Lee family to Korean political elites. Through the

Table 2.4 Children of Lee Mang-hee, first son of Samsung's founder

Child	Spouse	Education	Position
1st son	Daughter of a middle-class person	Korean University	Chairman of CJ
2nd son	Daughter of a politician	Taiwan University	CJ general director
Only daughter	Divorced	Seoul National University	Vice chairman of CJ

Source: Author's elaboration from Seoul Shinmun, 2005, pp. 100–138.

Table 2.5 Brothers and sisters of Hong Ra-hee, wife of Lee Kun-hee

Sibling	Spouse	Education	Position
1st brother-in-law	A daughter of the director of the Agency of National Security Planning	Seoul National University Stanford PhD	Owner of the JoongAng Ilbo group
2nd brother-in-law	A daughter of a politician	Seoul National University	Ex-high prosecutor
3rd brother-in-law	N/A	Seoul National University	CEO of Bokwang group
4th brother-in-law	N/A	Seoul National University	CEO of Phoenix Communication
1st sister-in-law	A son of ex-prime minister	Ehwa Women's University	Director of Samsung Culture

Source: Seoul Shinmun, 2005, pp. 31–34.

Hong family, founder Lee Byung-chul deepened connected to the Korean power elites. The children of Hong Jin-gi married children of chaebol groups and powerful politicians, such as Lee Hoo-rak, ex-chief head of the Agency for National Security Planning (the Korean equivalent of the CIA) under the Park regime, and Keun Jin-ho, an ex-cabinet member in the Chun regime (Ryu, et al., 2005, p. 338).

Hong Jin-gi made certain his six children received an elite education. All of them graduated from Seoul National University (the equivalent of Harvard University in the U.S.). He had four sons and two daughters. Hong Ra-hee, his first daughter, is the wife of Lee Kun-hee and holds several high positions in cultural foundations sponsored by Samsung. Hong Seok-hyun, his first son, is an owner of the JoongAng Ilbo group. Hong Seok-jo, his second son, was an ex-chief high prosecutor. Hong Seok-jun, his third son, was the vice chairman of Samsung SDI. Hong Seok-kyu, his youngest son, was the chairman of an affiliated firm of Bokwang group. Hong Ra-yong, his youngest daughter, married the second son of Rho Shin-yong, an ex-prime minister (Seoul Shinmun, 2005, pp. 30–34).

Lee Kun-hee and Hong Ra-hee have three children: son Lee Jae-yong; daughter Lee Pu-jin; and daughter Lee Seo-hyun (see Table 2.6), all of whom have held high positions within Samsung. Lee Jae-yong, the only son of Lee Kun-hee, married a daughter of Daesang, a second-tier chaebol conglomerate, but later divorced her. Lee Pu-jin, the first daughter of Lee Kun-hee, is married to an ordinary person from the middle class. The other daughter, Lee Seo-hyun, is married to the second son of the *DongA Ilbo*, one of the big three Korean daily newspapers.

Samsung's women have limited involvement in the daily management of the firms, in spite of their substantial share of ownership (Kim, 1997, pp. 57–69). The founder's eldest daughter, Lee In-hui, was responsible for Hansol, which focuses on both paper manufacturing and telecommunications. She did not have an official title, but was a powerful adviser. She married Cho Uhn-hae (1925–), a son of the owner of the Korea Hospital (renamed the Kangbuk Samsung Hospital) (Seoul Shinmun, 2005, pp. 118–132). Lee Byung-chul's second daughter, Lee Suk-hui, is married to Ku Ja-hak, the third son of the LG group, a first-tier chaebol conglomerate. Through this marriage tie, Samsung connected to other members of chaebol groups (e.g., Daelim, Hanjin and Doosan) and ultimately to ex-president

Table 2.6 Children of Lee Kun-hee, the owner of Samsung

Child	Spouse	Education	Position
Only son	A daughter of Daesang (a second-tier chaebol group)	Seoul National University Harvard	CEO of Samsung Electronics Company
1st daughter	A son of a middle-class person	Yonsei University	CEO of Hotel Shila
2nd daughter	The second son of the *DongA Ilbo*	Parsons New School for Design	Vice CEO of Cheil Textile

Source: Author's elaboration from Seoul Shinmun, 2005, pp. 22–30; Song, 2014.

Park Jung-hee, an ex-prime minister of Kim Jong-phil and an ex-cabinet member of Kim Dong-jo (Ryu, et al., 2005, p. 338).

The third daughter, Lee Sun-hui, is married to Kim Kyu, a professor in the communications department of SeoKang University. For a few years, her husband worked at a broadcasting firm, TBC, as a general manager. Lee Duk-hee, his fourth daughter, is married to a Samsung man, Lee Jong-ki, a general manager of JoongAng Ilbo (Yoizi, 1988, p. 83). Finally, Lee Myung-hui, his fifth daughter, is a major stockholder and a managing director of Shinsaegae, a second-tier chaebol conglomerate. Shinsaegae businesses include retail, department stores, civil construction, food processing, hotels and a system integration company. She is married to Jung Jae-un, the third son of the owner of Dong Bang Insurance. Unlike the founder Lee's other daughters, the eldest and the youngest have been actively involved in Samsung's businesses.

In summary, Lee Byung-chul used informal ties (e.g., blood, marriage and region) to establish a power bloc within the corporate structures of Samsung. Through regional ties, Lee Byung-chul connected to political elites in order to receive political favors. With marriage ties between the Lee family and Korean power elites, Lee cemented a power complex within Samsung's corporate structures. Further, Lee willed Samsung to his third son and allowed his other children to be involved in Samsung's businesses (Seoul Shinmun, 2005, pp. 15–150).

2.4. Samsung in the Korean media system

Samsung was the first member among chaebol groups to enter the Korean broadcasting and newspaper industries in the 1960s (Seo, 2003). Since then, it has increased its media holdings to include advertising, computer-mediated communication, video production, cable television, film and digital media industries (Kim, 2002).

Chronologically speaking, Samsung entered the Korean media market in 1963 when it 1) established the JoongAng television station serving Seoul and Pusan, Korea's second-largest city, and 2) founded the Tongyang Broadcasting Company (TBC) broadcasting FM radio in Seoul. Samsung later combined the JoongAng television station with TBC. In 1965, Lee Byung-chul and Hong Gin-gi co-founded the *JoongAng Ilbo*, modeled on Japanese daily newspapers such as the *Asahi*, the *Yomiuri* and the *Minitz* (Samsung, 1998). Hong Gin-gi was an ex-cabinet member in the Rhee Seung-man regime and the father of Hong Ra-hee, the wife of Lee Kun-hee, the current owner of Samsung. Hong Gin-gi and Lee Byung-chul maintained a close relationship with each other as personal friends, family members by marriage and business partners (Lee, 1986.; Yoizi, 1988, p. 85). Lee Byung-chul provided financial support for the *JoongAng Ilbo*, while Hong Gin-gi was involved in managing the newspaper (Samsung, 1998, p. 86, Seoul Shinmun, 2005, pp. 470–472). In 1966, Samsung further expanded its empire by establishing Samsung Everland, a theme park, which was the first amusement park in Korea.

In the 1970s, Samsung set up Samsung Publishing (1972) and Cheil Communication (1973), mainly to establish media holdings and support Samsung's corporations. Samsung owned almost 90 subsidiaries in the manufacturing industries. Each holding needed a publishing corporation to distribute its information to the public as well as to Samsung's subsidiaries. The role of Cheil Communication was similar to that of Samsung Publishing. In fact, Cheil Communication was the in-house advertising agency of Samsung that provided full services for its clients – from marketing strategies, advertising production and media planning to consumer research (Kim, 1994, p. 178; Samsung, 1998, pp. 460–462). Most of Cheil Communication's clients were Samsung's subsidiaries in the food, clothing, electronics, chemicals, machinery and construction industries.

The 1980s for Samsung was a decade of ups and downs. Samsung had to give up TBC, a broadcasting network, in 1980 because the Chun Doo-whan regime (1980–1987) would not allow chaebol groups to own network broadcasting stations. The Chun regime wanted to control the mass media and forcefully integrated TBC into the Korea Broadcasting System (KBS). Although Samsung lost TBC, it did not lose its other media businesses. At this time, Samsung jumped into the video business for two reasons: First, Samsung was a major manufacturer of visual devices (e.g., VHS and VCRs) and wanted to create more demand. Second, as the videotape market gradually increased, Samsung entered into video production. Its main customers were the general population since the two network broadcasting stations, Korea Broadcasting System (KBS) and Munhwa Broadcasting Company (MBC), directly produced television drama and entertainment shows and imported foreign movies and television drama to fill their schedules (Park, 1994;Choi, 1998).

In 1984, Samsung founded Starmax as a subsidiary of Samsung Corporation, a trade subsidiary of Samsung. Starmax, whose brand name was Dreambox, was responsible for producing movies on VHS and importing foreign films for customers after the Chun regime opened the Korean film market to Hollywood (Park, 1994). This experience in the video business helped Samsung recognize the potential growth of the film industry (Jin, 2005, p. 119). In the following year, 1985, Samsung established Samsung SDS, which has been responsible for developing software for computer-based communication, including Internet chatting, online games and e-commerce. Most of the customers have been private corporations and government institutions rather than individuals (Lee, 1997, pp. 123–134). In 1989, Samsung also established Cheil-Bozell, a joint venture with Bozell, a U.S. company responsible for facilitating joint ventures between Samsung and foreign companies in Korea.

In the 1990s, Samsung established Orange, brand name Nices, a recorded music subsidiary of Cheil Communication (Variety, 1997). When the Korean government launched cable television in 1993, Samsung was allocated only two cable channels: a paid channel, Catch One, and a documentary channel. Instead of establishing an independent holding, Samsung added a cable business to Cheil Communication, the advertising agency of Samsung. To prepare media content for the paid channel Catch One, Samsung made exclusive licensing agreements with Disney, Warner Brothers, Paramount, Twentieth Century Fox and Universal Studios. Samsung's basic cable channel, Channel Q (the Korean equivalent of the Discovery Channel), made program supply contracts with Japan's NHK, BBC and Discovery. Samsung also invested U.S. $60 million for a 7.6 percent stake of the independent Hollywood studio New Regency Productions to guarantee Korean distribution rights to films made by that studio (Shim, 2002).

Two years later, in 1995, Samsung reorganized its audio-visual businesses. They launched the Samsung Entertainment Group (SEG), which was responsible for incorporating the previously separate film, music and cable industries into a single unit. SEG also opened an annual Scenario Contest and Short Film Festival to showcase promising local directors and writers. They also co-produced films with foreign film directors and provided television drama and animation for network television (Variety, 1997).

SEG played a central role in applying advanced business know-how, including systematic planning, marketing and accounting, to the media subsidiaries under Samsung. For example, SEG held independent film festivals and film scenario contests with considerable cash prizes, supported young directors with degrees from prestigious film schools all over the world and hired competent staff members from diverse lines of business within chaebol groups (Shim, 2008). In 1995, CJ, a subsidiary of old Samsung, established CJ Media, which was responsible for cable television (Lee, 2008, pp. 92–94). In the film industry, CJ founded Dreamworks SKG, a film and drama importer from Hollywood in 1995 (Ahn, 2007, pp. 14–18). In 1997, CJ entered the film exhibition business by establishing Gold Village, the first multiplex theater in Korea (Ahn, 2007, pp. 22–23).

To summarize, Samsung, including the CJ and JoongAng Ilbo[15] groups, owned media holdings across the media industries from the 1960s to 1997 as seen in Table 2.7. Since these conglomerates entered the broadcasting industry in the 1960s, they have expanded into the printing, advertising, computer-mediated communication, recorded music and film industries.

These conglomerates maintained two tracks for their media holdings. Media operations in printing and broadcasting have played central roles in protecting the old Samsung's interests from political pressures, disseminating commercial

Table 2.7 The history of Samsung's media businesses

Period	Media Industries	Names of Media Holdings
1960s	Broadcasting	Tongyang Broadcasting Company (TBC)
	Newspaper	JoongAng Ilbo
1970s	Advertising	Cheil Communication
1980s	Video production	
	Recorded music	
	Computer-mediated communication	Samsung SDS
1990s	Film	Samsung Entertainment Group
	Advertising	Phoenix Communication
	Cable television	

Source: Author's elaboration from Lee, 1997; Kang, 1997; *Variety*, 1997.

information and entertainment to Korea and diluting the negative image of the old Samsung (Kim, 2005). Further, when the Korean government decided that the media industries would become part of its national economic strategies, Samsung changed its attitude about media to a more profit-oriented one (Kim, 2002). Samsung and CJ played a central role in grafting the Hollywood mode of production onto the Korean cable and film industries. By allying with media conglomerates, mainly from the U.S., Samsung and CJ distributed media products from developed countries for its cable channels, mastered media business know-how from Hollywood and implanted the logic of capital in the Korean cable and film industries (Shim, 2002; Economic Review, 2003).

Conclusion

The development of Samsung was rooted in changes to Korean political economy. From relatively humble beginnings, Samsung established its foundation during the post-colonial period (1948–1960); diversified from light industry and heavy chemicals, including electronics, to information technology during the authoritarian regimes (1961–1992); and upgraded to a transnational corporation under the civil government (mid-1990s to present). The Lee family has built up the Samsung Empire in Korea by connecting to Korean power elites and maintaining the tradition of family ownership and management. After founder Lee Byung-chul died in 1987, his heir, Lee Kun-hee, split Samsung into six corporations (Seoul Shinmun, 2005). Under the six new corporations, Samsung operated media businesses in advertising (Cheil Communication) and computer-based communications (Samsung SDS), as well as a theme park (Samsung Everland). CJ ran audio-visual corporations in the cable (CJ Media and CJ O-shopping), film (CJ Entertainment and CJ CGV), recorded music (Mnet) and game (CJ Internet) industries. Finally, JoongAng Ilbo held multiple media corporations in the printing (the *JoongAng Ilbo*), broadcasting (jTBC) and advertising (e.g., Phoenix Communication) industries.

Notes

1 Books related to the founder of Samsung include *The Autobiography of Hoam* (the pen-name of Lee Byung-chul) published by Samsung in 1986, *The Untold Story about Samsung* published by Lee Mang-hee (the first son of the founder of Samsung) in 1993 and *The Words Spoken by Hoam of Lee Byung-chul*, published by the Hoam Foundation in 1997.

2 The Samsung web sites I used are www.samsung.com; http://english.cj.net; http://joon gang.joins.com.

3 The yearbooks include Samsung (1988), Samsung (1998) and Cheil Jedang (2003).

4 My major economics resources include the following. Lee Jung-won (1989) focuses on how Samsung established its businesses from 1945 to 1960. Woo Jung-en (1991) examines the political logic of Korean financial structures during the authoritarian regimes. Kim Yong-rang (1993) deals with Samsung's diversification and its structure of ownership. Kang Chul-kyu (1997) elaborates on Kim Yong-rang's work, focusing on Samsung's role in the history of chaebol groups. Kim Eun-mee (1997, 1988) explores the collusion and conflict between the Korean state and chaebol groups. Finally, Bruce

Cumings (1997) investigates Korea's modern history from the early 1900s to the mid-1990s with respect to its international political economy in East Asia.

5 In sociology, Kong Jeong-ja (1989) deals with the marriage ties between chaebol groups and Korean power elites. Yoizi Isigawa (1988) investigates how Lee Byung-chul built up the Samsung Empire. Hong Duck-ryul (1993) analyzes the formation of the capitalist class in Korea by looking at the historical process of the Federation of Korean Industries, the inner circle of chaebol groups. Kim Yun-tae (2008) explores the state and chaebol groups from the 1960s to the 1990s.

6 In mass communications, Lee Jin-ro (1997) deals with the formation and growth of the Korean computer-based communication industry. Seo Hyun-jin (2003) analyzes how Samsung's ownership structure affected the media content of JoongAng-Ilbo in the 1960s. Kim Ju-hwan (2004) examines why Samsung owned a newspaper company (the JoongAng-Ilbo) and a broadcasting company (Tongyang Broadcasting Company) in the 1960s. Cho Kwang-myung (2004) explores marriage ties among the owners of the mainstream newspaper companies Chosun Ilbo, JoongAng Ilbo and DongA Ilbo. Finally, Seoul Shinmun (2005) examines the family history of chaebol groups, including Samsung.

7 The Samsung Trading Corporation in 1948 differed from the Samsung Corporation in 1951, despite their similar business, trading. The Samsung Trading Corporation was established by Lee Byung-chul and five other businessmen, including Cho Hong-je, a founder of Hyosung, a second-tier chaebol. The Samsung Trading Corporation went bankrupt after the Korean War broke out in 1950. In 1951, Lee Byung-chul established the Samsung Corporation (Yoizi, 1988, p. 79).

8 Tong-Yang Fire and Marine Insurance was sold by Hanjin, a chaebol group, in 1967. The other two firms merged with Samsung Life Insurance in 1989 (Yoizi, 1988, p. 79; Samsung, 1998; Kim, 1993, p. 170).

9 After acquiring the Dongbang Department Store, Samsung renamed it the Shinsaegae Department Store (Samsung,1998, p. 74; Kim, 1993, p. 169; Samsung,1998, p. 74).

10 This firm was merged with JoongAng Development in 1966 and has been responsible for all businesses related to Samsung real estate. Later, it was renamed Samsung Everland (Kim, 2005, pp. 109–115).

11 Later renamed the Kangbuk Samsung Hospital (Samsung, 1998, p. 176).

12 This nonprofit organization played a central role in supporting Samsung's family ownership (Yoizi, 1988, p. 81).

13 Samsung regained this corporation in 1994 (Samsung, 1998, pp. 76–81).

14 "Spin-off" is an economic term used when a division of a company becomes an independent business in the same industry (Kang, 1997, p. 43).

15 Both the CJ and JoongAng Ilbo groups were subsidiaries of Samsung by the 1990s.

References

Ahn, H.K. (2007). *A study on the power of major film distribution companies through vertical integration*. Seoul, Korea: Danguk University. Unpublished thesis. Korean.

Cheil Jedang (CJ). (2003). *The fifty years of Cheil Jedang*. Seoul, Korea: CJ. Korean.

Cho, K.M. (2004). *A research about marriage ties among the owners of Korean newspaper companies*. Seoul, Korea: Korea University. Unpublished thesis. Korean.

Choi, J.P. (2014). *History of Korean Chaebols*. Seoul, Korea: Hanam. Korean.

Choi, Y.S. (1998). The history of development of the Korean video industry. *Korea music and video yearbook 98* (pp. 101–102). Seoul: Recording Industry Association of Korea. Korean.

Cumings, B. (1997). *Korea's place in the sun: A modern history*. New York: W.W. Norton & Company.

Dodgson, M. & Kim, Y. (1997). Learning to innovate—Korean style: The case of Samsung, *International Journal of Innovation Management*, 1(1), 53–71.

Economic Review (2003). Samsungman power in Korean film. *Economic Review*, 1(21), 20–21. Korean.

Hoam Foundation. (1997). *The words spoken by Hoam of Lee Byung-chul.* Seoul, Korea: Hoam Foundation. Korean.

Hong, D.R. (1993). *The organization and class activities of large capitalists in Korea.* Seoul, Korean: Seoul National University. Unpublished dissertation. Korean.

Jin, D. Y. (2005). Political economy of communication industry reorganization: Republic of Korea 1987–2003. Urbana, IL: University of Illinois Press. Dissertation.

Kang, C.K. (1997). Diversification progress and the ownership structure of Samsung chaebol. In T. Shiba & M. Shimotani (Eds.), *Beyond the firm: Business groups in international and historical perspective.* (pp. 31–58). New York: Oxford University Press.

Kim, E.M. (1988). From dominance to symbiosis: Sate and Chaebol in Korea. *Pacific Focus*, III(2), 105–121.

Kim, E.M. (1997). *Big business, strong state.* New York: State University of New York Press.

Kim, J.B. (2005). *The corporate structure of Korea's chaebol groups.* Seoul, Korea: Nanam. Korean.

Kim, J.B. (2007). The circular ownership structure of 30 chaebol groups, *The Research of Economic Development*, 13(2), 171–201. Korean.

Kim, J.H. (2004). *Why Samsung owned the JoongAng-Ilbo in the 1960s.* Seoul, Korea. Yonsei University. Unpublished thesis. Korean.

Kim, K.K. (1994). *The globalization of the Korean advertising industry: History of early penetration of TNAAs and their effects on Korean society.* College State, PA: Pennsylvania State University. Dissertation.

Kim, S.S. (2002). *A Study of Korea's media ownership.* Seoul, Korea: Press Trade Union. Korean.

Kim, Y.C. (2010). *Thinking Samsung.* Seoul, Korea: Sahoipyungnon. Korean.

Kim, Y.R. (1993). *A study on the diversification and control structure of Samsung Chaebol.* Seoul, Korea: Seoul National University. Unpublished dissertation. Korean.

Kim, Y.T. (2008). *Bureaucrats and entrepreneurs: The state and the Chaebol in Korea.* Seoul, Korea: Jimoondang.

Kim, E. H. & Kim, W. (2008). Changes in Korean corporate governance: A response to crisis. *Journal of Korean Law*, 8(23), 23–46.

Kong, J.J. (1989). *The marriage ties of chaebol groups.* Seoul, Korea: Ehwa Women's University. Unpublished dissertation. Korean.

Lee, B.C. (1986). *The autobiography of Hoam.* Seoul, Korea: JoongAng Ilbo. Korean.

Lee, E.J. (2008). *The ownership of media companies in Korea.* Seoul, Korea: The Korean Press Foundation.

Lee, H.K. (2007). Influence of the vested companies on Chaebol's accumulation in Korea. *The Journal of Historical Management*, 22(1), 187–218.

Lee, J.R. (1997). *The study on the formation and growing process of the Korean computer mediated communication industry: Focused on the computer mediated communication companies.* Seoul, Korea: Kyunghee University. Unpublished dissertation. Korean.

Lee, J.W. (1989). *A study on the formation and structure of Samsung chaebol (1945–1960).* Incheon, Korea: In-ha University. Korean.

Lee, M.H. (1993). *Untold story about Samsung.* Seoul, Korea: Chungsan. Korean.

Park, H.S. (1994). Impact of new media technology on the Korean society: Changing pattern of communication. In H.D. Kang (Ed.), *International communication in Northeast Asia* (pp. 361–363). Seoul, Korea: Nanam. Korean.

Rowley, C. & Bae, J. (2003). Culture and management in South Korea. In M. Warner (Ed.), *Culture and management in Asia* (pp. 187–209). New York: Routledge.

Ryu, T.H., Kim, D. W. & Kim. D. M. & Jung, J.H. (2005). *The corporate governance, informal tie and marriage of chaebol groups*. Seoul: Korea, Nanam. Korean.

Samsung. (1988). *The history of Samsung during past fifty years*. Seoul, Korea: Samsung. Korean.

Samsung. (1998). *The history of Samsung during past sixty years*. Seoul, Korea: Samsung. Korean.

Seo, H.J. (2003). *A study about media management of chaebol groups including its reporting in the 1960s*. Seoul, Korea: Yonsei University. Unpublished Thesis. Korean.

SERI (2006). *The history of Samsung Economic Research Institute during twenty years*. Seoul, Korea: Samsung.

Shim, D.B. (2002). South Korean media industry in the 1990s and the economic crisis. *Prometheus*, 20(4), 337–350.

Shim, D.B. (2008). The growth of Korean cultural industries and the Korean Wave. In C.B. Huat & K. Iwabuchi (Eds.), *East Asian Pop Culture: Analyzing the Korean Wave* (pp. 15–31). Hong Kong: Hong Kong University Press.

Seoul Shinmun. (2005). *The pulse of chaebol*. Seoul, Korea: Moohan. Korean.

Song, S.H. (2008). Where is the succession of Samsung for Lee Jae-Yong? *The Wolgan Chosun* (pp. 96–113). Seoul, Korea: Chosun Media Group. Korean.

Song, W.G. (2006). Multilayers of chaebol's reform: The case of Samsung. *Trend and View*, 68, 173–201. Korean.

Song, W.G. (2014). *Corporate structure of Samsung group and management*. Presented paper at the discussion meeting supported by Korean Scandinavian Conference, Protection of Samsung' unfair labor working and The Assembly of Journalists for Economic Justice in October 14, 2014, Seoul, Korea. Korean.

Variety (1997). Samsung Entertainment Group. May 12–May 18, 1997, p. 54.

Woo, J.E. (1991). *Race to the swift*. New York: Columbia University Press.

Yoizi, I. (1988). *Lee Byung- chul and the empire of Samsung*. Seoul, Korea: The Editorial Room of Dolsam. Korean.

3 Concentration vs. competition in the neoliberal media

Do neoliberal policies concerning media bring about free media or not? Researchers emphasizing the positive functions of the market argue that neoliberal media laws and policies help the market facilitate competition. Public-oriented scholars state that a free market leads to forming centralized market structures. Despite stressing different aspects of market function, both sides share the belief that states as legal regulators would affect structures of media markets. Within the framework of this controversial debate, I examine the relationship between the roles of states as legal regulators and media markets in the Korean context. Korea is a good example with which to study this question because the Korean state institutionally and legally implanted a market-oriented ideology into the Korean media systems in order to develop the media as a national industry (Shim, 2008). Thus, I focus on the period between 1998 and 2014 when the Korean government reformed media systems under a neoliberal media model. I analyze government documents[1] and secondary resources in order to investigate neoliberal media laws and policies in relation to changes in Korean market structures.

This chapter is arranged in three sections. One covers media reforms including 1) the re-regulation of existing media laws and policies; 2) media privatization; and 3) the developmental model that transformed Korean media from a state-controlled system to market-driven one. The second section covers the outcomes of media reforms, specifically 1) the contribution of media industries to Korea's gross domestic product; 2) the patterns of media exports and imports; and 3) trends in the number of media companies. The final section investigates how these trends have shaped the structures of four media markets (advertising, broadcasting, newspaper and film), covering the changed patterns of market structures and the major players.

3.1. Neoliberal media reforms in Korea

Structural changes in the Korean economy affected media markets by the late 1980s, when Korea had been under the trade pressures from the U.S. The Korean state's march toward economic liberalization allowed foreign capital to enter the film distribution and advertising markets. By the mid-1990s, the Korean government had completely liberalized the advertising industry, thereby allowing transnational advertising agencies to compete with domestic players without any legal barriers (Yun, 2008). It also lowered legal barriers to the establishment of newspaper companies, thereby allowing chaebol groups (e.g., Hyundai and Hanhwa) to expand their newspaper businesses (Yoo, 1989). Further, the Korean state's new economic reforms encouraged chaebol groups to establish media holdings in the audio-visual industries in the mid-1990s.

The year 1998 was a milestone year in Korean media reforms associated with changes in economic policies. After the financial crisis in December of 1997, the Korean state had to make neoliberal economic reforms under the guidelines of the International Monetary Fund (IMF) and International Bank for Reconstruction and Development (IBRD). They included financial liberalization, deregulation of ownership and labor flexibility. The Korean state then proceeded with a full range of neoliberal media reforms that included lowering legal barriers to media ownership, activating mergers and acquisitions of media companies and privatizing state-owned media companies. These changed media laws and policies inevitably led to changes in market structures within and across media industries. Thus, in the following sections, I specifically examine the re-regulation of media laws and policies, the privatization of state-owned media companies and the adaptation of the developmental model for the media.

3.1.1. Re-regulation of media laws and polices

Since 1998, major liberalized reforms have centered on the broadcasting, newspaper and film industries. Between 1997 and 2001, the Korean government intensively revised about 70 percent of the existing media laws and regulations. The revised laws lowered ceiling limits to media ownership in the print and broadcasting industries and replaced licensing systems that encouraged private media ownership. They also removed protections that had forbidden foreign investment in print or broadcasting corporations, thereby putting them on an equal footing with the film and advertising industries in which foreign investment was already permitted. These liberalizing steps promoted the media industry as integral to the new neoliberal economic drive (Park, et al., 2007).

In 1999, the Korean government revised the Act on Registration of Periodicals, lowering legal barriers to media ownership in the printing industry and allowing foreigners to own up to 30 percent of total shares in a daily newspaper and up to 50 percent of total stock in a magazine and/or weekly newspaper. Concurrently in the film industry, the Korean government updated the Motion Picture Promotion Law. The revised regulation guaranteed the freedom of expression in motion pictures, replaced the registration system with the reporting system as the condition for the establishment for film companies and completely liberalized independent film production

Both 2000 and 2009 are considered milestones in the Korean broadcasting industry. Until the turn of the new millennium, Korea maintained a bipolar broadcasting system – that is, public and commercial broadcasting systems. Territorial broadcasting corporations were owned either by the Korean government or Korean capitalists. Three public broadcasting companies existed: the Korea Broadcasting System (KBS), the Munhwa Broadcasting Company (MBC) and the Educational Broadcasting System (EBS). The Korean state was the largest stockholder in these three networks. The Korean government held 100 percent of the total stock of both KBS and EBS. It also owned 70 percent of the total shares in MBC. The other 30 percent of MBC shares belonged to the Chongsoo Foundation, controlled by Park Geun-hye, president of Korea (2013– present). Although these three public broadcasting corporations belonged to the public broadcasting system, they had a dual financial system that collected television reception fees and earned revenue from commercial advertisement. Along with these three public companies existed other broadcasting stations (e.g., Seoul Broadcasting System, a national network, cable television, religious stations, local stations and digital satellite stations) that belonged to private commercial broadcasters who earned revenues from advertising (Jin & Shim, 2007).

While the bipolar broadcasting architecture was not dismantled, the Korean government revised broadcasting laws in 2000 and 2009. In 2000, the Korean government reorganized the entire broadcasting industry – including terrestrial, cable, satellite and digital television – under an umbrella regulatory scheme (Nam, 2008). More specifically, the Korean government replaced the licensing system of program providers (PPs) in cable television with an open registration system. It also allowed chaebol groups and foreigners to own up to 33 percent equity in both cable networks and a digital satellite television provider, as well as up to 100 percent equity in cable program providers. While the Korean broadcasting law did not allow first-tier chaebol groups and foreigners to own media holdings in the territorial television and radio businesses formally, cross-media ownership between territorial network broadcasters and cable channels was allowed (Yun, 2005). As a result, three players – chaebol groups, foreigners and territorial networkers – became the multiple system operators (MSOs) and multiple program providers (MPPs) in cable television, satellite and digital television.

Ten years later, in 2009, the Korean government again revised both the Act of Broadcasting and the Act on Registration of Periodicals covering newspapers and magazines. The effect of these revised laws was the Korean equivalent of the 1996 Telecommunication Act in the U.S. The Korean government here abolished the Maginot Line that had protected public interests from transnational media corporations (i.e., chaebol groups) in the broadcasting industry. In 1980 the Korean government had passed regulations forbidding cross-ownership between the newspaper and broadcasting industries in Korea (Kang & Kim, 1994). But in 2009, the legal barriers between the newspaper, news agency and broadcasting industries were abolished. Five new cable channels were issued to four newspaper companies (e.g., the *Chosun Ilbo*, the *JoongAng Ilbo* and the *DongA Ilbo* and the *Maeil Economic Daily*) and a news agency (Yonhap News, the state-owned news agency).

As seen in Table 3.1, an individual investor could own up to 40 percent of the total shares in a territorial television company, a comprehensive programming channel or a cable news channel. The comprehensive programming channel was

Table 3.1 Percentage changes in media ownership

Medium	Maximum Limit Per Person (%)		Newspaper and News Agency (%)		Chaebol Groups (%)		Foreigners (%)	
	By 2008	After 2009	By 2008	After 2009	By 2008	After 2009	By 2008	After 2009
National networks	30	40	No	10	No	10	No	No
Comprehensive programming channels	30	40	No	30	No	30	No	20
News channels	30	40	No	30	No	30	No	10
Cable TV			33	49			49	49
Satellite TV			33	49	49	49	33	49
IPTV content			No	49	No	49	No	20

Source: Author's elaboration of White Papers and scholarly works.

a new cable channel providing original news content for cable subscribers on top of entertainment programs, sports broadcasts and documentaries. The content of the comprehensive programming channel is similar to that of the territorial network. News agencies and newspaper enterprises could also run broadcasting stations and hold 1) up to 10 percent of total shares in the national media, 2) up to 30 percent of total stocks in the comprehensive programming channels and news cable channels and 3) up to 49 percent of total shares in the cable network, satellite digital television and program providers of Internet Protocol television (IPTV) industries.

Further, each member of a chaebol group could own up to 10 percent of total shares of the national broadcasters, up to 30 percent of total stocks in the comprehensive programming channels and news cable channels and up to 49 percent of total stocks in an IPTV's company. Finally, foreigners could own up to 20 percent of company shares in comprehensive channels, up to 10 percent of total shares in the cable news channel and up to 20 percent of total stocks in an IPTV's corporation. With this revised law, the Korean government institutionally entrusted relatively new media to chaebol groups and foreigner investors because they were able to own the national broadcasting stations, the comprehensive programming channel and the IPTV.

In sum, the Korean government reorganized existing media laws to cultivate the media as a national priority. Media reforms focused on relaxing the legal limits of media ownership in the broadcasting industry, permitting cross-media ownership between newspaper and broadcasting companies and abolishing pre-censorship of media content in the film industry. It also allowed foreign capital with TNCs able to become major stockholders or the largest stockholder in their Korean print, cable television and IPTV holdings. The Korean media were under the control of capital.

3.1.2. *Privatization of state-owned media companies*

Another step taken by the Korean government was to privatize state-owned media companies in the advertising, broadcasting and telecommunication industries. The state-owned media companies were 1) the Korea Broadcasting Advertising Corporation (KOBACO), the only broadcasting advertising agency; 2) the Munhwa Broadcasting Company (MBC), one of the public broadcasting companies; 3) Korea Telecommunication Cable Television (KTCA), the largest cable network system operator; and 4) Korean Telecommunication (KT), the only state-owned wired corporation. The plan to privatize these media enterprises was realized in the early 2000s with the exception of the MBC. Before reviewing the privatization of the three other media companies (KOBACO, KT and KTCA), let's explore why the Korean government failed to privatize MBC.

The Korean government failed to privatize the MBC for two main reasons. First, Korean civil society strongly resisted the privatization of the MBC, leading to animosity about the plan to privatize state-owned media companies. Thus, the Korean government had to give up the plan to privatize MBC. Second, there were political conflicts between the Korean government and Park Gun-hye, a political leader for the conservative party and daughter of the military dictator Park Jung-hee. The shares of MBC were held by the Korean government (70 percent) and the Chongsoo Foundation (30 percent). The Chongsoo Foundation was established by Dictator Park Jung-hee. After the military coup on May 16, 1961, Park seized the fortunes of Kim Ji-tae, including shares of the MBC, and then founded the May 16 Foundation. After Dictator Park was murdered by his successor in 1979, his first daughter, Park Gun-hye, returned much of the assets to Kim Ji-tae and his family members. However, she retained control of the May 16 Foundation, renaming it the Chongsoo Foundation (Yoo, 1994). Since then, Park Gun-hye has been the largest stockholder of this cultural foundation that held 30 percent of the total shares in MBC.

In the early 2000s, the government conceived a plan to privatize the MBC by selling publically the 70 percent of MBC stock it owned. However, Park Gun-hye, the largest stockholder of the Chongsoo Foundation, controlled the remaining 30 percent. The Korean government feared a worst-case scenario wherein the dictator's daughter might become the largest stockholder of the privatized MBC. Thus the Korean civil government suspended plans to privatize the MBC. Instead, the neoliberal government took steps to introduce a new media of comprehensive channels in 2009. Although comprehensive channels belonged to cable television, their media power would be equal to that of national broadcasting since about 86 percent of households in Korea subscribed to cable television networks.

Although the Korean government failed to privatize MBC, it did privatize each of the other three state-owned media companies: KOBACO, KT and KTCA. KOBACO was established by the Chun Doo-hwan regime in 1981. This state-owned company had been exclusively in charge of selling and allocating the total TV and radio advertising time in Korea. This state agency had also financially supported small- and medium-sized broadcasting corporations. However, foreign and domestic advertising agencies brought a lawsuit arguing that KOBACO was unconstitutional. Eventually, in 2008, the Constitutional Court ordered the Korean government to prepare alternatives to KOBACO and protect the interests of small broadcasting corporations. Following the Constitutional Court's decision, the Korean government started to discuss the introduction of privately operated sales agents or media representatives for broadcasters' advertising slots. These agents would buy media time or space from media owners and then sell it to national advertisers. The introduction of media representatives signaled the entrance of Korean broadcasting markets into the commercial era and away from the era of government control.

In addition, the Korean government privatized KT, the state-owned telecommunication company, and KTCA, the state-owned cable network company, due to trade pressure from the U.S. Both companies had earned large net profits over the previous few decades (Jin, 2006a). Since the late 1980s, the U.S. had pressured the Korean government to privatize KT in the name of bilateral trade liberalization. The Korean government had to accept American trading pressures as the U.S. was the largest country in Korea's export markets. The Korean government also needed money to install information technology infrastructures (Hyun & Lent, 1999). Under trade pressure and in order to prepare financially for a digital Korea, the Korean government privatized KT. However, it directly and indirectly controlled the process, including 1) how to sell the government's shares of KT, 2) when to sell them and 3) to whom they would be sold. As a result, foreign institutional investors and chaebol groups became the major stockholders in KT's shares. Foreign investors, including Brandes Investment Partners, a global investment advisory firm (6.39 percent), and Microsoft (3 percent), purchased 49 percent of the KT stock. Among members of chaebol groups, SK Telecomm, the largest mobile telephone company, acquired an 11.34 percent stake. LG Electronics, a first-tier chaebol, held a 2.27 percent share. Daelim, a second-tier chaebol group, owned a 1.3 percent share. Other major stockholders included individual and institutional investors (27.1 percent), KT employees and People Welfare Pensions in Korea (2.7 percent) (Jin, 2006a).

As the parent company of KTCA, KT controlled 100 percent of its stock. Thus, as KT was privatized, KTCA was liberalized by the Korean government as a matter of course. KTCA ran cable networking, broadband, media production and broadcast advertising businesses. The Korean government sold the KTCA through open bid to CJ Home Shopping, a media holding of the CJ group. In this way, the Korean government privatized state-owned media companies.

3.1.3. The developmental model for Korean media

A developmental model similar to those used by previous military regimes (1961–1987) to encourage growth in the Korean manufacturing industries was likewise applied to the cultural industries. But while the military regimes controlled chaebol groups by keeping tight reins on banking and financial resources, the civil government cooperated with chaebol groups to develop the media as a catalyst for the new economy. The Korean government began to involve itself in Korea's cultural industries to establish the infrastructures necessary for developing the media as a national economy. In 1999, the Korean government enacted the Basic Law on Promotion of Cultural Industries (BLPCI), which specified four major points: 1) the definition of cultural industry; 2) the designation of media companies as venture companies; 3) the institutional role of the Korean government; and 4) the introduction of new media venture funds between the Korean government and private financial institutions.

The BLPCI defined a cultural industry as one dedicated to cultural production, distribution and/or consumption. Under this umbrella were the industries of advertising, animation, broadcasting, character, digital media (e.g., digital multimedia content, computer-mediated communication and e-learning), film, games, play, print and recorded music. The BLPCI allowed the Korean government to designate prospective media companies in the game, recorded music, broadcasting and film industries as venture media companies. Venture media companies received tax favors when they imported media devices and financial favors when they borrowed investment from financial institutions. Third, the BLPCI permitted the Korean government to use the national budget to construct cultural clusters across the Korean Peninsula. Finally, the Korean government established investment associations with private financial institutions. Simply put, the BLPCI allowed the Korean government to exercise power over Korean cultural industries institutionally and financially. The following section details the institutional and financial roles of the Korean government related to Korean cultural industries.

The Korean government devoted its attention to establishing infrastructures for Korea's cultural industries. It constructed cultural clusters across the Korean Peninsula, educated specialized media human resources and introduced a programming quota system. The government also introduced the concept of the cultural cluster, defined as a multi-industrial complex in charge of researching and developing media content in the audio-visual media industries in order to build up media cities. Both government and private institutions were involved in this project to revitalize the local economy.

The Korean government constructed 13 cultural clusters by 2007. Chuncheon, located in the eastern part of the Korean Peninsula, focused on the animation business. Pusan, a southeastern city of Korea, specialized in motion pictures. Kwangju, Mokpo, Jeonju and Jeju, all southwestern cities, focused on computer-generated imagery (or 3D computer graphics) and mobile content. The central parts (e.g., Cheongju and Daejeon) were responsible for the gaming and edutainment industries. Edutainment combines education and entertainment to form a new content type mixing cartoon, character creation, animation, recorded music and games for digital devices (e.g., web-based and mobile). Another cultural cluster was at Pucheon, the suburban area of Seoul, and it focused on animation. Finally, Seoul, the capital of Korea, specialized in digital content for digital television, IPTV and mobile devices.

Another role of the Korean government was to train media specialists to provide stable human resources for the media industries. The number of educational institutions for media rapidly increased (see Table 3.2). These institutions were in charge

Table 3.2 Trends in the number of media educational institutions

Industry	Before 2003	2006
Broadcasting	4,587 (1990–2002)	10,208
Film	114 (1998–2002)	2,648
Game	313 (2001–2002)	1,262
Digital content	168 (2002)	37,108

Source: Park, et al., 2007, p. 29.

of running comprehensive curricula that ranged from planning, pre-production (e.g., storytelling) and production to post-production (e.g., editing) and marketing.

In 2006, 942 media education departments existed, including colleges (345), universities (347) and graduate schools (250). The departments were comprised of broadcasting (42.2 percent), animation (19.7 percent), recorded music (9.1 percent), gaming (9.0 percent), film (4.1 percent), character creation (1.8 percent) and Manhwa (cartoon) (1.6 percent). These departments introduced curricula at different educational levels as colleges were charged with cultivating media technicians. At the middle level, university curricula focused on media planning, production and marketing. Graduate schools were in charge of training top-level human resource personnel.

The Korea Advanced Institute of Science and Technology (KAIST) is one example. KAIST opened up the Graduate School of Culture Technology in 2005, providing an interdisciplinary education program encompassing cultural arts, sociology and media technology for graduate students (KOCCA, 2006). Moreover, the Korean government induced the universities to focus on specific media content rather than general content in order to enhance the quality of education. Each higher educational institution ran specialized curricula to turn out media professionals. For example, Sukmyung Women's University, located in Seoul, specialized in media content planning and scenarios for media production. Hoseo University taught animation graphics and design for game production. JoongAng University focused on virtual reality and human sensibility ergonomics.

A third policy adopted by the Korean government was a program quota system in the broadcasting industry to provide stable distribution among independent production companies across Korea and enhance the quality of media content made in Korea. The Korean government applied the program quota system differently to territorial broadcasting companies and non-territorial ones. All territorial broadcasting networkers broadcast media artifacts manufactured by Korean firms for at least 80 percent of total scheduled programming per day. Korean film ranged from 20 to 40 percent of total film shows. Korean animation covered 30 to 50 percent of total animation running time. And Korean popular music played for 50 to 60 percent of the total pop music airtime.

In addition, all non-territorial broadcasting networkers, including cable television, satellite and digital television, followed the programming quota system. They scheduled media products made in Korea for at least 50 percent of total shows per day. Korean film ranged from 30 to 50 percent of the total film running time.

Korean animation ran from 40 to 60 percent of total animation time. Korean pop music played from 50 to 80 percent of total pop music time. Moreover, the Korean government required all broadcasting networkers to allocate at least 15 percent of all scheduled programming during prime time from 7 to 11 every evening to Korean media artifacts manufactured by independent production companies.

Although the Korean government advanced promotional policies in the cultural industries, it failed to maintain consistency when media policies came into conflict with the interests of the national economy. The case of the free trade agreement (FTA) with the U.S. in April 2007 is a prime example. The FTA was a bilateral trade treaty between the U.S. and Korea, its omni-directional market openness ranging from basic necessities, electronic devices and automobiles to cultural products. The Korean government reduced the screen quota in the Korean film industry from 146 to 73 days per year in order to meet FTA regulations. While the screen quota system was intended to protect the domestic film industry, its reduction served the interests of U.S. trade and chaebol groups. Internally, chaebol groups, especially the first-tiered chaebol Samsung, LG and Hyundai, urged the Korean government to accept the free trade agreement with the U.S., the largest market in the world. Externally, the U.S. repeatedly required the Korean government to lessen (or abandon) the screen quota system as a condition of complying with the FTA (Jin, 2006b). Thus, the Korean government reduced the screen quota in the film industry in response to this dual pressure.

Because articles of the FTA specifically included revisions of Korea's media laws and policies, the Korea government had to revise related media laws and policies once again. Specifically, the Korean government allowed American media giants to hold 100 percent media ownership in Korean broadcasting or newspaper companies. Second, the Korean government extended the period of royalty payment from 50 to 70 years after an original copyright holder dies. Third, the Korean government reduced the obligatory programming time in the broadcasting channels from 35 percent to 30 percent for animation made in Korea and from 25 percent to 20 percent for Korean movies. Fourth, the Korean government increased the import restrictions of a country from 60 percent to 80 percent of a channel's programming. Finally, the Korean government abandoned the rights to expand the screen quota again in the future even if the industry hits a serious recession. These actions imply that the Korean government considered the media industry a negotiable card to increase U.S. exports.

In summary, the Korean government attempted to implant a developmental model in the Korean media industries, in spite of having shown an inconsistent stance in relation to pressures from both chaebol groups and the U.S. It constructed cultural clusters, with a focus on cultivating specialized human resources in universities to meet media industry needs, and introduced the screen quota system in the broadcasting industry.

The Korean government also established financial foundations for the growing media industries from multiple resources. The first resources came from the national budget. The Korean government allotted at least 1 percent of the national budget to cultural industries. This played a vital role in establishing the infrastructure for Korean cultural industries. This money was used for constructing the cultural clusters, growing professional resources and providing seed money for a promotional fund for Korean production companies. The second financial resource was promotional funds from three main sources: the national budget, box office sales and broadcasting advertising. This fund was to be used for loans to independent production companies; the modernization of cultural facilities or structural improvements to distribution in the audio-visual industries; co-production between Korean and non-Korean media firms; seed money to establish media venture funds; and foreign marketing costs to increase media exports.

The last financial resource was from investment associations, or media venture funds. The Korean government introduced this system in 1999 to resolve chronic financial difficulties. As seen in Table 3.3, members of investment associations could be the Korean government, chaebol groups with financial institutions or other private financial institutions. Generally, the Korean government contributed up to at most 20 percent of the individual accounts of the investment associations. The other 80 percent of the total invested money came from private financial institutions. Each investment association selected specified media content in the audio-visual media industries and then invested in media companies in these fields. Chaebol groups with investment holdings and venture capital in non-chaebol holdings provided financial resources for production companies in the audio-visual industry.

Although the Korean government exercised licensing rights regarding the establishment of investment associations, it was rarely involved in the decision-making

Table 3.3 Investment associations from 1999 to 2002

Name	Amount of Money ($ millions)	Year Established
Moohan	11.5	1999
Mearae Asset	10	1999
Dream Venture 1	13.5	2000
Dream Venture 2	5	2000
Cowell	10	2000
Tube 1	10	2000
Sovic	10	2000
MVP1	10	2000
Il-shin	5	2000
Venture Plus	10	2000
Han-neung	5	2000
Samsung Venture	15	2000
Peta Capital	10	2000
Century-on Venture	6	2000
Tube 2	10	2001
Dream Venture 3	8	2001
Dream Discovery	8	2001
Je-woo Investment	8	2001
Shin-Bo Investment	7	2001
KTB Network	10	2001
Moohan 2	10	2001
MVP2	10	2002
Total	201	

Source: Author's elaboration of White Papers.

process. These investment associations started to be established in 1999. The capital size of each investment association ranged from U.S. $5 million up to $13.5 million, and their members included the independent financial institutions (e.g., Moohan, Mearae Asset and Cowell), the financial holdings owned by chaebol groups (e.g., Samsung Venture, both Dream Discovery and Peta Capital of CJ) or both the Korean government and the financial institutions. These financial resources invested in motion pictures, games, television drama, animations, character creation, e-books and digital multimedia.

Shown here, the Korean government played a vital role in establishing the financial foundation for Korean cultural industries. It used the national budget to establish infrastructures for the media industries, raised promotional funds to modernize the old media machines and promote Korean media products in the global media market and allowed chaebol groups and financial institutions to become members of media venture funds.

In other words, the Korean government carried out media reforms institutionally and financially. Under the government's stated principle of "no-intervention, but support for the markets," it applied a developmental model to the Korean cultural industries. These promotional policies allowed the Korean government to construct media complexes across Korea, allocate at least 1 percent of the national budget and establish the investment association of media venture funds between the Korean government and private financial institutions.

Another key factor in the Korean government's support of its cultural industries is the commitment to creating a digital Korea. Since the early 1980s, the Korean government has continuously explored the economic possibilities of a digital economy that allows manufacturing industries to enhance economic efficiency (Lee, 1997). By the mid-1990s, the government had launched public digital projects, including improvements to the delivery of electronic services within the administration departments; the registration of newborn babies, real estate and automobiles; and the application of electronic services to the media industries (e.g., online newspapers, Internet chat and online communities). In the late 1990s, these public projects enabled the Korean government to consider information and communication technologies (ICT) as a potential new economy (Shim, 2008).

In the early 2000s, with the catchphrase that "Korea would be a global leader in the digitalized era," Korea launched an e-Government Special Committee to prepare a master plan for improving the delivery of information and services to individuals and businesses. Members of this commission included the prime minster, high government officials and digital experts from civil organizations. They focused on how to 1) link various government agencies and their activities via a networking system, 2) enhance the quality of administrative works within governmental agencies and 3) activate the participation of ordinary people in national affairs. The committee submitted a report covering e-procurement, home tax services, integrated social insurance, local government information systems, educational administrative information systems, digital signatures and e-seals. Based on the report published by the special commission, the Korean government launched the state-funded public project to establish the foundation of e-government, an electronic government system that included online processing of civil affairs and administrative information exchange via the Internet. The public project was to wire the public organizations from government agencies from both central and local administrations to the national assembly, the judiciary and even state-owned firms.

The Korean government also poured funds into the national budget to construct infrastructures that relied on ICT. For example, the Korean government poured in a total of 290.3 billion won (equivalent to U.S. $290.3 million) for computer networks at its major offices to foster speedy administrative measures and enhanced services. This project focused on linking up different public databases and streamlining electronic administrative procedures. Moreover, the Korean government installed digital broadband Internet facilities nationwide, including the introduction of commercial broadband Internet services across the Korean Peninsula. From 1998 to 2002, six telecommunication companies provided this service. KT occupied around 50 percent of the total broadband market, and five other companies (e.g., Hanaro Telecom, Thrunet, and Onse Telecom, Daecom and Dreamline) held the remaining markets. As a result, the number of broadband Internet subscribers increased from 0.37 million to 10 million, and the number of Internet users grew to account for more than 60 percent of the total population.

Further, the Korean government introduced new digital media, including digital satellite television and digital media convergence of telecommunication and broadcasting. In 2002, the Korean government launched digital satellite broadcasting (brand name Skylife), which aired on 94 channels. The major stockholders of Skylife were Korean Telecommunication, the privatized telephone company; Korea Broadcasting System, a public broadcasting company; and the Samsung group, the first-tier leader of the chaebol groups.

Later, the Korean government launched digital convergence media between telecommunications and broadcasting. Typical examples were digital multimedia broadcasting (DMB) in 2004 and IPTV in 2008. DMB is a personal pocket multimedia allowing people to enjoy media content, including film, television shows and online games, over portable devices. Two kinds of DMB exist: satellite DMB and territorial DMB. Both DMB types are available for both wired and wireless devices. Similarly, IPTV is an Internet-based television service that allows a user to search the Internet, send or receive e-mails, enjoy chats, make electronic bank transactions or purchase clothes on a high-definition TV screen. Unlike web television, IPTV asks the audience to use a television set linked to set-top boxes in order to watch television shows, to access the Internet and to use wired phone services through a single broadband connection. Digital convergence media allowed chaebol groups to expand their media businesses over digital media, as the Korean government issued licenses to run digital convergence media to the Korean monopoly capital. In other words, the Korean government constructed the infrastructure for a digital Korea and introduced the digital convergence between broadcasting and telecommunication. This inevitably allowed chaebol groups to earn big revenues and to increase the number of digital media outlets.

To sum up media reforms, the Korean government, with neoliberal thinking, reformed Korean media systems and carried out institutional and financial reforms using developmental models to grow media industries as a new national economy. Neoliberal policies transformed Korean media systems from a state-controlled structure to a market-oriented one, allowing capital (e.g., chaebol groups, foreign investors and mainstream newspaper corporations) to become the dominant players in the commercialized Korean media market.

3.2. The outcomes of media reforms for Korean economy

Korea's media reforms brought three big changes in total revenue, market sizes and the number of media companies. The total revenue from Korean cultural industries increased about nine times from 8 trillion 59 million won (approximately U.S. $859 million) in 1999 to 82 trillion 410 million won (U.S. $8,241 million) in 2011. As the total revenue from the Korean media industries consistently increased, cultural industries represented up to 6.2 percent of the total gross domestic product. The market size of each media industry generally increased, as seen in Table 3.4.

Audio-visual media industries expanded much more than the print industry. Both the recorded music and game industries saw a tenfold growth between 1999 and 2011. Other media industries, including film, broadcasting and advertising, doubled or tripled their growth in the same time frame. Secondary media industries (i.e., character creation and digital media) also showed significant growth. Although print media (i.e., newspapers, magazines and publishing) occupied the largest portion of total revenue in the Korean cultural industries, the growth rate of this industry was slower than most other markets.

The growth in media revenue and market sizes was related to the increase in the amount of media exports and imports. As seen in Table 3.5, the total amounts of both media exports and imports grew consistently in each media industry. Specifically, gaming media was the largest export, followed by broadcast media and recorded music and then by audio-visual exports. Gaming and film were among the biggest media imports into the Korean market. Completed import/export forms and licenses show trends for the majority of media. For example, the completed forms for Korean media exports increased from 42.2 percent of total media exports in 2006 to 45.9 percent of total exports in 2008. During the

Table 3.4 Changes of market size, 1999–2011 ($ millions)

Year	1999	2003	2006	2009	2011	Growth Ratio
Film	661	1,142	3683	3,306	3,457	523
Animation	930	405	288	418	551	−59
Recorded music	380	490	2,400	2,740	3,869	1,018
Games	900	1,500	4,500	6,580	9,202	1,020
Characters	3,220	4,808	4,509	5,358	7,214	224
Cartoons	N/A	759	730	739	757	Similar
Printed media	N/A	15,500	19,900	26,091	21,024	137
Broadcasting	3,020	7,100	9,700	10,680	14,550	482
Advertising	4,620	4,800	9,100	9,186	11,715	253
Digital content	N/A	1,300	1,180	2,036	2,828	217

Source: Author's elaboration of data from White Papers.

same periods, licensing media exports increased from 26.6 percent of total media exports in 2006 to around 36 percent of total media exports in 2008. However, the media exports of original equipment in manufacturing gradually decreased from 24.1 percent of total media exports in 2006 to 19.7 percent of total media exports in 2008. Media exports showed similar trends in the early 2000s.

It is also important to note that patterns of Korean media exports and imports show differences. Korean media exports outweighed Korean imports from Asian markets, while imports outweighed Korean exports to the U.S. While most Korean media exports were to Japan, China and Southeast Asia, the imports of media into the Korea market were predominantly from the U.S. As seen in Table 3.6, Japan was the largest consumer of Korean audio-visual media products with 26.2 percent of total media exports. China was the second largest with 24.5 percent of total exports. Media exports to Southeast Asia accounted for 22 percent of total exports. Other export amounts were to the U.S., the European Union and South America for a total of 27.3 percent of total exports in 2010. On the other hand, the U.S. was by far the largest country for Korea's imported media products. The U.S. accounted for 38.9 percent of total imports, followed by China (19.2 percent) and Japan (15.6 percent).

In addition, neoliberal media reforms generally led to an increase in the number of media companies. As seen in Table 3.7, the newly established media companies gradually increased in the audio-visual industries. Especially in the late 1990s and the early 2000s, creative artists started to establish media companies in the recorded music, film and digital contents industries.

There was a sevenfold increase in the number of media firms in the game industry, whereas film companies increased fourfold between 1998 and 2012 (see Table 3.8). The media companies in the recorded music and print industries doubled during the same period. Most media companies in the audio-visual media industries were

Table 3.5 Trends in total exports and imports ($ millions)

Year	1999		2004		2009		2011	
Industries	*Exports*	*Imports*	*Exports*	*Imports*	*Exports*	*Imports*	*Exports*	*Imports*
Film	5.7	28.7	58.2	66.1	14.1	73.6	13.5	53.3
Animation	81.6	3.6	61.7	80.0	89.6	7.3	96.8	6.9
Game	107.6	46.6	387.6	205.1	1,240.8	332.0	1,601.0	10.3
Recorded Music	10.6	4.2	34.0	20.5	31.2	11.9	83.2	10.3
Broadcasting	12.7	28.7	70.3	58.5	184.5	183.0	242.3	102.0
Total	218.2	111.8	611.8	430.2	1,560.2	697.8	2,044.0	182.5

Source: Author's elaboration of data from White Papers.

Table 3.6 Media exports and imports in 2010 (%)

Country	Japan	China	Southeast Asia	U.S.	E.U.	Others	Total
Export	26.2	24.5	22.0	13.2	8.8	5.2	100
Import	15.6	19.2	9.1	38.9	12.2	5.0	100

Source: White Paper from 2011, pp. 73–74.

Table 3.7 Numbers and percent of new media companies in each media industry

	1950s to 1980s	1990s	2000s
Cartoon	18 (19.1%)	35 (37.3%)	41 (43.6%)
Recorded music	28 (11.5%)	104 (43.0 %)	110 (45.5%)
Film	70 (11.9%)	205 (34.9%)	313 (53.2%)
Animation	19 (10%)	74 (38.9%)	97 (51.1%)
Character	39 (15.7%)	76 (30.7%)	133 (53.6%)
Digital content	11 (5.3%)	76 (37.3%)	117 (57.4%)
Total	185 (11.4%)	570 (36.8%)	811 (51.8%)

Source: Author's elaboration from White Papers.

Table 3.8 The evolution of media companies

Year	1999	2004	2009
Print	5,929, including 113 daily newspapers	6,810, including 135 daily newspapers	13,163, including 290 daily newspapers
Advertising	About 300	5,091, including 1,768 advertising agencies	4,532, including 1,501 advertising agencies
Film	1,146, including 367 production, 155 distribution and 409 exhibition	2,853, including 1,375 production, 315 distribution and 654 exhibition	4,380, including 2,365 production, 559 distribution and 715 exhibition
Recorded music	568 production, 104 distribution	N/A	1,266 production, 623 distribution
Games	450 production, 278 distribution	2,567 production, 1,001 distribution	3,317 production, 1,256 distribution
Broadcasting	30 TV networkers, 900 cable TV, 400 production firms	42 networkers, 451 cable TV, 1 digital satellite TV, 1 SDMB*, 6 TDMB*, 673 production firms	54 TV networkers, 383 cable TV, 1 digital satellite TV, 1 SDMB, 6 TDMB, 3 IPTV, 393 production firms

Source: Author's elaboration of data from White Papers.

Note: SDMB is the acronym for satellite digital multimedia broadcasting. TDMB stands for territorial digital multimedia broadcasting.

established after the 1980s. Over 80 percent of the total number of media companies were established between the mid-1990s and the early 2000s. However, there was a marginal decline in the number of firms in the advertising and broadcasting industries.

Interestingly, foreign capital was more interested in the cable television and advertising markets than the newspaper and film industries. It preferred the establishment of joint venture companies with chaebol groups (e.g., Samsung, LG and Hyundai) to direct managed subsidiaries. As seen in Table 3.9, transnational advertising conglomerates (e.g., Omni group, WPP group and Dentsu group) established joint ventures with media holdings owned by chaebol groups (e.g., Samsung, LG and SK). Foreign and domestic capital shared media ownership in these joint companies.

A similar pattern was found with cable television. As seen in Table 3.10, most foreign capital established joint companies with chaebol groups (e.g., CJ, Orion and Taekwang groups) or state-owned broadcasting companies (e.g., MBC). However, unlike advertising markets, foreign capital rarely established joint

Table 3.9 Transnational advertising agencies within chaebol groups in 2012

Advertising Group	Agencies Owned by Groups
Omni group	TBWA Korea; Lee & DDB
WPP group	JWT Adventure ; M-Hurb; Ogilvy & Mather Korea; Grey Worldwide; AlkiMedia; LG AD; Diamond Ogilvy
Interpublic group	McCann Erickson; FCB Korea; Universal McCann (Media)
Publicis group	Leo Burnett; WelcomPublis; Saatch & Saatch PLC
Dentsu group	Phoenix Communication; Dentsu Innovack
Havas group	Korad; Euro next; Euro RSCG 4D Korea
Hakuhodo group	Hakuhodo Cheil; Communication 21

Source: Author's elaboration of data from both White Papers and Kim & Cha (2009).

Table 3.10 Foreign capital in Korean cable TV in 2008

Business Field	The Korean names	Foreign capital	Nation	Start
System Operator (SO)	Curix	SSB-Aim Group	China (Hong-Kong)	1999
		Citi Group Global	The U.S.	1999
	Hyundai group	Creative Investment	The U.S.	2006
		Modern Investment	The U.S.	2006
	CJ group	AA Merchant Bank	Netherland	2005
		Sable Asia	Malta	2005
		Foross Cable Investment	Malta	2004
Program Provider (PP)	Daewon	Shogakukan Production	Japan	2001
			Japan	2001
		Toei Animation	Japan	2001
		TMS Entertainment Asatsu-dk	Japan	2007
	CJ group	Music on TV	Japan	2001
		MTV Asia	China (Hong-Kong)	1999
		NGC Network	The U.S.	2004
		Macquarie Bank	Australia	2008
	MBC	ESPN Asia	Singapore	2001
	GS group	MGM	The U.S.	2002
	Orion group	New Asia East Investment Fund	Singapore	2000
		Capital International	The U.S.	2000
		HBFS-B-TABM	Portugal	2004
	Taekwang	News Broadcasting	Japan	2005

Source: Author's elaboration of data from White Papers and Lee (2010).

cable television ventures with chaebol groups. Rather, they shared media owner-ship with the Korean-controlled conglomerates within media holdings owned by chaebol groups. Most foreign capital came from mutual funds across continents, including the U.S., Portugal, Hong-Kong, Malta and Japan.

The total number of media companies in the print industry increased from 6,785 in 1998 to 12, 072 in 2010. Daily newspapers increased from 108 in 1998 to 673 in 2010. Internet newspapers also increased from at most 50 in 1998 to 2,484 in 2010. In the advertising industry, agencies and production companies rapidly increased from at most 300 in 1999 to at least 2,184 in 2010. In the film industry, while the number of production companies increased from 116 in 1998 to 2,465 in 2010, the number of distribution companies increased from zero in 1,998 to 575 in 2010. Multiplex theaters grew from 1 in 1998 to 301 in 2010.

Similarly, the number of media channels in the broadcasting industry increased from at most 20 networks and 100 cable television companies in 1998 to 54 net-works, 6 territorial digital multimedia broadcasting (TDMB) companies, 1 sat-ellite digital multimedia broadcasting (SDMB) company, 200 cable television companies, 1 digital satellite broadcasting company and about 400 production companies in 2010. Among these media companies, a few leading companies were listed on the Korean stock markets, including 20 game companies, 20 broad-casting enterprises, 10 printed media companies, 9 recorded music firms, 9 film companies, 6 animation and character companies, 4 computer-mediated commu-nication firms and 2 advertising media firms.

These empirical figures show that neoliberal media reforms in Korea allowed the media industry to become a national economy contributing about 6 percent of the gross domestic product (GDP) in Korean economic sectors by 2012. The total amount of revenue from Korean cultural industries grew at least 10 times from 1998 to 2012. The growth of Korean media industries was associated with increases in media exports and imports as well as rapid growth in the number of media companies.

3.3. Market structures formed by media reforms

In the next section, I investigate the market structures that arose in the advertising, cable television, film and daily newspaper markets as a result of media reforms. I deal with the advertising market first, which played a vital role in financially supporting commercial media systems. After that, I examine the daily newspaper market, which manufactured public discourse in Korean society. The advertising and daily newspaper markets were associated with each other in terms of their information functions in the media. Additionally, I analyze the structures of both the cable TV and film markets, which played a central role in creating and dis-seminating popular culture.

3.3.1. Market structure in advertising

The Korean government started to liberalize the advertising industry in the late 1980s and completely liberalized the advertising markets into transnational advertising agencies (TNAAs) in the early 1990s. In spite of the liberalization of the advertising industry, in-house agencies owned by chaebol groups dominated the Korean markets in the 1990s. They occupied at least 80 percent of the total market shares, while TNAAs occupied at most 3.2 percent of the total market shares (Lee, 2008). However, these trends shifted during the periods of media reforms.

The size of the advertising market increased from about 4.6 trillion won (U.S. $4.6 billion) in 1999 to about 9.7 trillion won (U.S. $9.7 billion) in 2012. As seen in Table 3.11, the increase in broadcasting advertising markets (e.g., territorial television, radio and cable television) was much more significant than the print industry markets.

Cable television recorded the fastest growth rate, while territorial television registered the largest advertising revenue. Revenues in print advertising also increased. Much like the traditional media markets, new media markets also exhibited enormous growth rates. From 1998 to 2012, the Internet (e.g., computer-mediated communications) recorded a growth of 230 times its size. Others (e.g., sales promotion, digital satellite broadcasting, digital convergence media between broadcasting and telecommunication) also indicated about threefold growth.

While total advertising revenues expanded across all markets and platforms, advertising volume shifted from traditional (e.g., television and newspapers) to new media (e.g., Internet, satellite TV, cable TV, IPTV and DMB). The volume of television advertising consistently shrank from 38.1 percent of total advertising in 1999 to 23.0 percent in 2009. Similarly, newspapers advertising also shrank from 32.3 percent in 1999 to 20.7 percent in 2009. On the other hand, advertising in new media rapidly grew from 5.4 percent in 1999 to 28.3 percent in 2009. The shift in advertising focus suggests there has been a shift in media consumption among Korean audiences from traditional media to new media.

Another characteristic of the Korean advertising industry from 1998 to 2012 was the rapid growth of global advertising agencies, or transnational advertising agencies. Most TNAAs entered Korea's advertising markets, including the Publicis, Interpublic, WPP, Dentsu, Omnicom and Havas groups. These TNAAs either acquired in-house advertising agencies owned by chaebol groups or established

Table 3.11 Changed patterns of advertising, 1999–2012 ($ millions)

Media	1999	2002	2005	2008	2012
Television	1,492.1	2,439.4	2,149.1	1,899.7	1,930.7
Radio	175.1	278.0	268.3	276.9	235.8
Cable TV	128.1	234.5	436.8	860.0	1,321.8
Newspaper	1,805.5	2,020.0	1,672.4	1,658.1	1,654.3
Magazine	130	546.5	436.8	480.4	507.6
Internet	81.2	185.0	566.9	1,190	1,854.0
Others*	808.6	1,140.8	1,473.5	1,432.0	2,266.4
Total	4,620.6	6,844.2	7,003.8	7,797.1	9,770.6

Source: Author's elaboration of data from White Papers.

* Includes sales promotion (SP), outdoor, production and digital media convergence.

joint ventures with chaebol groups. In fact, after Korea's financial crisis in 1997, chaebol groups completely sold out or partially transferred stakes in their in-house advertising agencies to the TNAAs to save parent companies. For example, Grey Global Group (CCG), a British global agency, acquired Kumkang Communication, owned by the Hyundai group, in 1999. In the same year, TBWA, an American global agency, acquired Taekwang Multi AD, which was owned by the SK group. WPP, another British global agency, acquired LG AD, an in-house agency of the LG group, in 2002. Havas, a French agency, took over Korad, an in-house agency of the Haitai group, in 2004.

The second strategy exercised by TNAAs was to establish joint ventures with the chaebol groups' in-house advertising agencies. For instance, DDB founded Lee & DDB Korea with Daehong Communication, an in-house agency of the Lotte group, in 2000. Dentsu established Dentsu Innovack, a joint venture with JoongAng Ilbo, in 2001. Both Dentsu and JoongAng Ilbo co-owned Phoenix Communication. Consequently, about 100 TNAAs ran their advertising businesses in Korea in 2009, thereby increasing the market shares from 6 percent in 1998 to about 47 percent of total advertising markets in 2003. Global advertising agencies became major players in Korean advertising markets, thereby competing with in-house agencies owned by chaebol groups (Yun, 2008).

Interestingly, the restructuring of Korea's advertising markets allowed chaebol groups' in-house advertising agencies to dominate the market again in 2009. The market shares of chaebol groups' advertising agencies decreased from 1998 to 2003. However, they rebounded and increased their advertising market shares by 2005 when the first-tier chaebol groups (e.g. Hyundai, SK and LG) refused to renew advertising contracts with TNAAs after they established their new in-house advertising agencies (Hahm & Seo, 2011). In spite of intense competition between foreign and domestic agencies, independent advertising agencies were hardly ever among the top 10 producers. Chaebol groups regained lost ground and profited alongside TNAAs in the Korean advertising market.

The reemergence of chaebol groups in the Korean advertising markets was attributed to the fact that chaebol groups were major clients of advertising agencies and owners of major Korean advertising holdings. For example, Samsung Electronics was a subsidiary of the Samsung group, which controlled Cheil Communication, the largest advertising agency in Korea. SK Telecommunication, the largest wireless phone company in Korea, was a media holding of the SK group, which owned SK & MC. Hyundai Car and Kia Car were members of the Pan-Hyundai group, which held the Innocean. Other advertisers were subsidiaries of second-tier chaebol groups.

Through re-establishing in-house advertising agencies, chaebol groups regained their lost market shares. As a result, big money from both TNAAs and chaebol groups dominated Korea's advertising markets. They belonged to top 10 advertising agencies and increased market shares from at least 65 percent of the total advertising size in 2003 to 81.1 percent of the total market size in 2011. As seen in Table 3.12, agencies of chaebol groups included Cheil Communication (Samsung group), Daehong Communication (Lotte group), Innocean (Hyundai group),

Table 3.12 Advertising agencies and percentage market shares, 1999–2011

Rank	1999	Parent Company	2009	Parent Company	2011	Parent Company
1	Cheil (15.3)	Samsung*	Cheil (30.4)	Samsung*	Cheil (32.7)	Samsung*
2	LG AD (11.8)	LG*	Innocean (23.8)	Hyundai*	Innocean (27.5)	Hyundai*
3	Kumkang (11.7)	Hyundai*	HS AD (7.0)	LG* & WPP#	HS AD (4.8)	LG* & WPP#
4	Daehong (5.2)	Lotte*	Daehong (5.7)	Lotte*	Daehong (4.2)	Lotte*
5	Korad (4.8)	Haitai*	SK & MC (4.2)	SK*	SK & MC (3.4)	SK*
6	Phoenix (4.4)	JoongAng Ilbo* & Dentsu#	TWBA Korea (2.5)	OMNICOM#	TBWA Korea (2.4)	OMNICOM#
7	JWT Adventure (3.7)	WPP#	NongShim (2.3)	NongShim*	LBest (2.1)	LG*
8	Oricom (3.6)	Doosan*	Oricom (2.2*)	Doosan*	Hancom (1.5)	Hanhwa*
9	Universal McCann (2.9)	Interpublic#	People Works (2.0!)	Independent	Dentsu (1.3)	Dentsu#
10	Seoul (2.5!)	Independent	Hancomm (1.9*)	Hanhwa*	Welcom (1.2!)	Independent
	Total 65.9		82.00		81.1	

Source: Author's elaboration of data from White Papers.

Note:
* refers to in-house agencies of chaebol groups.
# refers to the advertising agencies owned by TNNAs.
' refers to the independent advertising agency.

Hancomm (Hanhwa group), Phoenix Com (JoongAng Ilbo group), NongShim (NongShim group), HS AD (LG group) and SK & MC (SK group). Three advertising companies (Innocean, HS AD and SK MC) were re-established by chaebol groups after 2005. Affiliates of TNAAs included LG AD, TBWA Korea, Korad, Kumkang Communication, Well Com and JWT Adventure. Independent advertising agencies included Seoul Advertising and Welcommunication. The Korean advertising market at the time was structured by the top 10 advertising agencies. The other about 1,500 small- and medium-sized advertising companies struggled to occupy the leftover market shares.

In summary, the Korean advertising markets were structured by top 10 advertising companies that were subsidiaries of both chaebol groups and TNAAs. Both domestic and foreign capital together occupied at least 65 percent of the total advertising market in 1999 and 81.1 percent in 2011. After neoliberal media reforms, Korea's advertising market became more oligopolistic than previous times.

3.3.2. Market structure of daily newspapers

Like the advertising markets, the Korean government had already liberalized the daily newspapers in the late 1980s. This led to an increase in the total number of papers from 85 in 1990 to 107 in 1997 (Yoo, 1989; Kwak, 2012). Liberal policies had encouraged chaebol groups and other Korean capitalists to establish paper companies or acquire them at the local and national levels. The Korean newspaper markets existed on two tiers in the 1990s. The first-tier group in charge of setting the public and national agendas consisted of national newspapers including general publications (covering social, economic and political issues), economic papers (focusing on economic issues) and sports papers. The top 10 papers included the *Chosun Ilbo*, the *JoongAng Ilbo*, the *DongA Ilbo*, the *Hankuk Ilbo*, the *KyungHang Shinmun*, the *Hankyoreh*, the *Nae-il Shinmun*, the *Munhwa Daily Newspaper*, the *Maeil Economic Daily* and the *Kukmin Ilbo*. The second tier consisted of the regional papers focusing on localized issues in the Korean Peninsula.

Chaebol groups held ownership at the national levels more than the regional level since the national papers played a more central role in framing the national discourse than the local ones. For example, at the national level, the Hanhwa group, a second-tier chaebol group, acquired the national daily *KyungHang* in 1990. The Hyundai group, a first-tier chaebol group, founded the national *Munhwa Daily Newspaper* in 1991. Chaebol groups also established local and national papers at the same time. For example, the Duksan group, a second-tier chaebol group, established the regional *Moodeung Ilbo* in 1988 and the national *Ilgan Today* in 1994. Two years later, the Line group, a second-tier chaebol group, purchased the *Moodeung Ilbo* from Duksan group (Kim, et al., 2000).

Korea's financial crisis, however, pushed chaebol groups to change the ownership structure of newspapers to save the parent companies. In 1998, the Hyundai group, which owned *Munhwa Daily Newspaper*, transferred its media ownership to the employees of the newspaper and two cultural foundations affiliated with Hyundai group. The Hanhwa group transferred its media ownership to the employees of the newspaper (Kwak, 2012). The Line group that owned the regional *Moodeung Ilbo* went bankrupt in 1998 (Kim, et al., 2000).

Following these fluctuations in the newspaper market, the number of companies gradually increased from 1998 to 2012. As seen in Table 3.13, the total number of daily newspaper companies at both national and local levels increased from 125 in 1998 to 290 in 2009. In fact, national newspapers nearly tripled in number, while local newspapers increased twofold.

Table 3.13 Number of daily newspapers, 1998–2009

	1998	2004	2009
National newspapers	55	58	152
Local newspapers	70	77	138
Total	125	135	290

Source: Author's elaboration of data from White Papers.

The rise in newspaper companies was associated with the injection of neoliberal laws and policies in the print industry. The Korean civil government relaxed regulations, allowing for the establishment of several media companies and a concentration of media ownership. The state rarely cared about news content. As a result, national and regional papers freely reported and criticized issues that involved the government, politicians and the president. News reporters covered government wrongdoing, any signs of misdeeds, abuse or corruption. Both national and regional papers, however, rarely criticized their big advertisers or their parent companies (Kwak, 2012, pp. 70–90).

It is important to note that the market situations of daily newspapers worsened because of a gradual reduction in readership and subscriptions. According to the Korea Press Foundation (2013), daily readership between 2002 and 2013 rapidly decreased to 33.8 percent from 82.1 percent of total paper readers. Daily subscriptions were similarly down, dropping from 64.5 percent to 20.4 percent of regular subscribers.

Worse yet, the newspaper industry had become polarized between "the big three companies" and other companies, as seen in Table 3.14. The big three companies – the *Chosun Ilbo*, the *JoongAng Ilbo* and the *DongA Ilbo* – were together dubbed "Cho-Joong-Dong." There were seven other national papers (e.g., the *KyungHang Shinmun*, the *Hankyoreh* and the *Nae-il Shinmun)* and a number of regional ones. In terms of market share comparison between the major three companies and others, Cho-Joong-Dong increased its market shares from 52.3 percent of total circulation numbers in 1998 to 67.7 percent in 2009. Although the number of companies increased more than twofold, from 125 in 1998 to 290 in 2009, Cho-Joong-Dong accumulated a monopoly of Korean daily papers.

In fact, the three companies of Cho-Joong-Dong had previously maintained a close relationship with the military regimes to receive favors (e.g., tax and financial rewards), thereby forming a patron-client relationship between the state and the owners of the three mainstream newspapers (Park, et al., 2000). The Cho-Joong-Dong also disseminated market-oriented ideology in the name of market supremacy to protect the private interests of big advertisers and chaebol groups. That is to say, the three major papers formed strategic alliances with the vested groups (Kim & Shin, 1994; Kwak, 2012). These power alliances between Cho-Joong-Dong and vested groups remained intact.

In addition, the three newspaper companies maintained concentrated family media ownership. The *Chosun Ilbo* was owned by the Bang family and its own cultural foundation. The Hong family and its relatives owned the *JoongAng Ilbo*, and the *DongA Ilbo* was controlled by the Kim family and its cultural foundation.

Table 3.14 Market share percentage in the daily newspapers (%)

Year	1998	2000	2002	2004	2006	2008	2009
Cho-Joong-Dong	52.3	64.3	67.5	65.0	56.6	60.9	67.7
Others	47.7	35.7	32.5	35.0	43.4	39.1	32.3

Source: Author's elaboration of data from White Papers and Kwak (2012).

These family-controlled newspapers tended to publish articles that served and protected their vested interests, including the interests of the ruling classes, the military regimes and chaebol groups. The newspapers also manufactured public opinion in favor of military leaders to make sure candidates who would serve their interests were elected president (Ryu, 1994).

In sum, the market structure of the daily newspapers worsened, polarization grew and the benefit-exchange mechanisms between Cho-Joong-Dong and the ruling classes strengthened. The big three mainstream papers encroached on 70 percent of the total circulation shares, while the other 287 daily papers competed against each other to appeal to the remaining 30 percent of the market. The widening gap in market shares between the big three newspaper companies and others led to severe inequity in print advertising. Advertisers preferred the big three papers with higher market shares to the other small- and medium-sized papers (Lee, 2009, 2011). Although the number of newspaper companies increased more than twofold during the 15 years of media reforms, Korea's newspaper market became highly concentrated.

3.3.3. Market structure in cable television

Since the mid-1990s when cable television initiated broadcasting services, the Korean government has consistently advanced technological innovation in the Korean broadcasting markets. Digital satellite television was launched in 2002. Digital media convergence between telecommunication and broadcasting (e.g., TDMB and SDMB) was introduced in 2005. Internet Protocol television and comprehensive cable channels were added to the national services in 2008 and in 2009 respectively (Kim, 2010; Jin, 2011). Korea expanded multimedia channels, leading to an increase in the total number of paid subscribers in the broadcasting markets. The total number of paid subscribers increased from about 7.8 million in 2001 to 23.36 million in 2010. Over 90 percent of Korean households began to use paid broadcasting services. The market share of cable TV, however, gradually decreased from 97.3 percent in 2001 to 64 percent in 2010. On the other hand, digital, satellite and Internet television subscriptions gradually increased. Thus, competition between cable and new technology companies intensified over the years.

In addition, the Korean media reforms led to a decrease in the number of cable TV companies. As seen in Table 3.15, the total number of media companies in the cable TV business decreased from 649 in 2004 to 398 in 2008. There has been a greater decrease in network operators and music system operators than in program providers and system operators. In contrast to cable TV, the number of media companies in network radio and television gradually increased during the same period. The number of digital convergence media companies remained stable.

Neoliberal media laws and policies were the main reason for the decrease in the number of media companies in cable TV. Deregulation allowed chaebol groups and foreign financial capital to expand their cable businesses through mergers and acquisitions (Jang, 2010). This meant that political power institutionally permitted the money play of both domestic and foreign capital. The two aggressively took over independent media companies in cable TV.

Table 3.15 Changed numbers of broadcasting companies, 2004–2008

		2004	2005	2006	2007	2008
Networkers (TV and radio)		43	43	46	50	53
Cable television	Total	649	524	443	412	398
	System operator (SO)	119	119	107	103	103
	Network operator (NO)	299	198	139	115	108
	Music SO	72	63	10	6	0
	Program provider (PP)	159	144	187	188	187
Digital satellite TV		1	1	1	1	1
Digital media convergence (e.g., TDMB and SDMB)		N/A	7	7	7	7
Electronic broadcasting		42	45	40	34	34
Total		735	614	531	498	490

Source: Author's elaboration of data from Fair Trade Commission, May 28, 2010, and White Papers.

Specifically, financial capital came from foreign institutional investors (e.g., Citigroup from the U.S. and Macquarie Bank from Australia), private property investors (e.g., New Asia East Investment and Foross Cable Investment), American cultural conglomerates (e.g., both Viacom and ABC-Disney) and Japanese cultural conglomerates (e.g., TMCs Entertainment and Music on TV). Foreign capital rarely established media subsidiaries in Korea, but rather invested in Korean-owned cable companies (e.g., chaebol groups, independent companies and the Korean state) (Lee, 2010). The most sought-after partners were chaebol groups with co-ownership of media holdings. For example, the Orion group cooperated with New Asia East Investment Fund, Capital International and HBFS-B-TABX; the CJ group shared its media ownership with Formosa Cable Investment, AA Merchant Banking, Music on TV, NGC Network and Macquarie Bank. Both the LG and Taekwang groups received foreign investments as well. The second most desirable partners were independent cable companies (e.g., Curix and CNM) that shared ownership and seats on boards of directors with them. Finally, foreign capital invested in media holdings owned by MBC, a public broadcasting network (Jang, 2010).

Cooperation between domestic and foreign capital brought about centralized market structures in cable TV. The first change was the emergence of multiple system operators (MSOs), multiple program providers (MPPs) or multiple system providers (MSPs). The appearance of these major players was related to the second change in centralized market structures of cable TV that centered on economic profits. The MPPs tended to recirculate media content among cable TV, digital satellite television (e.g., SDMB and TDMB) and IPTV. The MSOs could also sell broadband and Internet phone services. These MSOs and MPPs further invested in other paid broadcasting companies that offered digital media convergence and IPTV. Thus, the major players in cable TV were able to influence other paid broadcasting markets located at the top of their hierarchical structures. This economic potential was attributed to the appearance of a market structure centered around five to seven cable companies.

For example, the market structure of program providers (or cable channels) was polarized between the top five MPPs (e.g., CJ, Orion and the three territorial networkers) and about 150 other independent cable companies. The top five MPPs consistently increased their market shares from 33.2 percent in 2004 to 46.7 percent in 2008. Both the CJ and Orion groups became more powerful players than the territorial networks (e.g., MBC, KBS and SBS). The two groups ran motion pictures, animation, cartoon, sports, fashion and online game channels. The other three networkers rebroadcast their media contents to these cable channels.

Much like the structure of the program provider market, the cable system operating market was also concentrated among a few cable companies. The top seven MSOs (Taekwang, CJ, CNM, Orion, GS, Curix and C&B) occupied at least 80 percent of the total system operating market in 2010. Three of the top seven occupied at least 62 percent of the total cable system operating markets (Taekwang, 25 percent; CJ, 18.6 to 19.3 percent; and CNM, 18.3 percent). This triggered a tertiary hierarchical order with three meta-firms at the top, the four mid-size businesses at the second level and the remaining small business at the bottom. Further, unlike the market structure of program providers, the three territorial networkers were rarely involved in the cable system business.

In addition, a few chaebol groups (e.g., CJ, GS and Hyundai groups) became major MSPs with foreign capital. The appearance of MSPs in cable television started in 2001 when the Korean government allowed cross-media ownership between program providers and cable system operators. In 2001, the Orion group became a multiple system provider with eight cable channels and 6 cable system operators. The CJ group became an MSP with four cable channels and 13 cable system operators. The GS group was an MSP with a home shopping channel and 16 cable system operators. The Hyundai group was an MSP with a home shopping channel and 7 cable system operators. Eight years later, in 2009, the three chaebol groups (CJ, GS and Hyundai) were major MSPs occupying at least 40 percent of the total Korean cable TV market.

In other words, Korean cable TV became heavily concentrated among a few chaebol groups with foreign financial capital, as seen in Table 3.16. In the

Table 3.16 Market percentage of top four cable companies in 2009

Rank	MPPs	MSOs	MSPs
1	CJ group (31.9)	Taekwang group (27.8)	CJ group (26.7)
2	MBC (6.3)	CJ group (22.0)	Taekwang group (8.8)
3	SBS (5.4)	C&B (17.3)	GS group (7.5)
4	KBS (3.1)	Hyundai group (6.9)	Hyundai group (7.5)
Total	46.7	74.2	50.3

Source: Author's elaboration of government data from White Paper from 2011 and Jang (2010).

Table 3.17 Top seven MSOs and their percentage market shares

Names	Number of system operators (SOs)	Market shares	
		2008	*2009*
Taekwang group	22	25.9	25.9
CJ group	14	18.6	19.3
CNM	16	18.3	18.2
Hyundai group	10	8.3	8.5
C&B	12	5.6	5.3
Orion group	4	2.9	2.8
GS group	2	3.8	3.7
Total market shares by MSO	80	83.4	83.7
Single SO	22	16.9	16.3
Total of MSO	102	100	100

Source: Author's elaboration of data from governmental data and Jang (2010, p. 35).

program provider market, chaebol groups and three territorial networks occupied about 50 percent of the total market size and MPPs. In the cable system operating markets, the top seven companies held at least 80 percent of the total market size and MSOs (see Table 3.17). They were major MPPs and MSOs, thereby becoming MSPs. They represented big money in Korean cable TV.

3.3.4. Market structure in film

In accordance with a trade agreement with the U.S., the Korean government had liberalized the film distribution market and opened the doors to transnational media corporations by the late 1980s. Since then, American media conglomerates have established distribution branches in Korea, holding at least 80 percent of Korea's film market in the mid-1990s (Ryo, 2008). By the 1990s, Korean film markets were dominated by Hollywood studios rather than chaebol groups.

Against this market climate, since 1998, the Korean government has started to corporatize the film industry. Neoliberal laws and policies allowed for an increase in the number of film production, production and exhibition companies. This led to increased Korean film production and centralized structures for both distribution and exhibition markets (Park, 2005). The policy reforms displaced the dominance of Hollywood films in the Korean market and produced a limited competitive environment involving American cultural conglomerates and Korean media companies in the early 2000s.

3.3.4.1. Film production

During the period of media reforms, the number of film companies increased geometrically. As seen in Table 3.18, the total number of film companies grew fourfold from 1999 to 2011. The increase in production firms was much higher than that of distribution, importation and exhibition companies. The growth in the

Table 3.18 Changed numbers of film companies, 1999–2011

	1999	*2002*	*2004*	*2006*	*2009*	*2011*
Production	367	1,081	1,375	2,154	2,365	2,664
Importation	215	428	509	820	741	813
Distribution	155	290	315	435	559	641
Exhibition	409	557	654	983	715	829
Total	1,146	2,356	2,853	4,392	4,380	4,947

Source: Author's elaboration of data from White Papers.

number of film companies inevitably brought about an increase in the number of domestic film productions and a decrease in the number of imported films. The number of Korean film production companies increased from 49 in 1999 to 150 in 2011. On the other hand, the number of the imported motion pictures slightly decreased from 348 in 1999 to 289 in 2011. In sum, growth in the Korean film industry was associated with an increase in Korean film products.

Moreover, the increase in Korean film production can be attributed to economic investment by media venture funds established in 1999 by both the Korean government and financial institutions. The members of these investment associations included independent financial institutions (e.g., Moohan, Mearae Asset and Cowell), financial holdings owned by chaebol groups (e.g., Samsung Venture, both Dream Discovery and Peta Capital of CJ), the Korean government and other financial institutions. Although the Korean government invested at most 20 percent in individual venture capital investment associations, it typically entrusted the execution of capital to the financial institutions. Thus, each individual financial institution was in charge of managing total production costs with the goal of making profit. The total number of investment associations gradually increased from 2 in 1999 to 23 in 2007. Each association financially supported at least 45 Korean films and accounted for at least 40 percent of total production costs in the early 2000s.

Participation of the financial institutions in particular led to an increase in production and marketing costs. The cost of filmmaking grew exponentially between 1999 and 2012. Average production costs increased at least 130 times, and marketing costs grew sevenfold. However, 2006 was a point of attrition. From 1999 to 2006, the average costs of both production and marketing expanded exorbitantly. After 2006, both production and marketing costs stabilized.

In other words, Korean film production showed a heavy quantitative growth between 1998 and 2012. Investment associations for film production enabled film producers to manufacture blockbuster films, which led to an increase in production and marketing costs.

3.3.4.2. Film distribution

Before 1998, only American film distributors existed in Korea. They enjoyed the monopolized right to distribute both Korean and American motion pictures across the Korean Peninsula. After 1998, however, Korean film distributors appeared.

They included both second-tier chaebol groups (e.g., CJ group, Lotte group and Orion group) and independent distributors (e.g., Cinema Service, Korea Pictures and Chung-A-Ram) (Park, 2005). This was the beginning of an era of competition between Korean and Hollywood distributors. They released foreign and domestic motion pictures. In this segment, I analyze the nature of the changed film distribution market structure and then investigate the characteristics of both Korean and non-Korean motion pictures.

Table 3.19 indicates the general changes in the distribution market, including major players and market shares, from 2001 to 2010. The top five companies controlled Korea's distribution market. They included both American (e.g., Warner Brothers, Sony Pictures and Buena Vista, Buena Vista/Walt Disney and Twentieth Century Fox) and Korean distributors (e.g., CJ; Cinema Service, renamed Plenus; Orion; Korean Pictures; Chung-A-Ram; and Lotte). Among the Korean members of the top five, three companies (e.g., CJ, Orion and Lotte) belonged to chaebol groups. Independent distributors included Cinema Service, Korean Pictures and Chung-A-Ram. The top five distributors occupied 59.6 percent of the total market share in 2001 and 68.9 percent in 2010.

Between 2001 and 2010, the Korean film distribution market was volatile because of continuous mergers and acquisitions among members of the top five distributors. For example, Cinema Service was acquired by the Locus group in 2001 and renamed Plenus. The Locus group was an emerging media group that ran a variety of media businesses in film distribution and production, online gaming, recorded music and television drama and film studio production. However, the Locus group sold out all media businesses to the CJ group in 2004. Since then, CJ has become the first-ranked film distributor in Korea. In addition, mergers and acquisitions among Korean distributors affected Hollywood distributors. For instance, Walt Disney and Sony Pictures together established a joint venture

Table 3.19 Top five film distributors in 2001–2010 by market percentage

Rank	2001	2003	2007	2010
1	Cinema Service (22.6)	CJ (21.79)	CJ (29.7)	CJ (28)
2	CJ (14.7)	Plenus (18.70)	Orion (12.3)	Twentieth Century Fox (12.3)
3	Korea Pictures (13.2)	Warner Brothers (8.15)	Warner Brothers (11.3)	Sony Pictures and Buena Vista (9.9)
4	Warner Brothers (9.1)	Chung-A-Ram (7.63)	Sony Pictures and Buena Vista (9.8)	Lotte (9.8)
5	N/A	Buena Vista/ Walt Disney (6.40)	Lotte (8.6)	Warner Brothers (8.9)
Total market share of top five	59.6	62.67	60.4	68.9

Source: Author's elaboration of data from government White Papers from 2002, 2004, 2008 and 2011.

(Sony Pictures and Buena Vista) to expand their influence in Korea's distribution market. Mergers and acquisitions among chaebol groups and Hollywood distributors led to a centralized market structure. Together, they controlled at least 68.9 percent of the total market share.

As seen in Table 3.20, the top five distributors that released Korean motion pictures held market shares ranging from 68.9 percent to 90.5 percent. Most Korean films were distributed by Korean companies such as Cinema Service and the CJ and Orion groups. They held at least 80 percent of the total market share. American film distributors (e.g., Warner Brothers, Korea Pictures and Sony Pictures and Buena Vista) reached at most 9.9 percent of Korean film distribution. In the early 2000s, Cinema Service was the only distributor of Korean motion pictures. CJ acquired the parent company of Cinema Service, thereby making it the leading distributor in Korea.

Much like the distribution market of Korean motion pictures, the top five companies also controlled the distribution market of foreign motion pictures. The major distributors of foreign films were WBs, United International Pictures (UIP) and Twentieth Century Fox, CJ, Orion, New and Plenus. Top five distributors occupied at least 67.9 percent of the total market share in 2001 and 81.1 percent of the total market share in 2007. Although both domestic and foreign distributors controlled Korea's foreign film distribution market, market share trends between them looked different. Hollywood distributors gradually lost their market shares, holding 83.6 percent of Korea's total foreign distribution in 2001 and only 66.8 percent of this market share in 2007. Conversely, Korean distributors increased their market share from at least 16.4 percent in 2001 to 33.8 percent in 2007.

Taken together, chaebol groups and Hollywood studios controlled the Korean foreign distribution market. While chaebol groups had a greater market share in the distribution of domestic films, Hollywood distributors controlled the majority of foreign film distribution.

3.3.4.3. Film exhibition

By early 1998, independent movie theaters were in charge of the exhibition of all motion pictures in Korea. However, the CJ group opened a multiplex theater in the Gang-byun area of Seoul in 1998. Since then, chaebol groups (e.g., Orion, JoongAng Ilbo and Lotte) have expanded their media businesses into the film exhibition market. They constructed multiplex theaters in the downtown areas of several major cities and precipitated the fall of independent theaters. Hollywood studios have yet to venture into the exhibition market. As seen in Table 3.20, the

Table 3.20 Numbers of theaters and screens, 1999–2011

Year	1999	2003	2007	2009	2011
Number of screens	588	1,132	1,451	2,055	1,974
Number of theaters	409	302	314	301	292

Source: Author's elaboration of data from White Papers.

number of screens increased from 588 in 1999 to 1,974 to 2011. The total number of independent theaters, however, decreased from 409 in 1999 to 292 in 2012. While chaebol groups constructed multiplexes that could screen five or more movies, independent theaters typically consisted of a single screen in each theater.

Independent theatres collapsed because of the changing tastes of cinema audiences, who preferred the updated facilities of multiplex theaters to the old independent ones. Moreover, film exhibition was tightly linked to distribution. Distribution agreements typically required theater owners to provide at least five screens as a contract condition to release a motion picture. These two factors pushed the owners of independent film theaters to accept the commissioned management of major exhibitors (Park, 2005). As a result, the Korean exhibition market changed from an independent theater–oriented structure to multiple theater models, in charge of exhibiting about 95.6 percent of the total motion pictures exhibited in Korea in 2012. Eventually, multiplex theaters displaced small- and medium-sized movie theaters.

Let's look at the changed market situation from 2010 to 2012. In 2010, the top four film exhibitors controlled 83 percent of the total number of film screens and exhibited motion pictures at their own multiplex theaters. As seen in Table 3.21, CJ was the most prominent film exhibitor, owning 104 multiplex theaters and 806 film screens. Lotte was the second largest film exhibitor and owned 55 multiplex theaters and 478 film screens. Both JoongAng Ilbo and Orion also emerged as major exhibitors of films in Korea. Two years later, in 2012, JoongAng Ilbo acquired Orion, thereby becoming the third-ranked exhibitor. The Korean film exhibition market was now structured by three chaebol groups (e.g., CJ, Lotte and JoongAng Ilbo). Since 2003, these major exhibitors have begun to assert their influence by engaging in the business of commissioned management of independent movie theaters. Small- and medium-sized film exhibitors transferred the rights to manage their movie theaters to owners of multiple theaters in order to survive in the tough market situation. Both CJ and Lotte, however, paid more attention to commissioned management than JoongAng Ilbo.

Table 3.21 Major film exhibitors in 2010

Company		Total number of multiplexes	Total number of screens	Management Type	
				Direct management	Commissioned management
CJ	CGV	71	623	45	32
	Premus	32	183	10	15
Lotte		55	478	32	33
Orion		16	133	12	4
JoongAng Ilbo		31	240	7	26
Other multiplexes		32	199	0	0
Non-multiplex		69	147	0	0
Total		305	2003		

Source: White Paper published by the Korean cultural department in 2010, p. 255.

In summary, the Korean film exhibition market was structured by the top five exhibitors, which were all owned by chaebol groups. Since the end of 1998, a few chaebol groups (e.g., CJ, Orion and Lotte groups) have constructed multiplex theaters and also run the commissioned management of independent exhibitors around the Korean Peninsula.

Conclusion

Korea's media reforms brought three big changes to the media landscape: a shift in total revenues, market sizes and the number of media companies. The media industry became integral to Korea's national economy, accounting for approximately 7 percent of the country's gross domestic product in 2012. Total revenue from the media industries increased from U.S. $859 million in 1999 to $8,241 million in 2011. The rapid growth of the Korean media industries was associated with growth in media exports and advertisement market sizes, as well as an increase in the number of media outlets domestically. In spite of increasing quantitative growth in Korean media, the total number of media companies showed different growth tendencies in each of the four media markets. The number of media companies in three of the media markets (i.e., advertising, daily newspaper and film) increased, while the number of cable companies decreased.

Moreover, the fundamental changes in the media market systems led to the formation of oligopolistic structures by a few media companies: chaebol groups, transnational media corporations and the existing mainstream papers. They occupied from 50 to 80 percent of total markets shares in the four media markets. That is to say, chaebol groups, mainstream papers and transnational media conglomerates were able to determine what to produce, distribute and exhibit as well as what to not produce, distribute and exhibit. The polarization between these few big market controllers and the many small, independent media firms became more serious from 1998 to 2014.

Further, in all four media markets, chaebol groups held more market shares than the transnational media conglomerates. It seems that chaebol groups were the beneficiaries of centralized market structures formed by Korea's media reforms. However, chaebol groups and transnational media conglomerates cooperated with each other, shared media ownership and/or established joint ventures together.

Note

1 Data I analyzed *include* White Papers, published by the Ministry of Culture, Sports, and Tourism (MCST), and special reports, published by the Fair Trade Commission (FTC). The MCST is in charge of Korean media laws and policies, and its white papers report on Korean media market structures, revenues, imports and exports. The FTC supervises the Korean media market, including activities of chaebol groups, and its special reports reflect the economic activities of major media players across markets. While government sources constitute primary data, I review supplementary resources such as scholarly works and news articles for secondary data.

References

Hahm, S.W. & Seo, S.H. (2011). A study on the change of the concentration rate and share of advertising market in Korea. *Social Science Research Review*, 27(4), 343–370. Korean.

Hyun, D. & Lent, J.A. (1999). Korean telecom policy in global competition: Implications for developing countries. *Telecommunication Policy*, 23(5), 389–401.

Jang, H.S. (2010). A research of the integrated form between foreign capital and domestic finance in the Korean CATV: A case study of CNM. Paper presented at Special Conference by National Congressmen, at Committee of National Human Rights on September 8, 2010. Seoul, Korea.

Jin, D.Y. (2006a). Political and economic processes in the privatization of the Korea telecommunication industry: A case study of Korea Telecom, 1987–2003. *Telecommunications Policy*, 30(1), 3–13.

Jin, D.Y. (2006b). Cultural politics in Korea's contemporary films under neoliberal globalization. *Media, Culture & Society*, 28(1), 5–23.

Jin, D.Y. (2011). *Hands on/off: The Korean state and the market liberalization of the communication industry*. New York: Hampton.

Jin, D.Y. & Shim, D.B. (2007). Transformation and development of the Korean broadcasting media. In M. Patrick and I.A. Blankson (eds.), *Globalization and media transformation in new and emerging democracies* (pp. 161–176). New York: SUNY Press.

Kang, J.G. & Kim, W.Y. (1994). A survey of radio and television: History, system and programming. In J.W. Kim & J.W. Lee (Eds.), *Elite media amidst mass culture: A critical look at mass communication in Korea* (pp. 109–136). Seoul, Korea: Nanam.

Kim, C.H., Im, J.H., Song, K.J. & Kim, K.H. (2000). *Crisis of the Korean Local Newspaper in South Korea.* Seoul, Korea: Korean Press Foundation.

Kim, J.W. & Shin, T.S. (1994). The Korean press: A half century of controls, suppression and intermittent resistance. In J.W. Kim & J.W. Lee (Eds.), *Elite media amidst mass culture: A critical look at mass communication in Korea* (pp. 65–108). Seoul, Korea: Nanam.

Kim, K.K. & Cha, H. (2009). The globalization of the Korean advertising industry: Dependency or hybridity? *Media international Australia, Incorporating Culture & Policy*, 133, 97–109.

Kim, S.S. (2010). *Media markets and the public interests in Korea.* Seoul, Korea: Hanul Academy. Korean.

KOCCA. (2006). A study about the inter-relationship between regional development and cultural industry. Seoul, Korea: Korea Creative Contents Agency. Korean.

Korea Press Foundation. (2013). *The survey of press readers*. Seoul, Korea: Korea Press Foundation. Korean.

Kwak, K.S. (2012). *Media and democratic transition in South Korea.* New York: Routledge.

Lee, J.R. (1997). *The study on the formation and growing process of the Korean computer mediated communication industry: Focused on the computer mediated communication companies.* Seoul: Kyunghee University. Dissertation.

Lee, J.T. (2010). *Market situation of the Korean CATV and public interest.* Paper presented at special conference by National Congressmen, at Committee of National Human Rights on September 8, 2010. Seoul, Korea. Korean.

Lee, M.H. (2008). Transformation of the Korean advertising markets. In S.K. Yun (Ed.), *Korea's advertising* (pp. 69–98). Seoul, Korea: Nanam. Korean.

Lee, S.K. (2011). Input-output analysis of Korean newspaper industry. *The Journal of Korean Communication*, 15(1), 165–200.

Lee, Y.S. (2009). *Critical aspects on deregulation of cross-media ownership between newspapers and broadcasting: Media laws and policies on Lee Myung-bak regime.* Paper presented at spring meeting of Korean press and information, May 16, 2009. Seogang University, Seoul, Korea,

Nam, S. (2008). The politics of compressed development in new media: A history of Korean cable television, 1992–2005, *Media, Culture & Society*, 30(5), 641–661.

Park, E.Y. (2005). *The process of Korean film's corporation.* Seoul, Korea: Korean Film Foundation. Korean.

Park, J.W., Lee, B.M., & Rho, J.S. (2007). *The media policies of Rho administration.* Seoul, Korea: The Institution of Korea Culture and Tourism. Korean.

Ryo, W. (2008). The political economy of the global mediascape: The case of the South Korean film industry. *Media, Culture & Society*, 30(6), 873–889.

Ryu, H.H. (1994). *A conflict between a theory and practices within the Korean newspaper companies.* Seoul, Korea: Seungkwngkwan University. Dissertation.

Shim, D.B. (2008). The growth of Korean cultural industries and the Korean wave. In C.B. Huat & K. Iwabuchi (Eds.), *East Asian pop culture: Analyzing the Korean wave* (pp. 15–31). Hong Kong: Hong Kong University Press.

Yoo, Y.C. (1989). *Political transition and press ideology in South Korea.* University Minnesota. Unpublished dissertation.

Yoo, Y.C. (1994). Political economy of television broadcasting in South Korea. In J.W. Kim & J.W. Lee (Eds.), *Elite media amidst mass culture: A critical look at mass communication in Korea* (pp. 191–213). Seoul, Korea: Nanam.

Yun, S.K. (Ed.). (2008). The environmental changes in the Korean advertising industry. In S.K. Yun (Ed.), *Korea's advertising* (pp. 11–39). Seoul, Korea: Nanam. Korean.

Yun, S. M. (2005). *The research of media policies in Korea.* Seoul, Korea: Communication Books. Korean.

4   The Samsung media empire

Importantly, internal information on the structures and workings of chaebol groups was not available until 1998. In that year, the Korean government revised the Monopoly Regulation and Fair Trade Act (MRFTA), the Korean anti-trust law that regulated chaebol economic activities and corporate structures in Korean economic sectors. After 1999, chaebol groups were legally forced to reveal information about their corporate structures, including cross-shareholdings, lists of the members of board of directors, revenues and investments in chaebol affiliates. MRFTA defines chaebol affiliates as companies for which a person, his special relatives or a company controlled by him either 1) owns more than 30 percent of the company's issued shares or 2) substantially affects company management. According to articles 7 and 12 of MRFTA, the special relatives of a chaebol group include its top executive, his wife, his children, his close relatives and directors working in chaebol affiliates (Secretariat of National Assembly, 2010).

On the basis of MRFTA's characterization of chaebol groups, I analyze the establishment of the Samsung media empire and the familial ties existing among the corporate leaders of this conglomerate from 1998 to 2014 when the Korean government carried out a full range of neoliberal reforms. As discussed in chapter 2, Lee Kun-hee, the heir of the old Samsung group, reorganized Samsung to six enterprises (e.g., Samsung, CJ, JoongAng Ilbo, Shinsaegae, Hansol and Saehan). Each of these six corporations is considered a chaebol group based on the criteria of MRFTA. I refer to these six chaebol groups as the New Samsung groups. The six chairmen of the New Samsung groups are all special relatives of Samsung's founder, Lee Byung-chul.[1]

In particular, three of the New Samsung chaebol groups (i.e., Samsung, CJ and JoongAng Ilbo) have extensively expanded their media businesses in both the information and entertainment industries. In this chapter, I examine in detail how the owners of these three groups have used personal connections to expand their media businesses and control multiple media holdings within and across Korean media markets. I analyze both these media expansions and media ownership by the New Samsung groups, arguing that family capitalists have exploited economic ownership and the family ties to control media corporate structures.

My conclusions are based on extensive analysis of the annual reports and financial statements (the equivalent of 10-K reports in the U.S.) published by the

Financial Supervisory Service (FSS), the Korean government organization that oversees all media holdings of chaebol groups. In total, I gathered 173 annual reports and financial statements about the media operations owned by the three chaebol groups.[2] The data analyzed include information about 1) personal connections among the owners of the three chaebol groups and their families; 2) ownership structures existing between the parent company of each chaebol group and its media subsidiaries; 3) media expansion by the chaebol groups, including mergers and acquisitions; 4) members of the boards of directors; and 5) chaebol revenues. Additionally, I collected secondary data from news sources and scholarly works to elaborate upon and confirm my analysis of the governmental reports.

4.1. Overview of the Samsung group

Let's begin by exploring the central characteristics of the Samsung group's corporate structure, including its core businesses, ownership structures and management. In doing so, we will uncover the processes by which the Lee family, owners of the Samsung group, used Korea's financial liberalization to restructure Samsung and resolve inheritance issues among Lee family members while expanding its media empire.

Samsung owned multiple subsidiaries in five economic sectors: electronics (e.g., semi-conductors and digital devices), finance (e.g., insurance, securities and investments), manufacturing (e.g., machinery, petrochemicals and medicine), service (e.g., leisure, construction) and media (Song, 2011). Seven leading Samsung subsidiaries[3] controlled the sub-subsidiaries of Samsung in multiple Korean economic sectors. Specifically, Samsung Electronics and Samsung SDI supervised sub-subsidiaries in the electronic industry. Samsung Finance and Samsung Credit Card managed Samsung's affiliated holdings in the financial industry. Samsung Heavy Machine & Samsung Chemicals controlled heavy-chemical industry holdings, while Everland and Samsung Corporation focused on the service industry.

These seven leading subsidiaries were intertwined by virtue of a hierarchical, circular ownership structure within the Samsung group. This structure enabled the Lee family to control multiple subsidiaries while holding relatively small amounts of stock in each one (Song, 2011). In this context, the "Lee family" includes Samsung chairman Lee Kun-hee; his wife, Hong Ra-hee; their only son, Lee Jae-yong; and their three daughters, Lee Pu-jin, Lee Seo-hyun and Lee Yun-hyung.[4]

In 2013, the Lee family owned Samsung Everland, a de facto holding company of the Samsung group. Korean law had forbidden financial affiliates owned by chaebol groups to become major stockholders of a holding company or de facto holding companies within a chaebol group. The Korean government temporarily delayed the application of the law to Samsung. But eventually, the Lee family was forced to reorganize a portion of their shares in the financial affiliates of Everland. By 2013, two major stockholders from the financial industry, Samsung Insurance and Samsung Credit Card, were among Samsung's affiliates. To put some legal distance between Everland and its financial affiliates, the Lee family sold stock in these two Samsung financial affiliates to KCC.

At the same time, Samsung was eager to sell stock in Everland on the Korean stock market. To streamline this process, the Lees acquired the fashion business component of Cheil Industries, already listed on the Korean stock market, as well as rights to the brand name Cheil Industries. The Lee family then simply changed the name of their de facto holding company from Everland to Cheil Industries, and it became a publically traded company.

In spite of this name change, the Lee family did not lose controlling rights over Cheil Industries or the Samsung Empire. They remained the largest stockholder of Cheil Industries. Other major stockholders of Cheil Industries included a few leading Samsung subsidiaries (e.g., Samsung Electro-Mechanics and Samsung Corporation), Samsung's cultural foundations and KCC, an affiliate of the Hyundai group. Except for KCC, these leading affiliates play a vital role in the circular ownership structure of the Samsung group since they control over 5 percent of the total shares of Samsung's non-leading holdings.

Figure 4.1 illustrates this circular structure. Notice that the Lee family held 46 percent of Cheil Industries. In turn, Cheil Industries owned 19.4 percent of Samsung Insurance, the biggest life insurance company in Korea. Samsung Insurance owned 7.2 percent of Samsung Electronics, the world's biggest electronics company. And Samsung Electronics owned 35.3 percent of Samsung Card, Korea's biggest credit card company. This intertwining and circular ownership structure enabled the Lee family to ultimately control multiple Samsung subsidiaries across Korean economic sectors.

Another institutional control mechanism exercised by the Lee family over the Samsung Empire was the structural planning office. This was essentially the Samsung control tower responsible for managing all of Samsung's affairs. These included 1) personnel management; 2) financial affairs, including the owner's assets; 3) internal inspections regarding unfair deals within Samsung; 4) promotional and networking relationships; 5) information gathering about the power elites, both political leaders and highly placed officers in the National Tax Service

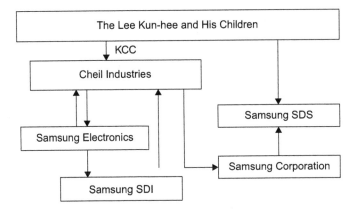

Figure 4.1 The ownership structure of Samsung group in 2014

and Public Prosecutors' Office; and 6) the applicable law (Seoul Shinmun, 2005). Members of this office were called the "selected Samsung men." Groomed to become chief executives and vice-executives of Samsung's affiliates after working at the structural planning office, they were power elites within the Samsung Empire (Kim, 2010).

This control tower was headed by Lee Kun-hee, the chairman and owner of Samsung. In the mid-1990s, Lee appointed Lee Hak-soo, an expert in financial affairs, as chief of the structural planning office. As an agent of Chairman Lee, Lee Hak-soo chose members of the structural planning office who were then approved by the chairman. Lee Hak-soo was involved in issues related to Samsung's affairs, including the reorganization of Samsung and the inheritance issues of the Lee family (Kim, 2010). He was also in charge of bribing political leaders (e.g., candidates for president and high officers at the National Tax Service, Public Prosecutors' Office, High Courts and the Supreme Court) to favor Chairman Lee's plans (Lee, 2012). The structural planning office controlled Samsung, and Chairman Lee controlled the structural planning office. By depending on such circular ownership structures and the structural planning office, the Lee family controlled the Samsung Empire and all its subsidiaries by the early 2000s.

Chairman Lee also took full advantage of Korea's financial liberalization to reorganize Samsung's structure and transfer the Samsung Empire to his children. This issue is important to our purposes for two main reasons. First, Samsung's reorganization explains the origin of the tight connections among the three chaebol groups currently evident in the corporate structures of Samsung's media holdings. Second, it also shows the relationship between financial liberalization and media expansion within the three chaebol groups. Thus, let us examine the relationship between Korea's financial liberalization and the reorganization of the Samsung group before analyzing the media expansion and media corporate structures of Samsung.

4.1.1. Financial liberalization and inheritance of the Lee family

In the 1990s, the Korean state had actively reformed the financial industry, introducing both convertible bonds (hereafter, CBs) and bonds with warrants (hereafter, BWs) and promoting the activation of mergers and acquisitions (M&As) among companies (Kim, 2007). While CBs are convertible into shares at a preset conversion price, WBs have an attached warrant entitling the purchaser to a certain number of shares of the borrowing company for a certain period of time at a price fixed in advance. The Korean state allowed both listed and unlisted enterprises to freely issue CBs and BWs. However, it rarely enacted specific provisions for these securities (e.g., the issuance volume, terms and transaction takes of CBs and BWs).

Utilizing legal loopholes, Chairman Lee began to transfer Samsung holdings to his children and family members in the 1990s. He used the structural planning office to determine which subsidiaries would be able to issue CBs and BWs and who would buy these newly issued stocks. The process went as follows.

Lee legally provided money for his children to buy new shares of unlisted Samsung holdings. Lee's children paid only the inheritance and gift tax to the National Tax Service. After that, they used their inherited money to buy CBs or BWs for the unlisted Samsung subsidiaries that would enter the Korean stock markets within a few months. Despite it being financially sound investment, most major stockholders of Samsung's affiliates gave up their rights to purchase these new shares. Lee Jae-yong and his sisters then purchased all the forfeited shares at relatively low prices and sold them on the Korean stock market after the new Samsung subsidiaries were listed. Lee Kun-hee's children made huge profits through these stock transactions, becoming the largest stockholders of Everland, then Samsung's de facto holding company, and the controllers of the Samsung Empire. The specifics of these transactions are as follows.

In early 1995, Lee Kun-hee handed over approximately 60 billion won (equivalent to U.S. $60 million) to his children. Lee Jae-yong and his sisters paid 16 billion won (equivalent to U.S. $16 million) for a gift tax to the National Tax Service. After that, they purchased 120,000 CBs of S-1, a safe security company under Samsung, at the price of 2.3 billion won (U.S. $2.3 million) just before S-1 was listed on the Korean stock market. Their purchase price for the stock in S-1 was 19,000 won (U.S. $19). A month later, S-1 was listed on the Korean stock market at 300,000 won (U.S. $300). Lee and his sisters sold out all securities of S-1, thereby making profits of about 33.72 billion won (U.S. $33.72 million). Again using their father's money, they applied the same "buy low, sell high" strategy to Samsung Engineering, a refinery, water treatment and energy subsidiary of Samsung. Having earned huge profits from these stock sales in early 1996, Lee Jae-yong and his sisters used the money to purchase all forfeited CBs issued by Everland, then an unlisted Samsung subsidiary.

In October 1996, members of the board of directors of Everland issued nearly 10 billion won (U.S. $10 million) in CBs. The major stockholders of Everland were the subsidiaries of the old Samsung, that is, JoongAng Ilbo, Samsung Electronics, CJ, Cheil Industries, Hansol, Samsung Cultural Foundation and Samsung Corporation. All major stockholders of Everland, except for CJ, forfeited the opportunity to buy the CBs of Everland. After three months, Lee Jae-yong and his sisters purchased all forfeited shares of Everland at 7,700 won (U.S. $7.7) per share. Shares of Everland could have been sold on the open market for at least at 85,000 won (U.S. $85). However, none of the major stockholders sold a single share of CBs issued by Everland. Lee and his sisters purchased all forfeited shares of Everland, making them its largest stockholders.

The case of Everland shows two intentions of Lee Kun-hee. First, Lee wanted to streamline inheritance issues among his family members. His brothers and sisters received businesses from the old Samsung at the cost of giving up rights to purchase the new CBs issued by Everland. They became owners of the new Samsung subsidiaries (i.e., CJ, Hansol, Saehan, Shinsaegae and JoongAng Ilbo). Lee's second intention was that his children would gain managerial control over the Samsung Empire by controlling Everland, the de facto holding company located at the top of Samsung's ownership pyramid.

Lee applied the same financial logic to reorganize Samsung's media holdings, which included Cheil Communication (an in-house advertising agency) and Samsung SDS, a Samsung subsidiary in the information technology sector. In 1998, Lee Jae-yong purchased forfeited BWs issued by Cheil Communication before it went public, thereby becoming its largest stockholder. Similarly, in 1999, Samsung SDS issued three-year BWs worth 23 billion won (U.S. $23 million). They then privately placed these BWs with Lee Jae-yong and his sisters at 7,150 won (U.S. $7.15) per share. Lee purchased 20 percent of the total BWs, and his sisters bought 45 percent of the total shares in Samsung SDS. They thereby became the major shareholders in this first-ranked, systematically integrated Korean company (Song, 2008). Cheil Communication was listed in 1998. Samsung SDS was not listed.

In summary, Lee Kun-hee, the top decision-maker of the Samsung Empire, utilized Korea's financial liberalization to restructure the old Samsung group into New Samsung groups (e.g., Samsung, Hansol, JoongAng Ilbo, CJ, Shinhan and Shinsaegae). He also used Samsung's three media operations (Everland, Samsung SDS and Cheil Communication) as channels to hand down an inheritance to his children.

4.2. Samsung's digital media expansion

Samsung was involved in the advertising and computer-mediated communication industries by the 1990s. As seen in Table 4.1, Everland was involved in Internet-incubating businesses. Samsung SDS was in charge of building up infrastructures for computer networking and computer-mediated communication, while Cheil Communication focused on the advertising industry. Since the late 1990s when Lee Jae-yong became the largest stockholder of Everland, a de facto holding company of the Samsung chaebol, these three media holdings have been involved in digital content–incubating businesses, or the "e-Samsung" project.

In the following sections, I examine the development of Everland's corporate structure, including its media businesses, ownership structures and boards of directors, as well as the corporate structures of Samsung SDS and Cheil

Table 4.1 Samsung's media businesses and its media holdings

Industry	Media Holdings	Businesses
Information technology	Samsung Everland	Digital-incubating businesses
Information technology	Samsung SDS	System integration Digital-incubating businesses Computer-mediated communication
Advertising Information technology	Cheil Communication	Advertising agency Advertising production Digital-incubating businesses

Source: Author's elaboration of data from the annual reports of Samsung's media holdings.

Communication. My goal is to show that Samsung's media expansions were driven by the same strategies of centralized, circular, family-based ownership seen in the rest of the Samsung Empire.

4.2.1. Internet-incubated center: Samsung Everland

Samsung Everland was originally established in 1963. It was in charge of managing Samsung assets with a focus on real estate and commercial buildings owned by the Samsung group. Since the 1990s, Everland has owned multiple holdings in environmental industries, real estate, food industries, resorts and media. The breakdown of revenues in Everland is as follows: leisure (27–43 percent); food (35–39 percent); real estate (23–27 percent); and environment (11–18 percent).

Everland rarely ran media businesses directly, but instead was a powerful investor in computer-mediated communication. Since Lee Jae-yong became the largest stockholder in Everland in the late 1990s, Everland has horizontally diversified its holdings into computer-mediated communication, a newspaper, online newspapers and a professional baseball team. Everland has paid greater attention to its Internet-incubating businesses, including the online newspapers, than its other media businesses. With strong support from Samsung's structural planning office, Lee Jae-yong established 14 joint venture companies with 9 subsidiaries of Samsung in order to develop digital software for Samsung devices. This was the so-called "e-Samsung" project. This project was more interested in investing in a wide range of digital content than others media products[5]. Lee was also involved in investment associations (e.g., KTB Investment Association, Software Development Investment Association and Media Valley) for small- and medium-sized digital firms. The number of companies in which he invested rose from 10 in 1999 to 65 in 2001. Everland was also a major stockholder in the *Hankuk Kyung-je Shinmun*, a daily economics newspaper, and its online affiliates.

Major stockholders of Everland included the Lee family, Samsung's leading subsidiaries and Samsung's cultural foundation. The Lee family together held at least 55.18 percent of total shares in Everland. Lee Jae-yong, the only son of Lee Kun-hee, was its largest stockholder with 25.1 percent of Everland shares. Since Everland was a de facto holding company of Samsung, Lee Jae-yong's majority shareholder status allowed him to inherit control of Samsung. Each of his three sisters held 8.37 percent of shares of Everland's total stock. When Lee Yun-hyung, the youngest sister, passed away in 2005, her stock (8.37 percent) transferred to Samsung's cultural foundation. Lee Kun-hee, the owner of Samsung, personally owned 3.72 percent of its total shares. Lee Jae-hyun, the owner of CJ, owned 1.52 percent of Everland's shares by 2005. Other major stockholders included Samsung's leading subsidiaries and cultural foundations.[6]

Taken together, the Lee family, Samsung's five subsidiaries, and its cultural foundations controlled 98.15 percent of the total shares of Everland. Although Lee family members were major stockholders in Everland, only Lee Kun-hee was a member of the board of directors, and only from 1999 to 2004. Except for these five years, no Lee family member has ever belonged to the boards of directors.

All members of the board of directors in Everland were Samsung men who came from the structural planning office of Samsung or Samsung's leading subsidiaries.

In sum, Everland got involved in more Internet-incubating businesses than other media businesses. Lee Jae-yong, the largest stockholder in this company, shared Everland's ownership with his two sisters, his father and the five leading subsidiaries of Samsung. In spite of this financial control of Samsung, the Lee family reserves seats on the board of directors for selected Samsung men from the structural planning office.

4.2.2. The digital constructor: Samsung SDS

Established in 1985, Samsung SDS was in charge of Samsung's information and technology businesses including system integration, computer-mediated communication and digital media investments. As one of Korea's pioneers into computer-mediated communication infrastructure, SDS played a central role in constructing the "digital Korea" that built e-government, e-commerce, e-finance and e-learning systems. The main clients of SDS came from the public sector (e.g., the National Tax Service, Incheon Airport, the National Prosecutors Office, the National Education Center and the Navy), finance (e.g., National Industrial Bank and National Farm Bank) and education (e.g., Myung Ji-University). SDS also ran computer-mediated communication under the brand name Unitel, which provided online chatting, online communities and online data services in the late 1990s. Important to our purposes, SDS ran Internet-incubating businesses associated with the "e-Samsung project" initiated by Lee Jae-yong.

SDS also invested in various online companies, including online securities (e.g., Ahn Chul-soo Lab), portal sites (e.g., NHN and Daum), online newspapers (e.g., the *DongA* and the *Hankuk Economic Daily*), e-learning (e.g., Credue), web design (e.g., Design Storm), e-medicine (e.g., 10 DR Implant), e-finance (e.g., Hankuk Information Certification), online data processing (e.g., Com Net+) and online text messaging (e.g., Yu-in Communication).

As a major investor in the digital industry, SDS developed two digital expansion patterns to support a digital Korea. First, SDS financially and technologically cultivated and supported in-house venture teams and allowed them to establish independent companies to be listed on the Korean stock market. NHN (brand name Naver), for example, was the first SDS in-house venture team. NHN became independent from SDS in 1999 and was listed in 2002. In 2012, the total revenue of NHN reached over 1 trillion won (equal to U.S. $1 billion). This revenue was equivalent to Korea's total advertisement expenses in 2012. NHN became the top-ranked portal site in Korea, providing online search services, online gaming, online advertising and online shopping.

SDS's second digital expansion pattern was to acquire promising online companies outside Samsung. For instance, SDS acquired Credue, an e-education company, in the late 1990s and listed it on the Korean stock market in 2006. Using these two patterns of investment, SDS increased its revenues by about 3.5 times from 550 billion won (U.S. $5.5 billion) in 1999 to 19.2 trillion won

(U.S. $19.2 billion) in 2012. Most revenue came from system integration (around 30–60 percent), systems management (about 20–30 percent) and education (10–20 percent).

The ownership structure of SDS was similar to that of Everland. The major stockholders were the Lee family, Samsung's leading subsidiaries and Samsung's cultural foundation. Between 1998 and 2005, the Lee family held 22.9 percent of SDS stock. Since 2006, that percentage has decreased slightly to 17 to 18 percent. Other major stockholders of SDS were Samsung's subsidiaries: Samsung Electronics (21.27 percent), Samsung Corporation (18.29 percent) and Samsung Electro-mechanics (8.44 percent).

Interestingly, two Samsung men owned SDS stock. Lee Hak-soo, the chief of the Samsung structural planning office, owned 4.5 percent of total shares in SDS. Lee In-joo, responsible for managing the assets of the Lee family, held 2.2 percent. As was the case with Everland, the Lee family did not take seats on the SDS board of directors. Most of the SDS directors came from Samsung's structural office and its subsidiaries, particularly Samsung Electronics, Hotel Shilla and Samsung Automobile.

Like Everland, SDS built up the infrastructure for information communication technologies and invested in digital media companies for the development of software.

4.2.3. Samsung advertising agency: Cheil Communication

Although Cheil Communication (renamed Cheil Worldwide Inc. in 2008) was the in-house advertising agency of Samsung, the company ran multiple media businesses. The media businesses covered advertising (e.g., advertising agencies, production, media planning and public relations), broadcasting (e.g., drama production and cable channels), recorded music (planning and music production) and film (e.g., production and exhibition). After 1998, Cheil reorganized its media businesses in accordance with Samsung's restructuring project. Under the reorganized Samsung, Cheil transferred most of its media businesses (e.g., cable channels, a film theater and an advertising agency) to the JoongAng Ilbo group. Cheil focused its energies on the advertising industry while still functioning as Samsung's in-house advertising agency. Cheil expanded its advertising sub-holdings, establishing companies like Essence Production (advertising production) and Hakuhodo-Cheil (advertising agency and advertising production for Japanese companies in Korea and Japan). Further, Cheil acquired several global and online advertising agencies in the global markets.

Since 1998, Cheil has become the first-ranked in-house advertising agency in Korea. Cheil held 20 to 30 percent of Korean advertising market shares. Regular clients of Cheil included Samsung's subsidiaries (e.g., Samsung Electronics and Samsung SDI) and old Samsung companies (CJ, Hansol and Shinsaegae groups).[7] The global growth of Cheil was dependent upon that of Samsung's affiliated companies. As seen in Table 4.2, Cheil acquired global advertising agencies across the world.

Table 4.2 Sub-holdings of Cheil Communication

Names of Sub-Holdings	Patterns	Businesses
Essence Production (1998)	Establishment in Korea	Broadcasting and advertising production
Hakuhodo-Cheil (2000)	A joint venture with Hakuhodo group from Japan	Advertising agencies
Samsung Advertising (2000)	Establishment in China	Advertising agency
BMB group (2008)	Acquisition in the U.K.	Advertising agencies
Barbarian group (2009)	Acquisition in the U.S.	Advertising agency for online advertisement
Herezie group (2010)	Establishment in France	Advertising agency and advertising production
McKinney Ventures (2012)	Acquisition in the U.S.	Advertising agency
Bravo Asia (2012)	Acquisition in China	Advertising agency

Source: Author's elaboration of data from annual reports of Cheil Communication.

Revenue from global markets reached 66 percent of Cheil's total revenue in 2012. Cheil owned about 30 global branches, including six global sub-holdings. They acquired five independent advertising companies on the global advertising market. Global Cheil acquisitions included Beattie McGuinness Bungay (a U.K. advertising agency) in 2008; Barbarian Group (a U.S. digital advertising agency) in 2009; McKinney Ventures (a U.S. advertising agency) in 2012; and Bravo Asia (an advertising agency in China) in 2012. Further, in 2010, Cheil established Herezie, a French advertising and production agency.

In addition, Cheil was a major investor in the "e-Samsung" project, contributing in the areas of advertising (e.g., Airmail, AD gate.com and BM Communication), online data gathering and processing (e.g., Valuenet, 365 homecare and Joy link Korea), online education (e.g., Credue), games (e.g., Battletop and N-forever) and online newspapers (e.g., *DongA* and *Hankyung*). Along with global advertising and online media expansion, Cheil made inroads into sports sponsorship. Cheil bankrolled professional sports teams/leagues (e.g., Chelsea in Europe and the NFL in the U.S.), the Beijing 2008 Summer Olympics, the Vancouver 2010 Winter Olympics and the 2010 Asian Olympics. It also sponsored individual athletes (e.g., Kim Yun-a, the 2009 and 2013 world champion in figure skating).

As a result, Cheil increased its revenue from 570 billion won (U.S. $570 million) in 1998 to about 2.4 trillion won (U.S. $2.4 billion) in 2012. The largest component of this business was advertising production, covering 29.94 to 74.1 percent of its total earnings. The second largest revenue percentage was generated from Cheil's advertising agency. Their revenue ranged from 17.88 to 70.06 percent of total company revenue. Marketing consulting generated at most 1 to 2 percent of Cheil revenue.

Ownership structure of Cheil showed similar patterns to other Samsung media holdings. Major Cheil stockholders were Lee family members and Samsung's leading subsidiaries. The Lee family held its shares only in 1998 and in 1999. Lee Jae-yong was the largest stockholder (29.75 percent), and Chairman Lee held shares under 5 percent of the total shares in 1998 and 1999. After that, the Lee family did not appear on the lists of major stockholders. In its place, a few leading Samsung subsidiaries and members of the old Samsung structure were major stockholders.[8] From 1998 to 2014, Samsung-affiliated companies consistently held at least 20 percent of Cheil shares. Cheil was controlled by Samsung in the same type of circular ownership as other Samsung subsidiaries. Moreover, domestic and foreign institutional investors intermittently owned Cheil shares. These included Korean institutional investors like National Pension, Hankuk Investment and Hyundai Investment, as well as foreign investors like Morgan Stanley, SSB-Small cap, Capital Group and Putnam.

Members of the Cheil board of directors included Samsung men, professors, lawyers associated with big law firms and formerly high-ranked political and economic officials. The total number of members of boards of directors in Cheil went from eight to nine, with a two-to-one ratio of Samsung men to Korean power elites. Samsung men served as chief executive and chief financial officers. These men were chosen mainly from the structural planning office of Samsung. The Korean power elites supervised financial audits and long-term strategies. They typically came from business schools (Seongkunkwan University, owned by Samsung, and National Seoul University), the National Tax Service, the Fair Trade Commission in charge of supervising chaebol group economic activities or the National Congress in charge of enacting political, economic and cultural regulations.

As in the case of other Samsung media holdings, familial connections have profoundly influenced the corporate structure of Cheil. Chairman Lee used Cheil as a channel to transfer Samsung's wealth to his only son, Lee Jae-yong. Three things have led me to infer that Cheil was involved with Samsung's transfer from Chairman Lee to "Lee Junior." First, Lee Kun-hee served on Cheil's board of directors only from 1998 to 2000. Second, Lee Hak-soo, chief of the structural planning office in Samsung group, was on Cheil's board of directors from 1998 to 1999. In addition to his position in the structural planning office, Lee Hak-soo was responsible for the Lee family's assets. Finally, Lee Jae-yong was the largest stockholder of Cheil in 1998 and 1999 with 29.75 percent of its total shares. The appearance of both Samsung chairman Lee and Lee Hak-soo of the Samsung structural planning office on the Cheil board of directors is suspicious. Chairman Lee rarely registered his name on the boards of directors within Samsung, but both he and his proxy, Lee Hak-soo, did so in the case of Cheil. These men took positions on Cheil's board of directors to facilitate passing Samsung down to Lee Jae-yong.

Marriage ties between the Lee family and the owner of the DongA media group are also relevant here. Lee Seo-hyun, the second daughter of Chairman Lee, married Kim Jae-yol, the second son of Kim Byung-kwan, the former chairman of the DongA media group. Both Lee Seo-hyun and her husband have been involved in the media management of Cheil, although they rarely owned shares of Cheil. Except for Lee Seo-hyun and her husband, no other members of the Lee family were involved in media management in Cheil.

In summary, Cheil was an in-house agency of Samsung in charge of its domestic and global advertising businesses. As a consequence of Samsung's global expansion, Cheil became one of the top 15 global advertising agencies. The ownership structure of Cheil was interlocked with Samsung's circular ownership structure. Based on this, the Lee family controlled Cheil indirectly since most members of its board of directors were either Samsung men or Korean power elites appointed by Samsung men.

4.2.4. Conclusions concerning the Samsung group

Chairman Lee Kun-hee, the owner of Samsung, exploited neoliberal economic reforms, including financial liberalization, to both 1) pass control of Samsung to his children and 2) expand its media businesses focusing on digital media content and advertising. From 1998 to 2014, Everland's diversified investments made it a major digital media investor. SDS expanded into businesses ranging from computer-mediated communication and systems integration to Internet-incubating businesses. Cheil expanded its media businesses in the advertising industry both domestically and globally.

The Lee family controlled these Samsung media holdings based on the inter-locked, circular ownership structure within Samsung. The three children of Chairman Lee were the largest stockholders in both Everland and SDS, but they rarely owned shares in Cheil. In spite of their controlling interests, the Lee family rarely served on boards of directors in the these three media operations. Instead, Samsung men under control of Chairman Lee occupied those board seats alongside Korean power elites. Owners of large corporations typically use seats on their boards of directors to connect to the power elite (Domhoff, 1990). The Lee family was no exception, using seats on Cheil's board to forge economically and politically beneficial connections.

4.3. Overview of the CJ group

Since 1997 when the CJ group was separated from the old Samsung group, it has diversified vertically and horizontally into distribution (i.e., logistics), finance, leisure, construction and pharmaceuticals. CJ has also expanded into media industries, thereby becoming a second-tier chaebol group in Korea. The number of its subsidiaries has increased from 13 in 1997 to 224 in 2012 (including 84 within Korea and 140 holdings across the world).

As was the case with other members of New Samsung, CJ's growth was closely associated with financial liberalization in Korea. CJ aggressively used Korea's financial liberalization to increase its number of subsidiaries within and across economic sectors. Recall that the Korean government allowed chaebol groups to issue BWs and CBs freely while loosening legal limitations on mergers and acquisitions among domestic and foreign companies. These political steps enabled CJ to tap into financial resources by issuing new shares in the form of BWs. Revenue from these bonds allowed CJ to purchase many other companies. Moreover, CJ invested in multiple Samsung subsidiaries in the trading (e.g., Samsung Corporation), electronics (e.g., Samsung Electronics and Samsung Electricity), military (e.g., Samsung Airspace), leisure (e.g., Everland, Hotel Shilla and Samsung Lions), petrochemical (e.g., Samsung Chemical) and machinery (e.g., Samsung Engineering) industries (Lee, 2011).

Simply put, Korean financial liberalization enabled CJ to expand its businesses and share ownership with Samsung across Korean economic sectors in Korea. As seen in Figure 4.2, the Lee family established hierarchical, interlocked, circular ownership structures within CJ that paralleled ownership structures in the entire Samsung Empire.

The following is the method by which the Lee family gained control over the entire CJ organization (Erri, 2011). The Lees[9] were the largest stockholders of CJ Corporation, a holding company of CJ. Lee Jae-hyun held the most stock in CJ Corporation, the largest stockholder of the CJ subsidiaries: CJ Jeil Jedang, CJ O-shopping, CJ CGV, CJ E&M and CJ Finance. CJ Jeil Jedang was in charge of sub-holdings in food processing and animal feed. CJ Finance was responsible for CJ's financial businesses. The three media holdings (e.g., CJ O-shopping, CJ CGV and CJ E&M) supervised CJ's media businesses in cable television, film, gaming, recorded music and digital convergence media across the telecommunication and broadcasting industries. This circular ownership structure between CJ Corporation and a few of its leading subsidiaries allowed the Lee family to control the CJ empire.

Unlike Samsung, the Lee family was actively involved in CJ's management, serving on its board of directors. Lee Jae-hyun, the owner of CJ, was the chief executive of CJ Corporation and CJ Jeil Jedang. Chairman Lee also was a member of the board of directors for several of CJ's holdings.[10] His elder sister,

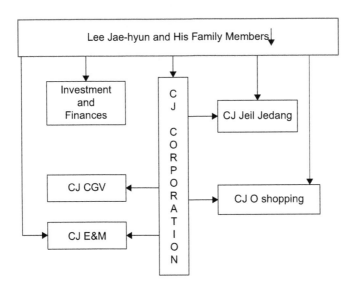

Figure 4.2 The ownership structure of CJ group in 2014

Lee Mee-kyung, was a vice-chairman of CJ E&M. His younger brother, Lee Jae-hwan, worked in CJ's media subsidiaries (e.g., CJ Mooter, Fortune Communication and Anypark). Other relatives of Chairman Lee were members of the boards of directors of several CJ subsidiaries. Along with taking board positions, the Lee family used the structural planning office to control the corporate structures of CJ.

In sum, CJ diversified horizontally and vertically within and across Korean economic sectors. The Lee family used a circular ownership structure between the parent company and its multiple holdings to control the CJ empire.

4.4. CJ's media expansion and ownership

CJ has diversified both vertically and horizontally into the audio-visual media industries, thereby establishing a media empire (see Table 4.3). The growth of CJ in Korean entertainment markets was linked to financial liberalization. It put CJ in a position to acquire other media companies, issue new stocks to foreign investors and list acquired media companies at Korean stock markets. In the cable television, film production, film distribution and exhibition, gaming and recorded music markets, CJ focused more on mergers and acquisitions than on the establishment of new media holdings. Through M&As, CJ increased its media holdings from about four cable channels and one broadband service company in 1998 to 30 media holdings in 2012.

The years 2014 and 2009 were milestones for CJ's media expansions. In 2004, CJ took over Plenus, which had multiple media operations in the gaming and film industries. By acquiring Plenus, CJ became the first-ranked film distributor and exhibitor, as well as a gaming company. The 2009 acquisition of On-Media enabled CJ to become the most powerful media company in the paid broadcasting markets (e.g., cable television, Internet TV, digital satellite TV, satellite digital multimedia broadcasting [SDMB] and territorial digital multimedia broadcasting [TDMB]). On-Media, owned by the Orion Group, had been the strongest competitor of CJ in these markets. Through the takeover of On-Media, CJ became the first-ranked company in the Korean entertainment markets.

Table 4.3 CJ's leading media holdings in 2010

Industry	Media Holdings	Businesses
Cable television	CJ O-shopping	Cable channels and media acquisitions
	CJ Media	Program (contents) providers
	CJ Hellovision	Cable networks, broadband service Internet phone
Recorded music	Mnet	Cable channels, music production, concerts and entertainment
Game	CJ Internet	Game production and distribution, including online games
Film	CJ Entertainment	Film financing and distribution
	CJ CGV	Film exhibition

Source: Author's elaboration of data from annual reports from CJ's media holdings.

CJ actively exercised M&A strategies to establish its media empire. CJ exploited seven media holdings[11] to expand its entertainment businesses. Specifically, CJ O-shopping (formerly 39 Home-shopping), CJ Hellovision (formerly Yangcheon Cable Television) and CJ Media (formerly SA management) played vital roles in expanding CJ's cable businesses. CJ O-shopping was a cable channel dedicated to the sale of manufactured products. It was also in charge of acquiring other cable companies. CJ Hellovision was responsible for cable network, broadband businesses and Internet telephone service. CJ Media provided media content for the paid broadcasting markets. Mnet was a leading recorded music holding for CJ. CJ Internet was involved in game production, distribution and development. CJ Entertainment ran film co-financing and distribution businesses, while CJ CGV exhibited Korean and foreign motion pictures. Among the seven media operations, four (e.g., CJ Media, CJ Entertainment, Mnet and CJ Internet) merged into CJ E&M in 2010. The other three media operations (e.g., CJ Hellovision, CJ CGV and CJ O-shopping) ran their businesses independently.

In addition, CJ was involved in media production in the entertainment industries. Their activities included 1) direct investment through CJ's financial holdings (e.g., CJ Venture Capital and Discovery Venture); 2) indirect investment by becoming members of media venture funds; and 3) a media constructor of which CJ owned 50 percent of the total shares. This enabled CJ to construct the East Pusan Theme Park, a specialized film media city in Korea.

In sum, CJ operated across many Korean economic sectors, including the media industry. Through active M&As, CJ diversified into the Korean entertainment markets, thereby establishing a media empire in Korea. In what follows, I explore in greater detail the corporate structures of CJ's media holdings in the paid broadcasting, recorded music, gaming and film markets.

4.4.1. M&As Machine: CJ O-shopping

CJ O-shopping played a central role in expanding CJ's cable businesses. CJ did not establish this cable company, but acquired it as 39 Home-shopping in 1999 upon the collapse of the Samgoo group in the aftermath of Korea's 1997 financial crisis. Upon acquiring 39 Home-shopping, CJ renamed it CJ O-shopping. The same year, CJ entered the cable network and broadband businesses by acquiring Yangcheon, a cable networking company, from the state-owned Korea Telecommunication.[12] Thus, CJ's cable network expansion was made possible by the media privatization policies of the Korean government.

CJ O-shopping purchased other companies in the cable networking and broadband markets, focusing on bigger cities instead of rural areas. About 70 percent of the Korean population lives in the apartment complexes of big cities. Moreover, CJ O-shopping acquired On-Media from the Orion group in 2009. On-Media was a multiple program provider, with 19 cable channels, 8 digital satellite television channels and 10 channels in IPTV, as well as a multiple system operator covering four local regions of Korea. CJ O-shopping transferred its cable networking business to CJ Hellovision in 2008, while transferring cable program services to CJ E&M in 2010.

Further, CJ O-shopping invested in Korea's media production companies. This cable company has held at least 10 percent of the shares of several media ventures.[13] Most CJ O-shopping revenues, however, came from home shopping sales (74 to 100 percent), Internet-related businesses (1 to 20 percent) and advertising (4.2 to 20 percent). Internet-related businesses included digital broadband service, digital high-definition broadcasting and Internet phone.

In terms of ownership structure, CJ Corporation was its largest stockholder with 30 to 40 percent of total shares. Other major stockholders varied. From 2000 to 2001, the Samgoo group held from 10.40 to 8.55 percent of total stocks. Foreign investors, mainly private equity funds, were temporarily major stockholders. These included Citi Corp. (6.84 percent) in 2000, T Rowe Price International (6.3 percent) and Sansar Capital Management (5.20 percent) in 2006 and Macquarie Bank IMM (5.07 percent) in 2008. Domestic institutional investors also were major stockholders. These included National Pension Service (8.81 percent) and Mirae Assets Management (7.67 percent) in 2012.

Most members of the CJ O-shopping board were members of the Lee family, Samsung men, CJ men and Korean power elites. The number of board members ranged from 4 to 10. Interestingly, the Lee family did not occupy the position of chief executive officer, but instead intermittently took seats on the board of directors. CJ O-shopping's chief executive officers were from Samsung and Samsung subsidiaries.[14] Generally, CJ men working at CJ subsidiaries were responsible for marketing strategies, while Samsung men supervised the finances. Korean power elites typically occupied two or three seats on the board of directors. Most of them were professors in the financial, management or communication departments of universities (Seoul National University and Korea University) or retired high officers in the Fair Trade Commission, the National Tax Service, the Ministry of Culture and Tourism or the commercial banks. Both the Fair Trade Commission and the National Tax Service supervised chaebol groups' economic activities, while the Ministry of Culture and Tourism was responsible for media laws and policies, including renewing the licenses of media companies.

In summary, CJ O-shopping played a vital role in expanding CJ's cable businesses. This cable company ran media businesses, including home-shopping sales, broadband services, media investment, media production and Internet-related businesses. CJ Corporation, a holding company of CJ, was its largest stockholder. Major members of its board of directors came from the Samsung and CJ groups, as well as the Korean power elites.

4.4.2. Cable network with foreign capital: CJ Hellovision

CJ Hellovision, which was independent from CJ O-shopping in 2008, ran cable networking businesses, broadband services and digital convergence services. Like CJ O-shopping, CJ Hellovision aggressively acquired other cable networking companies, thereby occupying at least 25 percent of the total Korean cable operating market share in 2012. CJ Hellovision was the second largest multiple system operator (MSO) in Korean cable television. CJ Hellovision acquired revenue from cable television subscribers (93 to 49. 2 percent), advertising (1 to 21 percent) and Internet-related businesses, including broadband users and Internet-related businesses (e.g., VoIP [voice over Internet Protocol], an Internet phone and IPTV) (1 to 23.5 percent).

CJ O-shopping was the largest stockholder in CJ Hellovision, with 46.01 to 87.2 percent of total stocks. Foreign institutional investors accounted for the second most shares held. In 2009, for example, Sable Asia held 13.32 percent of CJ Hellovision stock, and AA Merchant Bank owned 10.88 percent. Formosa Cable Investment held 7.98 percent of total shares. The third major stockholder was CJ Hellovision with 11.19 percent of total shares. This ownership pattern continued from 2010 to 2012.

Members of the board of directors in CJ Hellovision included both CJ men and foreign institutional investors from Lehman Brothers M.B. Groups, Banks Trust Company and the Royal Bank of Scotland. The CJ men either came from CJ's structural planning office or were the general directors of other CJ media holdings in charge of media management or marketing. Foreign directors were responsible for the financial audits and marketing strategies.

In sum, CJ Hellovision was involved in cable networking service, broadband and digital convergence. It was a joint venture company with foreign capital. CJ men and foreign investors from private financial institutions shared media ownership and seats on the board of directors.

4.4.3. Cable TV mecca: CJ Media

CJ Media (formerly SA Management) was established in 1999 when CJ acquired Look TV, a lifestyle cable channel, and DNG, a food cable channel. CJ Media provided media content for a variety of paid broadcasting services.[15] Genres broadcast by CJ Media included entertainment, music, documentary, food, sports and television drama. Its most popular genres, however, were film, fashion and animation channels. CJ Media reran their media content on17 digital satellite channels, 10 SDMB and TDMB channels and 10 IPTV channels.

In addition, CJ Media cooperated with American media giants to establish CJ NGC Korea, a joint venture with National Geographic, to rebroadcast documentary films to the paid broadcasting markets. It also acquired several cable channels in entertainment, music, rerun television drama, fashion, animation, gaming, film, sports and documentary. CJ Media's biggest acquisition was On-Media and its 19 cable channels.[16] In consequence of these expansions, CJ Media increased its number of cable channels to 41 channels by 2010.

Like other CJ media holdings, CJ Media was a powerful media investor in the audio-visual media industries. It was directly and indirectly involved in media venture capital, financially supporting media production companies. Moreover, CJ Media directly invested in other media companies promoting digital media convergence, entertainment agency and script development. For example, CJ Media owned: 0.12 percent of shares in TU Media, which was in charge of SDMB service; 0.35 percent of SK link, a music/sound company for the wireless industry; 12.99 percent of DY Entertainment and 2.31 percent of Phantom Enter-tainment, two entertainment agencies; 19.97 percent of A Story, a professional script company; 10.7 percent of Daewon Digital Broadcasting; and 12.07 percent of cable provider Dramamax. These media acquisitions and investments allowed CJ Media to become the most powerful multiple program provider (MPP) and media investor in Korea. However, CJ Media restructured its multiple media holdings into CJ E&M in 2010 in order to be listed on the Korean stock market.

Most of CJ Media's revenue came from advertising, cable subscriptions and media product sales. From 1998 to 2009, advertising revenue gradually decreased from 82 percent in 2000 to 50 percent of total revenues in 2009. Media product sales increased from 8 percent in 1999 to 32 percent of total revenue in 2007. Cable subscriptions slowly increased to 20 percent of total revenue in 2009 from 10 percent in 1999. CJ Media earned most of its profits from advertising and prod-uct sales rather than cable subscribers.

CJ Corporation, a holding company of CJ, was the largest stockholder in CJ Media from 1999 to 2012. Other major stockholders included CJ Entertainment, a media holding covering CJ's film production and distribution; domestic and foreign investors; and the Lee family. From 1999 to early 2010, before CJ Media integrated into CJ E&M, the company experienced major stockholder changes. Before 2001, CJ Corporation was the largest stockholder, holding 94.2 percent of total stocks. Other stockholders included foreign investor MTV Asia (2.44 per-cent), Goni Mechanics (1.74 percent) and Yong Distribution (1.24 percent). From 2002 to 2004, when CJ Media issued new BWs, CJ Corporation reduced its shares from 81.62 percent to 54.76 percent of total stocks, and CJ Entertainment (34.69 percent) became the second largest stockholder in CJ Media. Other stock-holders included Sony Music (6.02 percent to 3.40 percent), CJ Media (4.53 per-cent) and public broadcaster MBC (2.35 percent).

In 2005, CJ Media re-issued new BWs, allocating new shares to members of the Lee family.[17] As a result, CJ Media's ownership structure was changed. It included CJ Corporation (58.06 percent), CJ Entertainment (31.16 percent), Lee Kyung-hoo (3.24 percent) and Lee Mee-kyung (1.74 percent). The ownership structure of CJ Media was changed again between 2007 and 2009. Then, CJ Corporation became the largest stockholder, with at most 50.17 percent and at least 49.93 per-cent of CJ Media shares. Two other major stockholders were Korean institutional investor Shinhan Private Equity (16.59 percent) and foreign institutional investor Free Moris Private Equity (10.03 percent). CJ Media was formally integrated into CJ E&M in 2010.

Interestingly, CJ Media did not show any information about members of its board of directors. Korean law requires chaebol groups to disclose their own-ership structures, their investment in the Korean economy and the total stocks owned by the owners of the chaebol groups and their family members. However, the Korean government did not ask for the members of the board of directors in the unlisted subsidiaries owned by chaebol groups (Kim, 2005). I assume this is why CJ Media did not reveal the members of their board of directors in their annual reports and audit reports.

4.4.4. *K-pop center: Mnet*

Mnet was in charge of CJ's music businesses, including cable music channels, recorded music production, performance and media investment across the Korean recorded music industry. Historically, Mnet grew out of CJ Media Line, established by CJ as a sub-holding of CJ Media to enter the music industry in 2003. Between 2003 and 2006, CJ Media Line was renamed CJ Music. CJ Media issued new BWs in 2006 to take over Mediopia, a listed information technology company specializing in system integration learning and cable system operation. Late in 2006, the brand name of CJ Music was changed to Mnet. CJ changed this name to create a "back-door listing" of its music company on the Korean stock market.[18] It was a kind of free ride to evade strict financial regulations and save time and money in listing CJ's media company. The back-door listing created a legal cover for the company with cash flow. After that, CJ Media integrated its music businesses into Mediopia and renamed it Mnet.

Mnet was responsible for recorded music, musical performances (e.g., *Cats*, *Phantom of the Opera* and *Mama Mia*) and live concerts. This music company also invested in entertainment agencies (e.g., Gap Entertainment, Woolim Entertainment and Orange Shock), called "star manufacturing factories." Mnet was involved in recruiting potentially talented singers and training them to become popular stars. Like CJ's other media holdings, Mnet was a member of media investment associations.[19]

Since 2006, Mnet has continuously taken over media companies, including KMTV (a cable music channel); Good Concert (a record production company); Phoebus (a record production company); GM Planning (an entertainment agency); AD 2000 (a digital music production company); Seijong DMS (a digital music production company); and Gretech (an online game company). Moreover, Mnet cooperated with mobile service companies (LG Telecommunication, Korea Telecommunication Freetel and TU Media), a manufacturing company (Samsung Electronics) and a leading portal site (NHN) to increase revenues in the music download businesses. As a result, Mnet became the first-ranking music company in Korea but was integrated into CJ E&M in 2010.

Most of the revenue in Mnet came from recorded music, online music and advertising. The ratio of these three revenue streams were as follows: recorded music (33–44 percent), online music (21–34 percent) and advertising (27–35 percent). Although the three businesses accounted for relatively equal percentages of the total revenue in Mnet, revenue from recorded music gradually decreased from 44 percent of total revenue in 2007 to 33 percent in 2009. At the same time, revenue from online music gradually grew from 21 percent in 2007 to 34 percent.

In terms of ownership structure, CJ Corporation, a holding company of CJ, was the largest stockholder in Mnet. It held shares ranging from 20.4 percent in 2004 to 33.25 percent in 2010. Other major stockholders included CJ Media and Phoebus. CJ Media increased its stocks from 6.44 percent in 2006 to 15.07 percent in 2009. Phoebus, a subsidiary of Mnet, held 20.5 percent of shares in 2006 and dropped to 8.7 percent in 2009. Major members of the board of directors included people from CJ's structural planning office or media subsidiaries and representatives of the Samsung Audio and Visual Agency, a subsidiary of Samsung's Cheil Communications, as well as Korean power elites. As mentioned earlier, Cheil Communication withdrew from the Korean audio-visual media businesses in 1998. After that, those employed by Samsung Audio and Visual Agency continued to work at CJ media holdings, including Mnet. CJ men and ex-Samsung men occupied six board seats and supervised overall financial and marketing strategies. The other three seats were held by Korean power elites who were retired high officers of the National Tax Service and the Korean Blue House (the equivalent to the U.S. White House). They were the outside directors on the Mnet board.

In summary, Mnet was a media holding of CJ in charge of music production, distribution and investment. CJ Corporation, a holding company of CJ, was its largest stockholder. Most members of the board of directors were ex-Samsung men, CJ men and Korean power elites. The Lee family rarely occupied seats on its boards of directors. Mnet was closely interlocked with its parent company, CJ, in terms of ownership and management.

4.4.5. A center of Korean gaming: CJ Internet

CJ Internet was responsible for gaming businesses that developed, produced and distributed casual games, arcade games, board games, massively multi-player online role-playing games (MMORPG) and online games in Korea. Like CJ's other media holdings, CJ Internet invested in gaming venture funds (e.g., MVP Culture Fund, Online Game Revolution Fund and CJ Private Equity).

In 2004, CJ entered the Korean game industry by acquiring media businesses from Locus Holdings, a listed media enterprise with multiple media holdings in the gaming and film industries. Like Mnet, CJ used this acquisition and a backdoor listing to expand its gaming holdings. After consolidation, CJ integrated Locus Holdings with CJ Internet in order to list CJ Internet on the Korean stock market. As Locus Holdings was already the leading Korean gaming company with multiple game holdings, the acquisition of Locus Holdings allowed CJ Internet to become the most powerful player in the gaming industry.

After 2004, CJ Internet continued to increase its sub-media holdings. They acquired gaming companies including Media Web, Anypark, GameAlo and Aramaroo and Seed9. Media Web was the largest company controlling paid Internet cafés. Anypark and GameAlo were leading game developers working on game storylines, characters and marketing. Seed9 focused on developing characters within game products. Moreover, CJ Internet established two sub-media holdings. CJ IG was in charge of developing game content, and CJ Sports was in charge of professional gaming competitions.

CJ Corporation was the largest stockholder in CJ Internet, holding from 10.48 percent of total stock in 2004 to 27.45 percent in 2009. Other major stockholders included CJ Entertainment and foreign institutional investors. CJ Entertainment consistently owned around 9 percent of total shares. Foreign investors temporarily held CJ Internet shares.[20] Interestingly, Bang Jung-hyuk owned 5.08 percent of total shares. He was a founder of Net Marble, a top-ranked game portal site. He seemed to receive shares of CJ Internet as compensation when CJ Internet acquired Net Marble. Although Lee Jae-hyun, the owner of CJ, was not a major stockholder in CJ Internet, Chairman Lee held around 2 percent of total shares of CJ Internet.

In addition, Lee Jae-hyun served on the CJ Internet the board of directors. The number of members on the board fluctuated from 7 to 15. They included CJ men and the Korean power elites in roughly a two-to-one ratio. The CJ men came from CJ's structural planning office, CJ Corporation and CJ CGV, a film exhibition company. They were in charge of the financial and marketing aspects of CJ Internet and occupied seats on the boards of directors in CJ Internet sub-holdings. Korean power elites were the outside directors. Three kinds of outside directors existed in CJ: 1) retired high officers in the National Tax Service, the Korean Customs Service and the National Prosecutors' Office; 2) pioneers in Internet-mediated communication who had run portal sites like Yahoo Korea and Net Marble; and 3) professors in the communication departments of Korean universities.

To summarize, CJ Internet focused on the gaming industry. CJ Corporation was the largest stockholder of this gaming company, intertwined within the circular ownership structure of CJ. Like CJ Hellovision and Mnet, foreign investors were major CJ Internet stockholders. Similarly, the Lee family invited Korean power elites to serve on its board of directors. The media businesses of CJ Internet integrated with CJ E&M in 2010.

4.4.6. Entertainment top: CJ E&M

In 2010, CJ integrated five media holdings[21] into CJ E&M. Since then, CJ E&M has been a de facto media holding of CJ group. CJ E&M revenue came from broadcasting, advertising and subscription fees (45–55.6 percent), games (15.2–29 percent), films (12–15.7 percent) and other sources including recorded music (11.6–14.3 percent). Its largest stockholder was CJ Corporation (39.36–43 percent). Institutional investors (22.6 percent), foreigners (6.1 percent), CJ holdings (3.2 percent) and individual stockholders (26.6 percent) comprised the rest.

Membership on the board of directors ranged from seven to eight. Lee Jae-hyun, the owner of CJ, was directly involved in the management of CJ E&M as CEO. This is unique because the owners of chaebol groups tended to be reluctant to register their names on the boards of directors. Other members of the CJ E&M board were CJ men from the structural planning office, the ex-CEO of On-Media and Korean power elites. CJ men were responsible for setting up marketing strategies and executing financial plans. The ex-CEO of On-Media was in charge of managing the media businesses of On-Media. The Korean power elites included retired high officers from the National Tax Service, the Korean Tourist Corporation, the National Congress and the High Court; an ex-journalist; and a lawyer of Kim & Jang Law Firm, the largest law firm in Korea.

In sum, CJ E&M ran media businesses in paid broadcasting, gaming, film co-financing and recorded music. It was a de facto media holding of CJ after 2010 and therefore interrelated with CJ's circular ownership.

4.4.7. The headquarters of Korean film: CJ Entertainment

CJ Entertainment was responsible for co-financing, film distribution and investment businesses in the Korean film industry. Historically speaking, CJ established a film consulting company, IMM Consulting, in 1997, changing its name to SNT Global in 1999 and to CJ Entertainment in 2000. Behind these name changes, the Lee family deployed newly issued BWs to establish CJ Entertainment. Through monopolizing these issued stocks, the family acquired controlling rights in CJ Entertainment and then listed this company on the Korean stock market in 2002.

Like CJ's other media holdings, CJ Entertainment was an outcome of active M&As in the early 2000s. As discussed in chapter 2, the Korean film distributors were from small- to medium-sized film companies rather than chaebol groups at this time. Independent firms competed with Hollywood distributors. Against this backdrop, CJ established CJ Entertainment as a film distribution company and acquired Korean independent film distributors. The biggest M&A by CJ Entertainment was its acquisition of Cinema Service, which occupied 10 to 15 percent of total film distribution market shares in 2002. The acquisition of Cinema Service was related to the acquisition of Plenus from Locus Holdings in 2004. After acquiring Plenus, CJ reorganized its media businesses in accordance with its internal corporate structures. It transferred Cinema Service and Art Service, a production studio, to CJ Entertainment and Premus, an exhibition holding of Plenus, to CJ CGV.

Moreover, CJ Entertainment acquired independent film production companies (e.g., Myung Film) and digital distribution companies. As a result, CJ Entertainment controlled five sub-holdings in charge of supporting its main businesses, co-financing and distribution. They included CJ Nkino (e-tickets, online marketing and media production), Art Service (home video system, digital video disc and characters businesses), CJ Code (online video on demand) and CJ Entertainment America.

Like other CJ media holdings, CJ Entertainment was a powerful media investor in the Korean film industry. It co-financed several medium-sized production companies (Cidus, FHN, LJ Film, Object and MBC Production). The number of its co-financed motion pictures rose from 5 in 2001 to 12 in 2005. Moreover, CJ Entertainment indirectly invested in Korean motion pictures through membership in film media funds.[22] Further, CJ Entertainment individually loaned production costs to popular film directors like Kang Woo-seok and Chae Seung-jae, as well as to major production companies (e.g., Taewon Entertainment and Myung Film).

Interestingly, Japan was the largest export market for CJ Entertainment, holding at least 75 percent of its total exports. Other export countries included Thailand, Taiwan and Singapore. CJ Entertainment also imported the only motion pictures manufactured by Hollywood. It owned the 10-year exclusive rights to distribute film works manufactured by Hollywood's Dreamworks SKG, co-founded by director Steven Spielberg and CJ. It also owned 10-year exclusive rights to distribute films produced by Dreamworks SKG in the East and Southeast Asian film markets. Finally, CJ Entertainment provided motion pictures manufactured by CJ Entertainment and by Dreamworks for Korean public broadcasting companies, paid cable channels and digital media.

With this business model, CJ Entertainment earned revenue from motion pictures, ancillary media businesses and film exports. Its highest revenue came from film distribution, which ranged from at least 52.2 percent in 2003 up to 76.4 percent of total revenue. The second highest revenue percentage came from ancillary media markets, including the direct sales of VHS, DVD and video on demand (VOD), as well as indirect sales of motion pictures to the broadcasting channels. The ratio of revenue from ancillary markets increased from 8 percent of total incomes up to 28.6 percent. Lastly, the export of Korean motion pictures to East and Southeast Asian markets earned from 3.93 to 13 percent of the total CJ Entertainment revenue. CJ Entertainment was integrated into CJ Corporation, a holding company of CJ, in 2006 and then into CJ E&M in 2010.

In terms of its media ownership, CJ Entertainment's largest stockholder shifted from Lee Jae-hyun (24.05 percent) in 2001 to CJ Corporation (36.69 percent) in 2002. Lee Jae-hyun remained the second largest stockholder. Other major stockholders included domestic institutional investors like Hyundai Investment and the National Pension Service.

Like CJ's other media holdings, members of the board of directors in CJ Entertainment were composed of CJ men and Korean power elites. The CJ men came from the structural planning office of CJ and were in charge of the short- and long-term strategies, investment and marketing. Lee Jae-hyun was a member of the board of directors in only 2001 and then transferred his position to Shin Hyun-jae of the CJ structural planning office. Korean power elites were retired high officers from the National Tax Service and Public Prosecutors Office, as well as professors in the communications departments at the universities. They were the outside directors. In sum, CJ Entertainment, interlocked in the ownership structure of its parent company, was the most powerful film co-financer, distributor and investor in Korea.

4.4.8. The first multiplex: CJ CGV

CJ CGV, the first multiplex in Korea, ran a film exhibition business. The company was established by a joint venture between CJ Entertainment and Australia's Village Road Show in 1996. Because Village Road Show maintained its partnership with Warner Brothers and Goldman Harvest, CJ CGV benefitted from the transmission media management know-how from these global media giants. Two years later in 1998, this joint company constructed Korea's first multiplex theater at Kangbyung in Seoul. Since 1998, CJ CGV has continuously constructed multiplex theaters on 97 sites, operating 732 screens as of 2010.

CJ CGV controlled five sub-holdings, including a multiplex theater construction company (Premus Cinema), a digital cinema exhibition company (D-Cinema of Korea), a VHS/DVD rental company (Joycube) and two entertainment presentation system companies (CJ 4D Plex and Simuline). Like other CJ media holdings, CJ CGV invested in media venture funds.[23] CJ CGV expanded its theater business to China (11 sites with 78 screens), Vietnam (11 sites with 79 screens), Malaysia (1 site with 20 screens) and the U.S. (1 site with 4 screens). Its revenues come primarily from three sources: admission fees (63–74 percent), sales of foods at the theater cafeterias (15–17 percent), and advertising (10–11 percent).

The largest stockholder in this company changed from CJ Entertainment to CJ Corporation in 2006. This change was related to CJ's restructuring of its media businesses. Before 2006, CJ Entertainment was the largest stockholder of CJ CGV with 50 to 36.73 percent of its total shares. After 2006, CJ Corporation was the largest stockholder holding 36.73 to 40.5 percent of its total shares. Other major stockholders included domestic and foreign institutional investors. Korean institutional investors included the National Pension Service (5.43–9.07 percent) in 2006 and 2012, the Korea Investment Trust (5.9 percent) from 2010–2012 and USB Equity in Hana Commercial Bank (5.03 percent) in 2009. Major non-Korean stockholders included Asia Cinema Holdings (31.83 percent) in 2004, Franklin Mutual Advisers (7.36 percent) in 2005, Hermes Investment (6.20 percent) in 2009 and Small Cap World Fund (5.99 percent) from 2010 to 2012.

The seven-member board of directors of CJ CGV was composed of CJ men and Korean power elites. CJ men occupied four seats on the board, while the Korean power elites held three seats. The Korean power elites included retired high officers from the Fair Trade Commission or the Blue House, as well as professors from university communications departments. Although Korean and non-Korean institutional investors were major stockholders of CJ CGV, they were rarely involved in the management of CJ CGV.

To sum, CJ CGV built up multiplex theaters over Korea, China, Vietnam, Malaysia and the U.S. This film exhibition company was under control of the CJ group.

4.4.9. Conclusion of the CJ group

Financial liberalization and neoliberal media reform allowed the CJ group to diversify its media businesses within and across Korean media markets. Business areas of focus included the paid broadcasting, film, recorded music and gaming industries. Actively exercising financial strategies such as M&As and backdoor listings, CJ increased its media holdings on the Korean Peninsula from 5 to about 50 by 2012. In addition, CJ invested heavily in Korean commercial media contents and constructed "media cities." CJ established a media empire that controlled multiple media holdings in the entertainment markets and became the most powerful investor, distributor, exhibitor and constructor in Korea.

The Lee family used its ownership connections within CJ Corporation, a holding company of CJ, and a few leading media operations to control multiple media holdings. CJ Corporation was the largest stockholder of CJ's leading media holdings. The leading CJ media holdings had significant ownership overlap with CJ's other media holdings. For example, CJ O-shopping was the largest stockholder of CJ Hellovision. CJ Entertainment was the major stockholder of CJ CGV, CJ Media and CJ Internet. CJ Media was the major stockholder of Mnet. Through these interlocked ownership structures, the Lee family exercised its influences over multiple CJ media operations.

Most of the boards of directors in CJ's media holdings were populated by 1) CJ men working at the structural planning office of CJ and 2) Korean power elites. The CJ men were placed as proxies to protect the interests of the Lee family within CJ. The Korean power elites occupied the outside director board positions. Further, CJ cooperated with foreign media companies in the cable television and film markets, constructed multiplex theaters with a film exhibitor, established joint ventures with American media conglomerates and distributed imported media content made only in the U.S. over paid Korean media channels.

4.5. Overview of the JoongAng Ilbo group

The JoongAng Ilbo group became legally independent from the old Samsung group in 1999. Since then, the JoongAng Ilbo group has expanded to include holdings in the electronics (semi-conductors and liquid crystal display), finance (investments), retail (convenience stores), leisure (ski resorts, golf courses) and media (advertising, print, cable television and film exhibition) industries. As part of this diversification process, the JoongAng Ilbo group was divided into the JoongAng Ilbo and Bokwang groups at the end of 2005.

The Samsung, JoongAng Ilbo and Bokwang chaebol groups were linked by informal ties of blood and marriage among their owners. Samsung and JoongAng Ilbo were related by marriage between the Lee and Hong families. Lee Kun-hee, the owner of Samsung, married Hong Ra-hee, the first daughter of the Hong family. Here, "the Hong family" refers to those including Hong Seok-hyun, the largest stockholder of JoongAng Ilbo; his mother, Kim Yun-nam; his three brothers, Hong Seok-jo, Hong Seok-jun and Hong Seok-kyu; a younger sister, Hong Ra-yong; and his son, Hong Jeong-uk. JoongAng Ilbo was linked to Bokwang in terms of a blood relationship within the Hong family. As such, JoongAng Ilbo played an intermediate role between the Samsung and Bokwang groups.

Moreover, the JoongAng Ilbo group was connected to the owners of the old Samsung group, particularly Samsung Everland. By 1996, Hong Seok-hyun, a brother of Hong Ra-hee, was the largest stockholder of Samsung Everland. At the same time, Lee Kun-hee, the husband of Hong Ra-hee, was the largest stockholder of JoongAng Ilbo. However, the situation between JoongAng Ilbo and Samsung Everland changed. Both Samsung Everland and JoongAng Ilbo issued the new shares of CBs in 1996. Hong Seok-hyun abandoned the right to buy the newly issued CBs of Samsung Everland even though doing so would cause him to lose his position as the largest stockholder in Samsung Everland (Kim, 2010). Three years later, in 1999, Hong Seok-hyun became the largest stockholder in JoongAng Ilbo. At the same time, the Lee family members completely disappeared from the lists of shareholders in JoongAng Ilbo. This implies that the Lee and Hong families simply exchanged their stocks of Samsung Everland and Joon-gAng Ilbo. Subsequently, Lee Kun-hee reorganized Samsung in the late 1990s. Samsung Everland under Lee Jae-yong became a de facto holding company of the Samsung group. JoongAng Ilbo under the Hong family was independent from the old Samsung in 1999.

Taken together, the Hong family of JoongAng Ilbo was involved in the old Samsung as a major stockholder. This was rooted in the marriage between Chairman Lee Kun-hee and Hong Ra-hee, as well as a blood tie between Hong Ra-hee and her eldest brother, Hong Seok-hyun. Just how and why the JoongAng Ilbo group was associated with Samsung has been hidden in the official records.

Hong Seok-hyun, the largest stockholder of the JoongAng Ilbo group, divided its corporate structures into the JoongAng Ilbo group and the Bokwang group in 2005. He created Bokwang by transferring various holdings of JoongAng Ilbo in manufacturing, finance, service and advertising to his three brothers and his sister. As seen in Figure 4.3, the JoongAng Ilbo group was in charge of media holdings

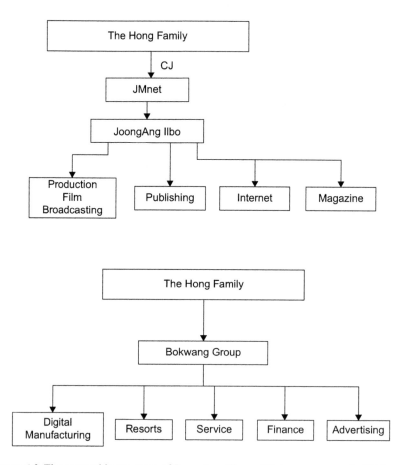

Figure 4.3 The ownership structure of JoongAng Ilbo and Bokwang groups in 2014

in the information and entertainment industries, while the Bokwang group was responsible for businesses in the advertising, digital manufacturing, finance and service industries. The Hong family controlled the corporate structures of both the JoongAng Ilbo and Bokwang groups at the same time. Hong Seok-hyun was the largest stockholder in JoongAng Ilbo, a de facto holding company of the JoongAng Ilbo group. His three brothers and a sister together were the largest stockholder of Bokwang, a de facto holding company of the Bokwang group. Both chaebol groups were controlled by the Hong family, relatives of the Samsung group's Chairman Lee.

4.6. Media expansions of JoongAng Ilbo

The JoongAng Ilbo group vertically and horizontally diversified and increased its media operations from at most 10 in 1998 to 48 media holdings in 2012. Their patterns of media expansion were similar to CJ's strategies. JoongAng Ilbo used active mergers and acquisitions, new shares (BWs) and back-door listings. This conglomerate aggressively acquired other companies (e.g., IS Plus, an entertainment and sports daily newspaper; Mega Box, a major theater multiplex) to enter the entertainment industries. It also issued BWs of its media holdings under the JoongAng Ilbo group[24] to prepare capital for the takeover of other media companies. Finally, JoongAng Ilbo used the back-door listing of J Content Tree to list its media holding on the Korean stock market.

The year 2005 seemed to be the turning point for the JoongAng Ilbo group's media expansion. Before 2005, the JoongAng Ilbo group diversified vertically within the advertising, print and computer-mediated communication industries. After 2005, the JoongAng Ilbo group diversified horizontally into the cable television, film and digital content markets. At this time, the JoongAng Ilbo group was reorganized into the JoongAng Ilbo and Bokwang groups to strengthen their strategies for media expansions. Hong Seok-hyun, the largest stockholder of the JoongAng Ilbo group, transferred both the manufacturing and advertising businesses of JoongAng Ilbo to his brothers and sisters under the new Bokwang group. Hong Seok-hyun retained control over the reorganized JoongAng Ilbo group.

Subsequently, both chaebol groups used different strategies for media expansions. JoongAng Ilbo fortified global partnerships with American media conglomerates News Corporation, Viacom and Time Warner in cable television and film exhibition. Bokwang strengthened its partnership with Japanese media conglomerate Dentsu in the advertising industry. As a result, the Hong family controlled both the JoongAng Ilbo and Bokwang groups and established a media empire. As seen in Table 4.4, the JoongAng Ilbo group was involved in the print, broadcasting, performance and computer-mediated communication markets, while the Bokwang group focused on the advertising market.

Specifically, both JoongAng Ilbo and J Content Tree played vital roles in chaebol media expansion. JoongAng Ilbo supervised the print and paper-related businesses, including online newspapers and media literacy. J Content Tree was responsible for the cable television, film and performance businesses. Under the

Table 4.4 Media businesses of JoongAng Ilbo and Bokwang groups in 2012

Parent Company	Leading Holdings	Sub-Media Holdings	Media Businesses
JoongAng Ilbo group	JoongAng Ilbo	JoongAng Ilbo	Daily newspapers
		JoongAng M&B	Weekly and monthly magazines
		JoongAng Books	Publishing
		J-cube Interactive	Online newspapers
		J P&R	Papers distributions
		A Printing	Paper printings
		Other holdings	Media literacy; agency businesses of newspaper's proofreading and editing
	J Content Tree	J-TBC	Comprehensive cable TV
		JoongAng Broadcasting	Cable channels
		Mega Box	Film exhibition
		JoongAng Entertainment	Film distribution
		Drama House	TV drama production
		Seol & Company	Plays and musicals
		A Story	Scripts for TV drama and film
		Free Egg	Entertainment
Bokwang group	Phoenix Communication	Phoenix Communication	Advertising agency
		PDS Media	Advertising agency
		Dentsu Innovack	Advertising agency
		CN Marketing	Advertising agency for small- and medium-sized companies
		KTF m How	Mobile advertisements
		Saatchi & Saatchi PCI	Advertising production for online and mobile advertisements
		Interworks Media	Advertising agency for online and mobile advertisements

Source: Author's elaboration of data from annual reports of the JoongAng Ilbo and Bokwang groups.

Bokwang group, Phoenix Communication ran advertising businesses, including an advertising agency, advertising production, media planning and online advertising. The media holdings of the JoongAng Ilbo and Bokwang groups owned multiple sub-media operations.

The ownership structures of both the JoongAng Ilbo and Bokwang groups were similar to the Samsung and CJ groups. These conglomerates maintained an interlocked and circular ownership structure between a de facto holding company and a few leading media operations. As an example, in 2012, JoongAng Ilbo was the largest stockholder of JoongAng M&B, J-cube Interactive, JoongAng Broadcasting and JoongAng Books. It was also a major stockholder of J-TBC. All of these media operations were not listed. Moreover, JMnet was a de facto holding company of the JoongAng Ilbo group. It controlled the corporate structures of J Content Tree, which, in turn, was in charge of the entertainment businesses of JoongAng Ilbo. Both JMnet and JoongAng Ilbo were categorized as special relatives in Korean commercial law because Hong Seok-hyun and his family members controlled both JMnet and JoongAng.

In sum, the JoongAng Ilbo group became independent from the old Samsung in 1999 through stock exchanges between Lee Kun-hee, the owner of Samsung, and Hong Seok-hyun, the owner of JoongAng Ilbo. After that, Hong Seok-hyun reorganized the JoongAng Ilbo group into the JoongAng Ilbo and Bokwang groups.

4.6.1. Dreaming the biggest media empire: JoongAng Ilbo

Samsung's founder Lee Byung-chul established the *JoongAng Ilbo* in 1965. The corporate name of this newspaper was also JoongAng Ilbo. By 1998, Lee Kun-hee, the owner of Samsung, was its largest stockholder. His brothers and sisters were also major stockholders in this newspaper company. His wife, Hong Ra-hee, rarely owned shares this newspaper company but was involved in the works of the newsroom. The *JoongAng Ilbo* was under the control of the Lee family as a subsidiary of Samsung group. However, in 1999, JoongAng Ilbo separated from the Samsung group. The largest stockholder shifted from Lee Kun-hee to Hong Seok-hyun, the brother of Hong Ra-hee (the wife of Lee Kun-hee).

Since 1999, JoongAng Ilbo has increased its media holdings from 6 print and computer-mediated communication operations in 1998 to 44 in the broadcasting, digital media between broadcasting and telecommunication, film, performance and print industries in 2012. From 1998 to 2014, JoongAng Ilbo established a media empire with one listed holding (J Content Tree) and 43 unlisted operations in Korea and a global branch in the U.S.

JoongAng Ilbo used three marketing strategies to increase its media holdings: the establishment of media holdings; the buildups of joint ventures with American media conglomerates; and active mergers and acquisitions. First, JoongAng Ilbo plied their existing media holdings to increase the number of media operations in the print and computer-mediated communication industries. Their existing media holdings served two purposes: 1) as the sub-center of media expansions and 2) as the channel to generate revenue in media-related businesses.

First, JoongAng Ilbo established several online sub-media holdings under the name Joins that were in charge of publishing the online newspapers. The newly established online holdings focused on developing specialized media content (i.e., cars, real estate and golf). Another example is JMN U.S.A. JoongAng Ilbo entered the daily paper market in the Korean-American communities in Los Angeles in 1999. A few years later, JoongAng Ilbo expanded JMN U.S.A. to New York, Chicago, Washington and Atlanta. In the Korean markets, JoongAng Ilbo deployed their existing media holdings to enter ancillary markets. For example, Korean

Institution focused on copyediting articles published by small newspaper companies. JoongAng Design was responsible for running the editing businesses of newspapers. A Printing printed articles published by small newspapers and magazine companies. AJIT Academy developed foreign languages textbooks and media-literacy education tools for teenagers' essay tests.

JoongAng Ilbo also established joint ventures with American media conglomerates in computer-mediated communication and broadcasting. For example, JoongAng Ilbo established a joint venture with Microsoft, Joins-MSN, to run portal site businesses. It also founded a joint venture J-TBC with Time Warner and the News Corporation. J-TBC was a comprehensive cable channel that provided news, drama, motion pictures and documentaries for its subscribers. Cartoon-Network Korea was a joint venture with Turner Broadcasting, a media holding of Time Warner. JoongAng Ilbo cooperated with FOX Television Studio, a media holding of News Corporation, to co-produce television drama and own the exclusive distribution rights over the nine Asian countries.

The final strategy used by JoongAng Ilbo to expand its media businesses was to acquire other media companies. In 1999, JoongAng Ilbo took over Channel Q and Catch One, two cable channels from Cheil Communication. Since then, JoongAng Ilbo has acquired several media companies, including Seol & Company in plays and musical performances; Cinus in film exhibition; Drama House in drama production; A Story in professional script writing; AHIT in film development; J Content Tree (renamed from IS Plus) in sports and entertainment; JoongAng Broadcasting in cable television; and JoongAng Mobile & Broadcasting in digital mobile content.

Like other media holdings owned by the Samsung and CJ groups, JoongAng Ilbo was a powerful media investor in media production companies. Some of its prominent investments include *Money Today*, an economic daily newspaper; the *Metro*, the most widely circulated free daily newspaper; Yonhap News, a news agency with the largest market share among the news agencies; A Story, the first professional script company; Skylife, the only Satellite Digital Television; e-Channel, an information-based cable channel; Free Egg and i-Popcorn, animated video sharing; Daeduk Net and Korea Wisenet, online data processing companies; Tigen, a hobby site; and e-Pursi and FutureBook, e-publishing companies. Moreover, JoongAng Ilbo was a major member of Korean media venture funds that focused on producing digital media content fitting into portable media, plays and performances.[25]

Finally, JoongAng Ilbo was involved in the construction of the digital media city in Seoul, Korea. It focused on the development of digital media content (e.g., games, virtual realities and 3D motion pictures). JoongAng Ilbo owned 25.81 percent of total shares in DMCC Project Financial Investment, which was in charge of collecting capital to construct the digital media city in Seoul. It also held 22.73 percent of total stock of DMCC Management, which supervised the digital media city.

In terms of revenues, most of JoongAng Ilbo's revenue came from the print markets (advertising and subscription fees), ranging from 93 percent of total revenue in 1999 to 83 percent in 2012. JoongAng Ilbo focused on the information industries of print and computer-mediated communication.

The ownership structure of JoongAng Ilbo showed a variety of changes from 1998 to 2014. I categorize the changes of JoongAng Ilbo into three patterns: 1) the time of the ownership transition from the Lee family to the Hong family; 2) co-ownership between the Hong family and the Lee family within the CJ group; and 3) the establishment of JoongAng Media Network (JMnet). The first period was from 1998 to 2002, when the Lee family within the old Samsung transferred media ownership in JoongAng Ilbo to the Hong family. In 1998, Hong Seok-hyun, a brother-in-law of Lee Kun-hee, was the largest stockholder in JoongAng Ilbo with 21.5 percent of total shares. With 20.3 percent of total shares, Lee Kun-hee was the second largest stockholder. Hansol and its holding were the third largest stock-holders with 18.4 percent of total stock. Other stockholders were CJ Corporation (14.71 percent) and Cheil Fabrics (8.6 percent), Samsung Corporation (3.9 per-cent) and 14 Samsung men (8.4 percent). In 1999, the Hong family replaced Lee Kun-hee and took over the three subsidiaries of the old Samsung (Cheil Fabrics, Samsung Corporation and Samsung Electricity). By 1999, the names of Lee Kun-hee and the leading subsidiaries of the old Samsung disappeared from the lists of stockholders in JoongAng Ilbo. Four years later, in 2003, Hansol and 14 Samsung men replaced the Yumin cultural foundation, which owned 19.99 percent of total stocks in JoongAng Ilbo. Yumin was the pen name of Hong Jin-kee, the father of Hong Seok-hyun.

The second change of ownership structure in JoongAng Ilbo occurred from 2003 to 2008. For these five years, JoongAng Ilbo was owned by Hong Seok-hyun and CJ's subsidiaries (i.e., CJ Corporation, CJ Construction or CJ Olive Yong). Hong Seok-hyun was the largest stockholder with shares ranging from 36.79 to 43 percent of total stocks. The second largest stockholders were CJ's sub-sidiaries with about 26 percent of total shares. The final ownership shift occurred in 2009. Both the Hong family and CJ's subsidiaries together established JMnet. This was a limited liability company and a de facto holding company of the Joon-gAng group. Major stockholders in JMnet were JoongAng Ilbo, Hong Seok-hyun and CJ's subsidiaries. Thus, JMnet was economically controlled by both the Hong family and CJ's Lee family. Hong Seok-hyun was the largest stockholder of Joon-gAng Ilbo, and Lee Jae-hyun was the largest stockholder of the CJ subsidiaries within the hierarchical ownership structure of each chaebol group. JMnet also was the largest stockholder of J Content Tree, the only listed holding of JoongAng Ilbo.

The board of directors of JoongAng Ilbo was composed of Hong Seok-hyun, a few JoongAng Ilbo men and Korean power elites. The ratio of JoongAng Ilbo men to Korean power elites was about two to one. The term "JoongAng Ilbo man" refers to those working in high positions at JoongAng Ilbo or its media subsidiar-ies (e.g., chief editor, chief executive officer and chief executive financial officer). The Korean power elites included an ex-prime minister, retired high officers in the High Court or the Public Prosecutors Office and a chief executive officer of Daum, a leading portal site in the Korean computer-mediated communication industry.

Two interesting points were found regarding members of the board of direc- tors of JoongAng Ilbo. First, a few JoongAng Ilbo men held multiple seats on the board of directors in JoongAng Ilbo media holdings such as JoongAng Broadcast- ing, JoongAng M&B in the weekly and monthly magazines, Cinus in film exhibi- tion, JoongAng Books in publishing and IS Plus (renamed J Content Tree) in the sports and entertainment businesses. The second point is that Hong Jeong-do, the son of Hong Seok-hyun, was involved in media management. Like Lee Kun-hee in Samsung, Hong Seok-hyun attempted to transfer the JoongAng Ilbo group to his son because the owner of a chaebol group traditionally tended to train his potential heir in the art of management.

In summary, JoongAng Ilbo was a media producer, distributor, exhibitor, inves- tor and constructor in Korea. This company deployed three strategies (e.g., active M&As, the establishment of media operations and joint ventures with American cultural giants) to increase its media holdings. Both the Hong family and CJ's Lee family controlled the corporate structures of JoongAng Ilbo. These family mem- bers shared seats of the board of directors with Korean power elites.

4.6.2. The second base for Samsung entertainment: J Content Tree

J Content Tree was a media holding of the JoongAng Ilbo group responsible for its entertainment businesses. This company was a producer, distributor and exhibitor that owned eight sub-media operations. They include: JoongAng Media Chan- nel Q (TV drama production and drama exports), Drama House (TV drama pro- duction), Seol & Company (plays and musical performances), Mega Box (film exhibition), Cinus Entertainment (film distribution), J Content Hub (digital media content fitting into the portable media devices), IS Ilgan Sports (online and offline newspapers for sports and entertainment) and JoongAng Ilbo Cultural Businesses in the secondary media markets.

In 2005, the JoongAng Ilbo group acquired *Ilgan Sports*, a daily sports and celebrity newspaper. In fact, this newspaper had been owned by the Jang family of the Hankuk media group. This media group had belonged to a major newspaper among the top four in the daily market. However, the 1997 financial crisis forced *Hankuk* to shrink its market power, as its parent company was under financial cri- sis. Thus, the Jang family took over Hangil Trade, a listed company on the Korean stock market, to resolve their financial difficulties. This was a back-door listing. Like the CJ group, the Jang family of the Hankuk media group used the back- door listing to list *Ilgan Sports* on the Korean stock market. But unlike CJ group, listing *Ilgan Sports* didn't help the financial situation of the Hankuk media group. This pushed the Jang family to issue CBs of *Ilgan Sports* in 2003. JoongAng Ilbo purchased about 11 percent of total CBs for *Ilgan Sports*.

The action taken by JoongAng Ilbo brought about conflicts between the Joon- gAng Ilbo and Hankuk media groups, which had long been print media com- petitors. Lee Kun-hee, the owner of Samsung, met with Jang Jae-gu, the owner of Hankuk media group, to resolve this conflict (Lee, 2003, August, 27). Lee's action indicates the JoongAng Ilbo group was under control of the Samsung group as Lee rarely got involved in the issues of M&As except as they related to his family.

Two years later, in 2005, JoongAng Ilbo became the largest stockholder of *Ilgan Sports*. JoongAng Ilbo renamed *Ilgan Sports* IS Plus in order to use IS Plus as a media hub to expand its entertainment media businesses in drama production, cable channels, digital media contents and performance. Four years later, in 2010, IS Plus issued new CBs to acquire the film exhibition company Mega Box, one of the top three film theaters in Korea. In 2010, IS Plus was renamed J Content Tree.

As J Content Tree focused on entertainment businesses, revenues from media production and film exhibitions rapidly increased to about 72 percent of its total revenue in 2012 from approximately 6 percent in 2006. From 2009 and 2010 alone, revenues from media production increased from 27.6 percent to 37.3 percent of total revenues. Similarly, revenue from film exhibition grew from 35.4 percent in 2008 to 56.2 percent of total revenues in 2010. On the other hand, revenues from advertising and subscription fees from print media reduced from 90 percent of total revenue in 2006 to at most 25 percent in 2012. The changes of revenue showed that J Content Tree was no longer merely a sports and celebrity newspaper, but a media hub of the JoongAng Ilbo group in the entertainment markets.

The media ownership in this company was flexible. From 2006 to 2011, Joon-gAng Ilbo was the largest stockholder. It held shares ranging from 28.47 percent of total stocks in 2006 to 20.38 percent in 2011. Three years later, in 2014, the largest stockholder in this company changed from JoongAng Ilbo (11.1 percent) to JMnet (11.3 percent), a company co-established by the JoongAng Ilbo and CJ groups. The change occurred because the CJ and JoongAng Ilbo groups cooper-ated in Korea's entertainment markets. Other major stock holders with at least 5 percent of total stocks varied. From 2006 to 2008, Jang Jun-ho, ex-largest stock-holder of *Ilgan Sports*, was the second largest stockholder with about 8 percent of total stocks. Other major holders were Phantom Entertainment, an entertainment agency, with 5.49 percent of total shares; JoongAng M&B with about 5.3 percent of total stocks; and Hong Seok-hyun with 6.37 percent of total stocks. However, after 2008, Jang Jun-ho did not own any stock in IS Plus.

The board of directors of J Content Tree was composed of four or five mem-bers. They included representatives of the Hong family (i.e., Hong Seok-hyun and Hong Jeong-do), a chief executive officer of the *Hankuk*, JoongAng Ilbo men and Korean power elites. Between 2006 and 2008, the Hong family was rarely involved as members of the board of directors. However, two JoongAng Ilbo men participated as members of the board of directors. In 2006, a financial expert from Daeshin Stock Company was the chief executive officer. From 2007 to 2008, a chief executive officer of the *Hankuk* occupied the position of chief executive officer. However, since 2009, Hong Seok-hyun and Hong Jeong-do have been members of the board of directors. Korean power elites held positions as outside directors. They included an ex-prime minister, a chairman of Korea Broadcasting System an advisory lawyer for the Ministry of Culture & Sports Department and a retired high officer of the Korean national courts.

In sum, JoongAng Ilbo acquired J Content Tree from the Hankuk media group, thereby establishing an entertainment hub for the JoongAng Ilbo group in the broadcasting, film and digital media between broadcasting and telecommunication industries. The JoongAng Ilbo and CJ groups controlled J Content Tree. Only the Hong family participated in media management.

4.6.3. *Advertising with foreigner capital: Phoenix Communication*

Phoenix Communication was a listed advertising company under the Hong family. Phoenix ran an advertising agency and specialized in advertising production, sales promotions and online advertisement. This advertising company was involved in all aspects of marketing including executing, planning, producing and advertising events. Phoenix owned six sub-holdings, which included PDS Media (advertising production); Dentsu Innovack (advertising agency for Japanese companies in Korea and for Korean enterprises in Korea); CN Marketing (advertising business for small- and medium-sized companies); KTF m How (mobile advertisements); Saatchi & Saatchi PCI (online and mobile advertisements); and Interworks Media (online and mobile advertisements).

Phoenix and its media sub-holdings were established by the old Samsung, JoongAng Ilbo, Bokwang and transnational advertising agencies (TNNAs). The history of Phoenix's media expansions shows its transition from the old Samsung group to the JoongAng Ilbo and Bokwang groups, as well as cooperation between chaebol groups and TNNAs in the Korean advertising market. In 1996, Cheil Communication, an in-house advertising agency for the old Samsung group, established Phoenix with the Dentsu media group from Japan. The investment ratio between the old Samsung and Dentsu group was one to one. After JoongAng Ilbo separated from the old Samsung in 1999, this advertising agency was under the JoongAng Ilbo group. Six years later, in 2005, Phoenix was under control of the Bokwang group.

Similarly, media sub-holdings of Phoenix were established through cooperation between the JoongAng Ilbo group and TNNAs. In 1999, Phoenix established two sub-holdings of PDS Media and Dentsu Innovack with transnational advertising agencies. PDS Media was co-founded by Phoenix, the Dentsu group and the Leo Burnett Group in order to do advertising production. Dentsu Innovack was also a joint venture between Phoenix and the Dentsu group to provide an advertising agency for Japanese enterprises in Korea. In 2001, Phoenix and Dentsu Innovack co-acquired a Korean advertising agency, Whal-in, in order to focus on advertising for small- and medium-sized companies. After that, Phoenix renamed Whal-in CN Marketing. Three years later, in 2004, Phoenix co-established KTF m How with two partners, a Korean wireless carrier and the Dentsu group, to enter the mobile advertising market.

At the end of 2005, Hong Seok-hyun, owner of the JoongAng Ilbo group, transferred Phoenix and its sub-advertising holdings to the Bokwang group controlled by his two brothers and sister. Since then, these advertising holdings have belonged to subsidiaries of the Bokwang group. Further, in 2006, Phoenix founded a joint venture of Saatchi & Saatchi PCI with Saatchi & Saatchi for online and mobile advertising. Finally, in 2008, Phoenix established Interworks Media to focus on digital advertising for the digital convergence media between telecommunication and broadcasting industries. Phoenix was cooperating with the JoongAng Ilbo and Bokwang groups, as well as with TNNAs.

Regular clients of Phoenix included subsidiaries of the JoongAng Ilbo and Bokwang groups, Nestle Korea, P&G Korea, Fuji-Xerox, the Korean Ginseng Public Company and a few cosmetics companies. Most revenue for Phoenix came from its advertising agency and advertising production, including production and sales promotion. Revenue from its advertising agency businesses gradually reduced from about 56 percent of total revenue in 1998 to about 25 percent in 2012. On the other hand, revenue from advertising production gradually increased from about 44 percent of total revenue in 1998 to approximately 75 percent in 2012. Phoenix's focus was on advertising production rather than advertising agency.

In terms of ownership structure in Phoenix, its largest stockholders were Hong Seok-kyu, chairman of the Bokwang group, and the Dentsu group. Both Hong Seok-kyu and Dentsu held the same percentage of shares in Phoenix. Foreign institutional investors that were temporarily major stockholders include Goldman Sachs International and Armor Capital. Although Hong Seok-kyu and Dentsu owned the same percentage of shares, Hong Seok-kyu exercised managerial rights over the corporate structure of Phoenix. Members of the board of directors included Hong Seok-kyu, two Dentsu men from Dentsu group, a few directors from sub-holdings of Phoenix and two financial experts. Unlike other media holdings of the JoongAng Ilbo group, Phoenix did not invite the Korean power elites to serve as outside directors.

To summarize, Phoenix was an advertising holding for the Hong family and the Dentsu group that focused on advertising production in Korea.

4.6.4. Conclusion of the JoongAng Ilbo group

Since becoming independent from Samsung in 1999, the JoongAng Ilbo group has diversified horizontally and vertically in the Korean information and entertainment industries, thereby establishing a media empire with about 40 media holdings. This media empire was controlled by both the Hong family and the Lee family. This means that JoongAng Ilbo used the family connections to establish a media empire.

4.7. The establishment of Samsung media empires

The Lee family exploited Korea's financial liberalization to reorganize Samsung's corporate structures and establish Samsung's media empire. Lee Kun-hee, the largest stockholder of the old Samsung, transferred its subsidiaries to his brothers and sisters, as well as the brother of his wife, thereby building up the New Samsung groups. Members of New Samsung groups, mainly the three chaebol groups Samsung, CJ and JoongAng Ilbo, expanded the Korean information and entertainment markets, as seen in Figure 4.4. The Samsung group focused on

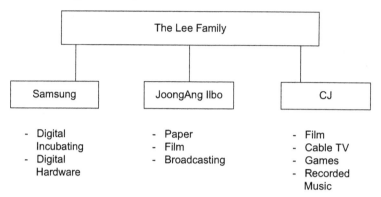

Figure 4.4 Samsung media empires in 2014

advertising and computer-mediated communication. The CJ group expanded in the paid broadcasting and film markets. The JoongAng Ilbo group expanded its media businesses in paid broadcasting markets, media production, performances and film exhibition. The three chaebol groups were all major media investors in media production. They also constructed media cities across the Korean Peninsula. In other words, Samsung established its media empire in the era of Korean media marketization.

Using both informal ties (e.g., blood and marriage ties) and economic circular ownership, the Lee family established a Samsung media empire controlled by the Lee family. This was accomplished under the influence of Lee Kun-hee, the owner of the Samsung group. His nephew, Lee Jae-hyun, was the owner of the CJ group. A brother-in-law of Lee Kun-hee, Hong Seok-hyun, was the owner of the JoongAng Ilbo group. Neither Chairman Lee Kun-hee nor his three children shared media ownership of the CJ or JoongAng Ilbo groups. The Hong family within JoongAng Ilbo rarely held ownership within the CJ or Samsung groups. This implied that each owner within the Samsung media empire seemed to exercise independent rights to control multiple corporate structures within the Samsung, CJ and JoongAng Ilbo groups.

Nonetheless, members of the Lee family shared economic ownership of core holdings in both the CJ and JoongAng Ilbo groups. Lee Jae-hyun, a niece of Chairman Lee Kun-hee, became a major stockholder of Samsung Everland (later renamed Cheil Industries in 2014), a de facto holding company of Samsung group, by 2005. Also, CJ's holdings under Chairman Lee Jae-hyun were major stockholders of JoongAng Ilbo, a de facto holding company of the JoongAng Ilbo group from 1998 to 2010. JMnet, a de facto holding company of the JoongAng Ilbo group, was co-established by CJ and JoongAng Ilbo by 2011. Another example of shared media ownership was A Story. Ownership of this professional script company belonged to both CJ and JoongAng Ilbo.

As implied earlier, the Lee family rarely shared media ownership with other members of chaebol groups. The Lee family maintained exclusive ownership of other chaebol groups rather than looking to either foreign capital or American media conglomerates. Moreover, the Lee family shared human resources within its media corporate structures. For example, Samsung men working at the structural planning office of Samsung participated in media management of CJ's media operations with positions on their boards of directors. Samsung men, considered agents of Samsung's Lee family, also participated in CJ's economic management as members of boards of directors in CJ's manufacturing holdings. This is to say that the CJ group played a mediating role in linking the Samsung group to the JoongAng Ilbo group in the Korean economic sectors and media businesses.

Similarly, the three chaebol groups cooperated with each other in mergers and acquisitions in the Korean media markets. Three prime examples included 1) J Content Tree, 2) Plenus and 3) On-Media and Mega Box. The first example showed the persistence of a close relationship between the JoongAng Ilbo and Samsung groups in spite of their no longer being joiner under the old Samsung group. In 2003, JoongAng Ilbo became a major stockholder of *Ilgan Sports*, owned by the Hankuk media group, which brought about a tacit conflict between the Hankuk media group and the JoongAng Ilbo group, longtime competitors in the Korean daily paper market. A year later, in 2004, Lee Kun-hee, the owner of Samsung, met the owner of the Hankuk media group. Although specific information about this meeting was not disclosed, JoongAng Ilbo successfully acquired *Ilgan Sports* in 2005 and then renamed it J Content Tree. Using J Content Tree, the JoongAng Ilbo group expanded its media businesses to drama production, cable channels, film exhibition and distribution, plays and digital media content.

Other examples reflecting cooperation between CJ and JoongAng Ilbo were M&As of Plenus and On-Media and Mega Box. CJ acquired Plenus in 2004, thereby becoming the first-ranked Korean film distributor and entering the Korean online game market. Interestingly, by 2002, Hong Seok-hyun had become a major stockholder in Plenus. Two years later, in 2004, the CJ group successfully acquired Plenus. Another important example was the acquisition of On-Media and Mega Box. Both On-Media and Mega Box had been owned by the Orion group, a second-tier chaebol group. Hong Seok-hyun, the owner of JoongAng Ilbo, had been a major stockholder of the Orion Cinema Network (cable television brand name On-Media). In 2009, the CJ group acquired On-Media. Three years later, in 2012, JoongAng Ilbo acquired Mega Box, thereby becoming the third-ranked film exhibitor in Korea.

Interesting examples of connections between the CJ and JoongAng Ilbo groups were found in the case of the comprehensive cable channel. In 2010, the Korean government was collecting applicants for licenses to operate comprehensive cable television from Korean media businessmen. As mentioned in chapter 3, the media power of comprehensive cable television was equal to that of the national territorial station. Comprehensive cable television broadcast content in all genres, including news, sports and drama. However, the CJ group did not apply for this license. Instead of the CJ group, the JoongAng Ilbo group applied for and obtained a license for comprehensive cable TV in 2010.

The examples mentioned here reflect the Lee family's family connections that allowed it to expand its media businesses within and across media markets. Visibly, CJ and JoongAng Ilbo cooperated with each other to establish the media empires controlled by the Lee family. Behind the scenes, Samsung supported the media expansions of the JoongAng Ilbo group because Chairman Lee resolved the conflict caused by the tension between the JoongAng Ilbo and Hankuk media groups.

However, the Lee family used different patterns in each chaebol group to manage media holdings. Within Samsung, the Lee family was reluctant to join the boards of directors of Samsung Everland (later renamed Cheil Industries in 2014), Samsung SDS and Cheil Communication. Instead of the Lee family, Samsung men were members of boards of directors in these three media holdings. The Lee family within CJ was intermittently involved in the management of CJ's media holdings, especially when CJ established leading media operations or acquired big media companies. Most of the board members in CJ's media holdings were CJ men working at the structural planning office of CJ and Korean power elites. Finally, the Hong family consistently held board membership in media holdings owned by both the JoongAng Ilbo and Bokwang groups.

Further, the Lee family commonly invited Korean power elites from political, economic and cultural institutions to serve as outside directors on their boards. The three chaebol groups seemed to prefer retired high officers from the Public Prosecutors Office, National Tax Office or Fair Trade Commission as outside directors. The owners of large corporations used corporate structures to connect to the power elites in a given society, and, in keeping with this, the Lee family used the seats on the board of directors in Cheil to connect to the Korean power elites (Domhoff, 1990). The Lee family was able to coalesce their power in connection to Korean power elites within the media corporation structures of the three chaebol groups.

Taken together, the Lee family used personal and family connections to expand their media businesses and control multiple media holdings, thereby becoming the emperors of the Samsung media empires in Korea.

Notes

1 For instance, the chairman of CJ is Lee Jae-hyun, Lee Byung-chul's grandson. The chairman of Samsung is Lee Kun-hee, the third son of Lee. The chairman of JoongAng Ilbo is Hong Seok-hyun, whose sister, Hong Ra-hee, is married to Lee Kun-hee, the founder's son and chairman of Samsung (Seoul Shinmun, 2005).
2 See http://dart.fss.or.kr.
3 The seven Samsung subsidiaries are: Samsung Electronics, Samsung SDI, Samsung Finance, Samsung Credit Card, Samsung Heavy Machine & Samsung Chemicals, Everland and Samsung Corporation.
4 She died in 2005.
5 Digital media investments at this time ranged from e-finance (e.g., Value Net and All@), data processing (e.g., 365 homecare), web portals (Empass), web design (e.g., Design Storm), e-medicine (e.g., 10 DR Implant), e-learning (e.g., Credue), e-commerce (e.g., i-market Korea), 3D (Inooka) and e-security (e.g., Hauri and secu-i) to online gaming (e.g., Battletop and N-forever).

6 Major Everland stockholders besides Lee family members included Samsung Credit Card (14 percent), Samsung Capital (11.62 percent), Cheil Industries (4 percent), Samsung Electro-mechanics (4 percent), Samsung SDI (4 percent) and Samsung's cultural foundations (0. 88 percent).
7 Other major clients included SKT (the largest wireless carrier in Korea), KT (a privatized wired and wireless carrier), Hite (a beer-manufacturing company), Dong-Seo Food (Korea's largest soft drink company) and Koreana (a cosmetics corporation). Samsung's subsidiaries (e.g. Samsung Electronics, Samsung SDI and Samsung SDS) were also Cheil clients in the domestic and global markets.
8 These included Samsung Electronics, Samsung Corporation, Cheil Industries, Samsung Insurance, Samsung Fire Insurance and JoongAng Ilbo.
9 The Lee family within CJ includes eight persons: Lee Jae-hyun (the owner of CJ), his wife (Kim Hee-jae), his two children (Lee Kyung-hoo and Lee Sun-ho), a sister (Lee Mee-kyung), a brother (Lee Jae-hwan), a sister in-law (Min Jae-won) and an uncle (Son Kyung-sik).
10 These holdings include CJ System, CJ CGV, CJ GLS, CJ Food Ville, CJ O-shopping and CJ E&M.
11 These holdings include CJ O-shopping, CJ Media, Mnet, CJ Hellovision, CJ Internet, CJ Entertainment and CJ CGV.
12 KT was a state-owned wired and wireless carrier.
13 These ventures include Discovery Broadcasting and Film Venture Associations, CJ Investment for Broadcasting and Film Venture Associations, Benex Digital Cultural Contents Associations.
14 These included Samsung Corporation, Samsung Fire Insurance and Samsung Electronics.
15 These include cable TV, digital satellite TV, TDMB, SDMB and IPTV.
16 As previously noted, CJ O-shopping took over On-Media and then transferred it to CJ Media.
17 Lee family members who benefitted from this BW release were Lee Mee-kyung, a sister of CJ's owner, and Lee Kyung-hoo, only son of owner Lee Jae-hyun
18 A back-door listing is a reverse takeover or reverse merger by which a privately held company, which may not qualify for the public offering process, purchases a publicly traded company (Investopedia.com, 2013).
19 These include CJ Game Investments, KTF-CJ Music and Michigan Global Contents.
20 Foreign investors in CK Internet included T. Rowe Price International (8.75 percent) in 2004; Willington Management (7.41 percent) in 2005; MiraeAsset Private Equity (8.39 percent) from 2005–2006; and Templeton Asset (6.4 percent) in 2009.
21 These media holding were CJ Media, CJ Entertainment, CJ Internet, Mnet and the division of media contents in CJ O-shopping.
22 The film media funds include IMM Cultural Contents; CentryOn Visual Investment 1•2; K&J Entertainment; ISU Entertainment; Discovery Fund; Tube Entertainment; Chicken Run Foreign Consortium; and CJ Film 3•5•6.
23 These media venture funds included CJ Venture Investment 9, Bennex Film Venture and Master Image.
24 The holdings include JoongAng Ilbo, JoongAng M&B and Ilgan Sports.
25 Venture funds include IMM Media Venture Fund, YeonYang Venture Fund and Company K-Partnership.

References

Domhoff, W. (1990). *The power elite and the state: How policy in made in America*. New York: Aldine de Gruyter.
Erri. (2011). How CJ maintains its Empire. *Economic Reform Report, ERRI*, 8, 1–27. Korean.

Investopedia. (2013). www.investopedia.com/

Kim, J.B. (2005). *The corporate structure of Korea's chaebol groups*. Seoul, Korea: Nanam. Korean.

Kim, S.J. (2007). Samsung republic. *Hwanghae Munhwa*, fall, 25–44. Korean.

Kim, Y.C. (2010). *Thinking Samsung*. Seoul, Korea: Sahoipyungnon. Korean.

Lee, E.J. (2011). How CJ maintains its empire. *Economic Reform Report*, ERRI, 8, 1–27. Korean.

Lee, S.H. (2012). *X-file of Lee Sang Ho on the Lee family of pan-Samsung*. Seoul, Korea: Dong Asia. Korean.

Lee, Y.T. (2003, August 27). Lee Kun-hee met Jang Jae-gu. The *MediaToday*.

Secretariat of National Assembly. (2010). *A study about policies about chaebol groups from 1980s to 2000s*. Seoul, Korea: National Assembly. Korean.

Seoul Shinmun. (2005). *The pulse of chaebol*. Seoul, Korea: Moohan. Korean.

Song, S.H. (2008). Where is the succession of Samsung for Lee Jae-Yong? *The Wolgan Chosun*, pp. 96–113. Korean.

Song, W.G. (2011). *Founder Lee and his influences over Samsung*. www.economyinsight.co.kr/news/articleView.html?idxno=478 Korean.

5 A family media monopoly

The neoliberal media model has allowed existing media companies to transform into cultural giants with multiple holdings under centralized ownership. These giants inevitably became the major players in oligopolistic media markets (Kunz, 2007). Controlling high market shares, cultural conglomerates are able to determine what to produce (or not), how to distribute (or not) and how much to spend on media content within and across media markets (Meehan, 2005). Schiffrin calls this power "market censorship." Media giants set the rules of production and focus on creating marketable products that will support their economic positions, often at the expense of the public good (2000, 2006).

The nature of market censorship is similar to that of media monopoly (Bagdikian, 2000, 2004) because large media enterprises censor the free flows of media content in the market and affect media activities of independent companies. Media monopoly can install barriers to entry into the market, thus reducing competition, restricting consumers' choice of media outlets and shifting the prevailing definition of information from being a public good to a privately appropriable commodity (Keane, 1991; Soley, 2006). By controlling the circulation of cultural commodities, cultural conglomerates attempt to control the means of communication in a society. Thus, in neoliberal democracies, the largest threat to free expression comes from large corporations with high market shares rather than government suppression of speech (Mazzocco, 1994; Atkins, 2006).

Market censorship is linked to media ownership because of connections between market structures and media ownership. Media owners of cultural conglomerates can directly influence media markets through their media holdings, which can indirectly affect the activities of other companies in the media markets (Murdock, 1982, 1990). Media owners also tend to bind their power to the knowledge (or media content) produced by their media holdings in order to exercise their power over a capitalistic society (Jansen, 1988). I call this power "corporate censorship" (Jansen, 1988; Murdock, 1990; Schiller, 1991). With their high media market shares, cultural conglomerates control the production, construction and distribution of news and entertainment content. For good or ill, this gives conglomerates like Samsung the power to determine what information the public receives, the form in which it is received and how it is publically interpreted. Thus, corporate censorship is a tool of capitalist control over the media.

In this chapter, I trace how and why corporate censorship works in the relation-ship between structures of media markets and ownership. I focus particularly on the corporate censorship of the Lee family, focusing on the emerging issues from the four media markets in a Korean context. To do this, I analyze government data from both White Papers published by the Ministry of Culture Sports and Tourism (MCST) and special reports published by the Fair Trade Commission (FTC). By 2014, 16 White Papers existed. They reflect the changed structures of the four media markets and identify the major market players and their market shares. Also, 50 special reports were available regarding the media businesses of the Samsung, CJ and JoongAng Ilbo chaebol groups over the four media markets. Further, I gathered secondary sources from scholarly works and newspaper arti-cles. These data epitomize how and why media owners from the Lee family have exercised corporate censorship over the four media markets.

5.1. Market censorship in neoliberal Korean media

In this section, I first analyze issues emerging from the interactions between the daily newspapers and advertising markets. I then examine issues relating to the structures of the cable television and film markets in order to show how and why the Lee family exercised corporate censorship over the Korean information and entertainment markets.

5.1.1. Information monopoly under chaebol groups

Since the late 1990s, the Korean paper markets have been structured by the top three companies, the *Chosun Ilbo*, the *JoongAng Ilbo* and the *Dong A Ilbo*. The three companies were called Cho-Joong-Dong in Korea. Cho-Joong-Dong's increased market power was based on sacrifices of independent paper distribu-tors, as well as illegal actions of the Korean paper monopoly. In fact, Korean media law prohibits newspapers from distributing copies for free or giving lavish gifts to subscribers. However, Cho-Joong-Dong ignored the Korean media laws. The *JoongAng Ilbo* engaged in more unfair actions than the *Chosun Ilbo* and the *Dong A Ilbo*, such as providing free papers for six months or U.S. $100 gift cards or bicycles for new or regular subscribers (Cho, 2004). These actions by the three players pushed other national papers to imitate their marketing strategies to survive and keep their subscribers. Losing subscribers brought about a double loss of both advertisement money and subscription fees. The Korean daily market became an arena of war for increased market shares by the national papers.

The Fair Trade Commission, in charge of investigating unfair activities in media companies, investigated these alleged unfair practices in the daily market in 2004. Seven national newspaper companies were found to have given away a total of 799 bicycles to lure subscribers through their 26 distribution branches. The *JoongAng Ilbo* doled out 380 bicycles, the greatest number among the news-papers inspected. The *Chosun Ilbo* and the *Dong A Ilbo* followed with 183 and 121 bicycles respectively. Next were the *Hankuk Ilbo* (49), the *Hankyoreh* (10) and the *Segye Times* (6). The FTC imposed fines for delivering newspapers for free for prolonged periods and giving away gifts beyond a certain value when customers signed on for long-term subscriptions (Seo, 2004). However, these illegal sales and promotions rarely disappeared.

Interestingly, the financial resources for the sales promotions did not come from the pockets of the *Chosun Ilbo*, the *JoongAng Ilbo* or the *Dong A Ilbo*, but rather from sacrifices of small distributors or branch managers. They were not regular employees of these three companies, but were subcontracted to deliver papers to subscribers. These small distributors had to renew their distribution contracts annually. But a condition of renewal was to have met a certain quota in previous years. If they failed to fulfill the quota, their contracts would be cancelled. Based on contract conditions, small distributors were required to send a certain fee to the three companies per month (Cho, 2002). This shows that branch managers were ultimately under the control of Cho-Joong-Dong. The *JoongAng Ilbo*, for example, unilaterally increased its fees from U.S. $500 to $5,000 per month and forced 500 branch managers to pay the costs of sales promotions. Similar patterns were evident at the *Chosun Ilbo* and the *Dong A Ilbo*. The centralized market shares held by the three companies allowed for the exploitation of branch managers.

Worse yet, major revenues of the three paper companies have decreased. The revenue percentage of both advertisement and subscription fees decreased from 87.5 percent of total income in 1999 to 74.5 percent of total income in 2007. During the same period, other income sources, including advertising articles, increased from 12.5 percent of total revenue in 1999 to 25.5 percent in 2007 (Lee, 2010). The increased percentage of other revenue was due to the increased number of advertising articles in the papers in the form of special sections and advertiser-friendly articles on topics ranging from real estate, cosmetics, credit cards, motoring, education and travel to golf, food and drinks (Kim, 2008).

These advertising supplements were mostly based on public relations materials offered by advertisers of the chaebol groups. Even journalists, especially those who belonged to economic or information technology departments, rarely checked the accuracy of the information in PR materials. Newspaper articles no longer reflected the public's interest in social justice, but rather represented the private interests of the major advertisers, mainly chaebol groups. That is to say, the newsroom was under the pressure of capital.

Chaebol groups especially used advertisement money to manufacture amicable public opinions. For example, the owner of the Hyundai group, Jung Mong-ku, was arrested on suspicion of tax evasion in 2006. At that time, the Hyundai group atypically funneled advertising money into the national daily papers, especially Cho-Joong-Dong, until the day when Chairman Jung Mong-ku was given a suspended sentence. Similarly, national papers, especially Cho-Joong-Dong, published articles on the chaebol groups' roles in the Korean economy, the contributions of chaebol owners to the Korean economy and the necessities of market-initiated policies in the economy. Journalists rarely reported the illegal tax-evasion and exploitative activities of chaebol groups in the Korean economy (Lee & Che, 2007).

Similar patterns were found in other chaebol legal cases (i.e., with the Doosan, Samsung and Hanhwa groups; see Erri, 2008, 2010). Korean journalists gave up the role of watchdog for Korean society. Lee Jung-hwan, a media critic, stated that journalists were no longer seeking truth and justice for Korean society, but were little more than domesticated salary-men (Lee, 2010). Ironically, these examples show that the biggest obstacle to freedom of speech in the Korean press is the capital of major advertisers rather than state power.

Importantly, Cho-Joong-Dong manipulated public opinion to enter the cable market by aggressively propagating articles about the reintroduction of cross-media ownership between the newspaper and broadcasting industries (Yang & Kim, 2008). In July of 2009, responding to Cho-Joong-Dong, the Korean government revised existing print and broadcasting laws and reintroduced cross-media ownership between papers and broadcasting companies. At the same time, Cho-Joong-Dong established new broadcasting holdings with chaebol groups and American cultural conglomerates. The *Chosun* founded Chosun TV. The *Dong A* established Channel A. The *JoongAng Ilbo* instituted JTBC. One year later, in 2010, Cho-Joong-Dong successfully grabbed the comprehensive cable channel.

After that, Cho-Joong-Dong sold bundle advertisements for its papers and cable channels. However, advertisers were reluctant to give big advertising money to the top three's cable channels due to low ratings. Each cable channel of Cho-Joong-Dong earned at most 1 percent of the audience in 2012. Moreover, Cho-Joong-Dong pressured the Korean government to raise the television subscription fee for public broadcasting and to deregulate advertising items about previously forbidden content. In this way, Cho-Joong-Dong tried to turn its deficits in the cable businesses into a national tax from the pockets of the public. This is why Cho-Joong-Dong were called the cultural gangsters of Korea.

In summary, the centralized market structure of the daily papers brought about three issues: 1) worsening of the market polarization between Cho-Joong-Dong and the other papers, including the progressive and local papers; 2) leaning advertising dollars in the direction of Cho-Joong-Dong in spite of the increased number of paper companies; and 3) marginalizing investigative news regarding unfair actions of major advertisers, mainly chaebol groups. This meant the Korean daily papers rarely published articles to form public discourse, but instead overflowed with advertising supplements. The cultural doors to enter Korean society were shut down in a neoliberal authoritarian Korea.

5.1.2. Cable monopoly under speculative cartel

Unlike the daily paper market, foreign capital, mainly from institutional investors, got involved in Korean cable television. It invested in cable companies owned by the chaebol groups (e.g., the CJ, Hyundai, LG, Orion and Taekwang groups). Under the neoliberal model, chaebol groups with foreign capital aggressively acquired small- and medium-sized cable companies with a focus on both relay cable operators and system operators. Both chaebol groups and foreign capital focused on cable system operation's market potential. Cable system operators earned profits from paid subscription fees, advertising revenue, broadband and Internet phone services. By 2012, at least 87 percent of total households in Korea were paid subscribers of cable television.

Moreover, cable television was located at the top of the pyramid in paid broadcasting markets because media products shown on cable channels were rebroadcast to digital media (e.g., digital satellite television, Internet Protocol television [IPTV], satellite digital multimedia broadcasting [SDMB] and territorial digital multimedia broadcasting [TDMB]). These economic benefits induced chaebol groups with foreign capital to seek aggressive mergers and acquisitions (M&As). As a result, the number of cable system operating companies decreased from 748 in 2002 to 199 in 2009. Eight cable operating companies occupied 84 percent of the total market shares in 2014. Independent cable system operators collapsed, and chaebol groups with foreign capital controlled Korea's cable system operating market.

However, foreign capital rarely got involved in the cable program provider (PP) market responsible for content production. Since 2001 when the Korean government replaced the licensing system of PPs with an open registration system, only chaebol groups like the CJ, Taeyoung and Orion groups have acquired independent cable companies with a focus on popular cable channels (e.g., recorded music, film and animation). They thereby became the powerful multiple program providers (MPPs) with up to 50 percent of total market share in 2010. As examined earlier, the chaebol groups were also major multiple system operators (MSOs).

Although foreign capital rarely invested in the cable content market, it was able to influence cable program providers through partnership with the chaebol groups. For example, powerful multiple system providers (MSPs) CJ Media and On-Media played a vital role in manufacturing a phenomenon called "med," a term combining the Korean words for American TV series. Both CJ Media and On-Media were major Korean buyers of Hollywood studio content. They imported Hollywood's products in the form of an output deal in which they owned priority import rights to Hollywood products in Korean media markets under specific conditions of prepayment. CJ Media and On-Media monopolized the rights to import media products made in the U.S. into Korean audio-visual markets. After importing American drama, both MSPs broadcast over 30 American shows on their cable channels every week. For example, the women's cable channel On Style re-ran the entire six seasons of *Sex and the City*. OCN, a cable film channel, broadcast episodes of *C.S.I. Crime Scene Investigation* continuously for 24 hours (Kang, 2007). These imported American dramas were also rebroadcast on other digital media channels (e.g, digital satellite television, IPTV, SDMB and TDMB). The Korean MSPs maintained a symbiotic relationship with American cultural conglomerates. Korean cable companies imported American media products to fill their cable channels and recycled them at the digital media outlets.

Against this background, the number of cable production companies slightly increased from 159 in 2003 to 187 in 2009. However, this increase was meaningless because of the hierarchical structure of cable television. Cable production companies, under control of MSOs, provided legal marketplaces for independent producers. Structurally, however, cable production companies were only subcontractors of the MSOs who owned the absolute rights to set programming. Theoretically, independent producers could sell their works to other digital media. But this was not easy for program providers with poor financing because MSOs held about 87 percent of total paid broadcasting market shares. MSOs also were multiple program providers rebroadcasting media content to other digital media outlets. In addition, MSOs transferred the costs of sales promotion to independent production companies. Because MSOs owned programming rights over the cable channels, independent producers involuntarily accepted the unfair actions by MSOs in order to survive in the hostile marketplace. If small production companies refused to pay costs of promotional sales to increase the number of subscribers, they would lose the chance to broadcast their content on the cable channels.

MSOs were the gatekeepers of cable production and distribution. As such, they were able to limit media access and control cable users much as they controlled independent production companies. MSOs often changed broadcast schedules without notifying cable users when some media products recorded high ratings. MSOs also changed the popular cable channel products from basic and expanded basic to premium services. The more the audience watched cable channels, the higher their subscription fees. Market controllers of MSOs dealt with cable users as their means to earning profits. MSOs even forced cable users into bundled services with cable channels, broadband and Internet phone services. Because there was no option to select another company, cable users had no choice but to agree to the limited products presented by MSOs.

The unreasonable activities by MSOs were designed to limit free competition among media companies. Chronic exploitation by MSOs eventually made cable production companies give up their other media interests, thus blocking new entries into the cable production market. Even MSPs with multiple cable channels and cable system operators refused to transmit media content to other digital media like SDMB, TDMB, IPTV and satellite digital television. Korean broadcasting regulations recommended that multiple program cable providers re-transmit media content to digital media in order to guarantee access to non-cable users. However, the market controllers ignored the legal recommendations and then stopped re-transmitting media content to other digital media companies altogether.

In summary, Korea's cable markets were structured by chaebol groups in joint ventures with foreign capital and/or American cultural conglomerates. Chaebol groups were the visible entities directly exercising corporate censorship over the cable television systems and channels. Foreign capital American cultural conglomerates were the invisible hands over the Korean cable markets, exerting influence with advertising dollars. By controlling market structures, domestic and foreign capital have exploited cable production companies, restricted free competition among media companies and limited the access of media users in cable television.

5.1.3. Motion picture monopoly by chaebol groups

The Korean film distribution and exhibition markets were centralized by chaebol groups and Hollywood studios. In the distribution market, both market controllers were more concerned with distributing foreign motion pictures than Korean ones. The distribution ratio between foreign and domestic motion pictures was approximately eight to one. In the film exhibition market, chaebol groups dominated Hollywood studios. They were major investors in Korean motion picture productions and production companies. Chaebol groups were indirectly involved in the production process as major members of film venture funds.

Chaebol groups especially focused on vertical integration between the film distribution and exhibition markets. In the distribution market, chaebol groups like CJ, Orion and Lotte aggressively acquired independent companies (Cinema Service, Chung A-Ram and Myung Film), thereby increasing their market power from zero to 89.7 percent of total distribution market shares between 1998 and 2006. These top three became market controllers to the detriment of Korean independent distributors. In the film exhibition market, CJ, Orion and Lotte constructed 263 multiplex theaters across the Korean Peninsula from 1998–2012. This increased the number of film screens from 507 in 1998 to 2,081 in 2012.

The increase in the number of multiplex theaters led to a decrease in the total number of film theaters from 409 in 1999 to 292 in 2011. The main reason was the vertical integration between major distributors and exhibitors within three chaebol media giants. Major film distributors required independent theaters to have at least five screens. At that time, most small theaters had just one screen. To receive newly distributed motion pictures, independent theaters gave the rights to their theaters' management over to the chaebol groups. This was called the commissioned management of film theaters. Although the independents owned the property rights to their theater buildings, their theater businesses became branches of the chaebol groups' film exhibitions. Small- and medium-sized theaters collapsed, becoming subcontractors to the CJ, Orion and Lotte groups in accordance with annually or bi-annually renewed contracts. The three chaebol groups created a monopoly in the Korean film exhibition market.

In 2012, the CJ group occupied 44 percent of the total shares in the exhibition market. It owned both CJ CGV and Premus, with 922 film screens, 858 multiplex theaters' screens and 64 independent film exhibitors under commissioned management. The Lotte group was second with 645 film screens, including 55 independent film exhibitors under commissioned management. It held about 31 percent of total market shares. The third-ranked exhibitor was Mega Box, owned by the JoongAng Ilbo group, with 424 screens. Mega Box experienced ownership changes from the Orion group to Macquarie Investment to the JoongAng Ilbo group. This multiplex held about 20 percent of total market share. The total market share of the top three film exhibitors reached 75.2 percent of the total exhibition market in 2012.

In fact, most revenue in Korean film markets came from admission tickets, which ranged from about 74 percent of total revenue in 2001 up to 78.55 percent in 2005,

Table 5.1 Percentage of film revenue

	2001	*2002*	*2003*	*2004*	*2005*
Admission tickets	74.00	75.00	76.00	77.32	78.55
Video	12.10	12.18	7.97	6.41	3.05
DVD	0.25	1.38	1.20	2.31	1.09
Television	5.08	4.90	3.56	4.77	4.31
Online	0.14	0.34	0.48	0.28	0.35
Exports	7.10	3.43	9.67	7.95	12.30
Other	1.34	2.77	2.03	0.96	0.35
Total	100	100	100	100	100

Source: Fair Trade Commission (June 2, 2008), p. 4.

as seen in Table 5.1. The other income was from film exports (3.43–12.30 percent), video rental services (3.05–12.10 percent) and TV (3.56–5.08 percent).

Taken together, the chaebol groups CJ, Orion, JoongAng Ilbo and Lotte vertically and simultaneously diversified into the co-financing, distribution and exhibition markets. They thereby became centralized market controllers as small- and medium-sized distributors and exhibitors collapsed. The chaebol media conglomerates set the rules regarding what to produce, distribute, exhibit and release. Further, chaebol groups exercised corporate censorship, causing the social and cultural problems of the 1) formation of cartels to control the prices of admission tickets; 2) establishment of exploitative structures over film producers; and 3) development of disturbing market orders.

CJ Entertainment, Lotte Entertainment and Mediaplex, the top three film distributors, attempted to control admission prices beyond the legal boundaries. The Korean government suggested guidelines for ticket prices on an annual basis; however, this was not a legal obligation for film exhibitors. Film exhibitors generally provided several discounted services (e.g., membership discount, credit card rewards and early/late admission tickets) for cinema audiences. However, in 2007, the top three sent an official letter saying they would not distribute motion pictures if exhibitors continued to offer discounted admissions. Consequently, discounted services for movie audiences disappeared. In addition, the top three exhibitors, CJ CGV, Lotte Cinema and Mega Box, forced local independent exhibitors to increase ticket prices. Prices were flexible according to regional areas, tending to be more expensive in big cities than local areas. Consequently, the overall price of theater admission increased from U.S. $7 in 2001 to U.S. $9 per movie-goer in 2009.

The second problem caused by the centralized distribution market was the exploitation of producers by CJ, Orion and Lotte. Because chaebol groups were the most powerful film investors, distributors and exhibitors, they were involved in the production processes, including film production and content, production costs, film screening periods, film running times, places to release motion pictures and even the ratio of dividend profits from popular motion pictures. For example, a production company with an original synopsis contacted one of the three chaebol groups and private financial institutions at the same time to acquire total production costs. The three chaebol groups tended to provide 50 percent of the total production costs for a Korean film to the production company under certain conditions. These included 1) acquisition of the other 50 percent of production costs by each production company, 2) scenario revisions often emphasizing human stories and diluting political aspects of films, 3) main actors or actresses, 4) payment of commissions and 5) a six-to-four ratio of dividend income between investor and producers.

These conditions reflected the chaebols' exploitative structures used with exhibitors, distributors and producers. As seen in Table 5.2, exhibitors wielded the most power in the industry and earned 50 percent of the total admission income per Korean film. The other 50 percent of the total admission income was divided among distributors, investors and producers. Distributors acquired 10 percent of the remaining 50 percent of admission incomes. Investors deducted the total production costs and also obtained their invested capital. The ratio of dividend profits between investors and film producers was six to four. Worse, if film producers violated the conditions of contracts, their portion of dividend profits was reduced from four to two. Thus film producers, subject to the greatest exploitation, received only 6 percent of the total admission profits per Korean film. This hierarchical structure, established by the three chaebol media groups, forced independent film producers to become subcontractors of the three chaebol groups or give up film production.

Take the example of the Korean blockbuster *May 18*. This film dealt with the resistance of ordinary people in the Kwangju Uprising in May 1980 against the military Chun Doo-hwan regime. It cost over U.S. $10 million to produce

Table 5.2 The ratio of dividend profits among producers, investors, distributors and exhibitors

Motion picture	Total costs of a motion picture U.S. $4 million
	Dividend incomes in the ratio of 6 to 4 between investor and producers
	Distribution commission: 10 percent
	Exhibition commission: 50 percent
	Total admission tickets: 2.5 million
	Average admission price: U.S. $5.4 per audience
Exhibitors	Profits: U.S. $6.75 million (2.5 million * U.S. $5.4 * 0.50)
	Commission = 50 percent of the total admission income
Distributors	Profits: U.S. $0.675 million (U.S. $6.75 million * 0.10)
	Commission = 10 percent of the remaining 50 percent of the total admission income
Investors	Profits: U.S. $1.25 million
	Deduction of total production costs U.S. $4 million from U.S. $6.075 million and then obtained U.S. $1.25 from 60 percent of U.S. $6.075 million
Producers	Profits: U.S. $0.825 million

Source: Fair Trade Commission (February 21, 2008), p. 15.

and sold over 730 million admission tickets in 2007. Nonetheless, Planning, the production company for *May 18*, went into bankruptcy in spite of the immense profits of the co-financer and distributor, CJ Entertainment, as well as the exhibitor, CJ CGV, which were controlled by the CJ group (Lee, 2009). A similar pattern is found with the film *Nom, Nom, Nom*, the highest grossing film in Korean theaters in 2008. Media critic Kwak Byung-chan argues that the three chaebol groups were the biggest player, growing their profits while degrading the creativity of film producers and the quality of Korean motion pictures (September 17, 2012).

In addition, the three chaebol groups tried to manipulate market demands with their distributing and exhibiting power. For example, *The Typhoon* set one of the higher box office records in 2006. It was distributed by CJ Entertainment and exhibited by CJ CGV. At that time, this film was released at 540 screens over the Korean Peninsula, over 30 percent of the total number of screens in Korea. The number of screens obtained by *The Typhoon* was higher than the Hollywood blockbuster *King Kong*, seen only on 370 screens (Im, 2006, January 13). A similar pattern was found with the movie *Thieves*, which set the highest box office record in 2012. This film was distributed and exhibited by the Orion group. *Thieves* occupied about 1,072 screens over the Korean Peninsula, about 50 percent of the total number of screens in 2012.

The monopoly power of chaebol groups blocked low-budget films in the Korean exhibition market. Even *Pieta* (2012), directed by Kim Ki-duk, showed at a mere 140 screens within Korea before director Kim won the Golden Lion Award at the Venice Film Festival in 2012. This film was an extremely low-budget film that only cost U.S. $0.13 million from director Kim Ki-duk's own pocket. After the Venice Film Festival in 2012, the three chaebol groups increased the number of screens from 140 to 330. However, a month later, Kim decided to give up releasing his film to the Korean multiplex theaters to allow space for other low-budget films. However, his intended goodwill was to no avail. In fact, it was impossible for independent or experimental producers to get the chance to release their films at the multiplex theaters (Power, 2012).

Korean film markets were monopolized by the CJ, Orion and Lotte chaebol groups. They dominated Hollywood studios in both the distribution and exhibition markets. Their Korean film monopoly was able to set the rules at Korean film markets. This led to increased ticket prices, exploitation of film producers and marginalization of film artists with high originality in the Korean film markets.

In sum, the Korean information and entertainment media monopoly was forged by chaebol groups with transnational media conglomerates and/or foreign capital. Chaebol groups with transnational media conglomerates exercised their power over the daily papers as the major advertisers, thereby setting the public agenda and polluting newsrooms for the private interests of capital. They also speculated in cable television using foreign capital and aggressive M&As. Further, only chaebol groups set the rules in the film production, distribution and exhibition markets. They perpetuated chronic exploitative structures over the film producers, perturbing market orders and manipulating the flow of motion pictures.

5.2. Corporate censorship by the Lee family

The Lee family was the richest family in Korea. Lee Kun-hee, the owner of Samsung group, was the richest man in Korea. His youngest sister, Lee Myung-hee, was the richest woman in Korea and the largest stockholder of Shinsaegae group. His nephew and owner of the CJ group, Lee Jae-hyun, belonged to Korea's 20 richest. The economic power of the Lee family controlling pan-Samsung groups contributed to 14.70 percent of the Korean gross domestic product in 2005, as seen in Table 5.3. Pan-Samsung groups included the Samsung, CJ, Hansol, JoongAng Ilbo and Shinsaegae groups.

Among the members of pan-Samsung groups, Samsung, CJ and JoongAng Ilbo owned multiple media operations with high market shares within and across the Korean information and entertainment industries. As investigated in chapter 4, the three chaebol groups together established media empires across and within the Korean information and entertainment industries. The Samsung group focused on advertising (Cheil Communication) and computer-mediated communication (Samsung Everland and Samsung SDS). JoongAng Ilbo controlled media holdings in the advertising (Phoenix Communication), daily paper and computer-mediated communication (JoongAng Ilbo), cable television (JTBC) and film (J Content Tree) markets. The CJ group owned multiple media operations in the cable television (CJ Home-shopping, CJ Media, CJ Hellovision and Mnet), film (CJ Entertainment and CJ CGV) and game (CJ Internet) markets.

These media operations controlled by the Lee family dominated all four media markets. Both Cheil Communication and Phoenix Communication were always in the top 10 advertising agencies. The *JoongAng Ilbo* was part of the Korean newspaper monopoly known as Cho-Joong-Dong. Both CJ Media and CJ Hellovision were market controllers in cable television, located at the top of the hierarchical paid broadcasting markets. CJ Entertainment was the most powerful film distributor. J Content and CJ CGV were the most powerful film exhibitors. Simply put, the Lee family's economic and cultural power made them able to exercise corporate censorship over the Korean information and entertainment markets. I will now discuss the Lee family's impact on each of these markets.

5.2.1. The Lee family and information markets

The Lee family used economic and media power to control the information markets. Methods used by the family included 1) advertisements, 2) lawsuits against journalists, 3) social networking between the Lee family and journalists and 4) its media holdings. With both advertisements and lawsuits, the Lee family attempted

Table 5.3 Percentage of pan-Samsung groups in the Korean GDP

Year	1990	1992	1994	1998	2000	2002	2004	2005
Percent	7.32	8.84	12.19	15.38	13.44	12.41	13.64	14.70

Source: Kim (2007).

to control newsrooms under financial difficulties. With social networking, the Lee family built a press castle for the private interests of the Lee family in Korean society. With its media holdings (the *JoongAng Ilbo*, Cheil Communication and Phoenix Communication), the Lee family directly published articles supporting its private interests, diluted the news regarding scandals of the Lee family and got involved in the presidential elections of Korea. The Lee family applied their economic and cultural power over Korean journalism to manufacture public opinion for their private interests.

First, the Lee family deployed advertisements to influence Korean journalism. In the Korean paper markets, pan-Samsung groups including Samsung, CJ, Shinsaegae and Hansol were powerful advertisers. Let's take the example of the Samsung group. Samsung's power over the Korean daily newspapers was absolute in the commercial newspaper market (Kim, 2008). As seen in Table 5.4, Samsung's advertisements in major national daily papers accounted for 10.94 percent of the annual incomes per national paper.

Samsung paid more advertising money to the three mainstream papers, together nicknamed Cho-Joong-Dong, than to minor papers. The three were very conservative papers maintaining pro-chaebol news and an anti–North Korea tone. The percentage of the annual income of Cho-Joong-Dong attributable to Samsung advertising ranged from at least 8.14 to 12.47 percent of the total revenue. Samsung also financially supported minor newspapers like *Hankuk*, *Hankyoreh* and *KyungHang* that tended to maintain a critical tone about the unfair economic actions of chaebol groups, including Samsung. However, Samsung stopped their regular advertisements in both *Hankyoreh* and *KyungHang* in 2009 because the two progressive newspapers critically reported about the Samsung X-file and the Samsung Scandal (Kim, 2008).

The Samsung X-file in 2005 and the Samsung Scandal in 2007 are examples of Samsung's exercise of power without responsibility. Both cases reflected Samsung's power over Korean society, including in the political, economic and media realms.

The Samsung X-file was disclosed on July 21, 2005. Lee Sang-ho, an investigative journalist of the Munhwa Broadcasting Company, one of the public broadcasting companies, reported on the Samsung X-file. This term was coined as a name for 280 wiretapped recordings conducted by the National Intelligence Service (NIS) at the end of 1997. The X-file tapes contained dialogues between Samsung's vice chairman Lee Hak-soo, the head of the structural planning office of Samsung, and Lee's brother-in-law, Hong Seok-hyun, the owner of JoongAng Ilbo. The dialogues included five points: 1) the existence of a slush fund for

Table 5.4 Percentage of Samsung's advertisement in national papers

Newspaper	Hankuk	Hankyoreh	JoongAng	Chosun	Dong A	KyungHang
2007	5.37	5.45	8.14	9.67	8.23	5.17
2009	4.54	0.02	10.94	12.47	10.44	0.03

Source: Erri (2010, p. 25).

presidential candidates in 1997; 2) Samsung's involvement in creating the public image of the presidential candidate in the ruling party in 1997; 3) lists of the Korean power elites connected to Samsung; 4) the amounts of bribes; and 5) Samsung's attempt to acquire the Kia group in 1997 (Lee, 2012). Samsung's X-file reflected the cozy relationships among Korea's political elites, the Lee family, the prosecuting authorities and the courts.

The Samsung Scandal was another example of illegal connections between the Lee family and Korean power elites. In October 2007, Kim Yong-chul, ex-member of the Samsung structural planning office and an internal lawyer for Samsung for seven years, turned whistleblower. He made three main points: 1) Chairman Lee and his top aides belonged to the structural planning office and illegally ordered transactions allowing Lee's son to acquire the Samsung group through Samsung's subsidiaries at unfair low prices; 2) Samsung regularly bribed Korean power elites in the government, the courts and the media; and 3) Samsung trained Samsung executives to serve as scapegoats to protect the Lee family. All Samsung executives were expected to do illegal lobbying and bribery, buying people with Samsung money (Choe, 2007). Kim also disclosed that the JoongAng Ilbo group was not independent from Samsung on the practical level because the structural planning office of the Samsung group was consistently involved in the businesses of the JoongAng Ilbo group.

The Samsung X-file and the Samsung Scandal resulted in the appointment of a special prosecutor to investigate during a three-month probe by parliament. The special investigation disclosed that 1) Samsung created hidden money within its corporate structures by borrowing bank accounts in the names of Samsung executives; 2) Chairman Lee was in breach of fiduciary duty for incurring losses to Samsung while helping his son gain control of the Samsung group; and (3) Chairman Lee evaded taxes on income from the trading of Samsung group unit stocks channeled through accounts held by other executives.

In both these circumstances, Samsung used the carrot and the stick to manipulate public discourse to favor the Lee family. First, Samsung attempted to control the Korean papers through advertisement. They increased advertising money to the daily papers, especially Cho-Joong-Dong, which published Samsung-friendly articles. On other hand, Samsung stopped their regular advertising in newspapers critical of Samsung's unfair actions in the Korean economy. Both Samsung and its subsidiaries stopped their regular advertisements without notifications. For example, both the *Hankyoreh* and the *KyungHang* critically reported about Samsung's tax evasions, creation of slush funds and suppression of trade unions. Samsung stopped their advertisements and financial sponsorships of both newspapers from 2007 to 2010. Both the *Hankyoreh* and the *KyungHang* had to refuse anti-Samsung ads. For example, Samsung whistleblower Kim Yong-chul published a book called *Thinking about Samsung* in 2010. However, he did not get a chance to advertise his book in the Korean national newspapers, even those newspapers critical of Samsung (Ahn, 2010).

Consequently, anti-Samsung articles, especially those critical of the Lee family, gradually disappeared from the Korean newspapers. The newsrooms submitted to threats from Samsung capital. Korean journalists had to practice self-censorship about the major print advertisers, including Samsung and the chaebol groups, in order to keep their jobs. Journalists became salaried yes men rather than social watchdogs. This opened the door for promotional articles about the roles of chaebol groups while the real news about chaebol corruption, misuse of power and marginalization of oppressed labor went untold.

In addition to advertisements, Samsung deployed Strategic Lawsuits against Public Participation to intimidate critical journalists. For example, Samsung brought several lawsuits against Kim Yeon-kwang, editor of *Monthly Chosun*, and Lee Sang-ho, a reporter for MBC. In 2005, both journalists extensively published about the Samsung X-file. Both journalists also criticized the old practices of the NIS's illegal wiretapping. However, the Korean prosecuting authorities with the sole right to indict the case in the courts ignored the illegal actions of the Lee family in the Samsung X-file. Instead, they investigated the illegal wiretapping conducted by NIS, arguing that the information-gathering works of journalists should be done within the boundaries of the law. They indicted the two journalists on charges of violating the Communication Privacy Protection Law. Korean prosecuting authorities eventually cooperated with the Lee family, allowing them to use lawsuits to block information about the Samsung X-file. Both journalists were harassed by the endless trials, and Samsung continued on with business as usual.

The Samsung group used a similar strategy to control the progressive online newspapers that lacked capital funding. In early 2008, *Pressian*, a financially unstable online paper in Korea, published an investigative story saying that the Lee family built up a slush fund through Samsung Electronics, the biggest electronics company in Asia and a leading subsidiary of Samsung group. *Pressian* was accused of defamation and business interference by the Samsung group. By the end of 2012, this case was still in the courts. Samsung used Strategic Lawsuits against Public Participation (SLPP) in order to silence the critical journalists. This costly lawsuit created a fearful environment within newsrooms, taming Korean journalists and fortifying self-censorship of reporters.

A third way Samsung exercised corporate censorship over Korean journalism was by using personal ties between Samsung and journalists. This social networking was based on Samsung's granting of favors to certain journalists, including financial support for foreign research, grants for special reports, information-gathering works and high-paid jobs within Samsung subsidiaries. This social networking enabled Samsung to create a press castle that was usually invisible, but effective at the critical time. Two examples from the early 2000s illustrate the power of Samsung's social networking over Korean journalism.

The first example was the closing down of the *Sisa Journal* in 2006. On the surface, this was due to labor strife between the owner, Keum Chang Tae, and journalists of the *Sisa Journal*. However, the real issue was Samsung's invisible, but very sticky, power of social networking. This weekly paper had a good reputation for high quality. Unlike daily newspapers, the *Sisa Journal* was financially sound. It rarely depended on advertising income, but had large subscription revenue. It seemed that the *Sisa Journal* was free from Samsung. However, Keum Chang

Tae, the owner of the *Sisa Journal*, had been the chief editor of the *JoongAng Ilbo* in the early 1990s. After retiring from the *JoongAng Ilbo*, he became the owner of the *Sisa Journal* in 2003.

On July 15, 2006, journalists from the *Sisa Journal* attempted to publish a critical article about the internal power misuses of vice chairman Lee Hak-soo, head of the structural planning office of Samsung. However, Keum ordered the chief editor to delete the article. When the chief editor refused, Keum stopped the printing process and replaced the article on Lee Hak-soo with Samsung advertisements. Journalists of the *Sisa Journal* filed vigorous protests against the owner's actions. However, the owner fired all journalists participating in six months of sit-down strikes and shut down this independent paper in 2006. A few months later, the owner, Keum, re-published the *Sisa Journal* with several advertisements sponsored by the Samsung group and news sanitized by capital. The voices looking for the truth and justice had disappeared. The case of the *Sisa Journal* shows Samsung's invisible control over the Korean newsroom through connections between the media owners and top executives of Samsung.

Samsung also attempted to control the newsroom at the practical level. Samsung peeked into the news intranet of MBC, a public broadcasting company, for several years. MBC's news intranet was a cyber place to collect all news before broadcasting publicly. The news intranet was the heart of the newsroom in the digitalized era. In November 2010, MBC found an IP address linked to the intranet of Samsung Economic Research Institution (SERI), a research institution of Samsung group. A chief researcher of SERI had consistently looked into the news intranet of MBC. He was an ex-journalist of MBC by 2005 when MBC reported on the Samsung X-file. That same year, he changed jobs from a journalist at MBC to a chief researcher at SERI. Although Samsung said his action was due to personal misbehavior and unrelated to Samsung, there was no investigation as to why a Samsung man and ex-journalist of MBC peeked into the internal newsroom of MBC or how he used the information he found (Cho, 2010).

The final way Samsung manipulated public opinion was through its media operations. The Lee family owned two major advertising agencies, Cheil Communication and Phoenix Communication, as well as a daily paper, the *JoongAng Ilbo*. In the advertising market, both advertising agencies were in charge of spending the advertising money of pan-Samsung groups to the Korean news companies, including digital media. Cheil Communication focused on advertising with businesses related to the Samsung, Hansol and CJ groups. Phoenix Communication paid more attention to advertising businesses of the JoongAng Ilbo and Bokwang groups. Both Cheil Communication and Phoenix Communication occupied from at least 19.70 percent in 1999 to 35 percent in 2012 of Korean total advertising market shares. The Lee family gradually increased its media influences over the Korean information industries through its advertising holdings.

In the print market, the *JoongAng Ilbo* was responsible for disseminating the market-oriented ideology in general and the private interests of the Lee family in particular. In fact, the *JoongAng Ilbo* was a vanguard for the Lee family in Korean journalism history. It published articles for the private interests of the Lee family during the authoritarian regimes and maintained this tendency into neoliberal authoritarian Korea. I will explain this with the example of the Samsung X-file, which aptly shows the role of *JoongAng Ilbo* relative to the pan-Samsung groups. On July 24, 2005, when the Samsung X-file was disclosed, JoongAng Ilbo chairman Hong Seok-hyun was a Korean ambassador to the U.S. At that time, Chairman Hong dreamed of becoming the future president of Korea after becoming the United Nations general secretary (Lee, 2012). However, reports of the Samsung X-file in the Korean papers forced Chairman Hong to resign as Korean ambassador to the U.S. and give up his ambitious dreams. Thus, Hong Seok-hyun returned to his position as chairman of the JoongAng Ilbo group.

Under these circumstances, the *JoongAng Ilbo* skillfully twisted the news regarding the Samsung X-file. The *JoongAng Ilbo* rarely dealt with issues concerning the cozy relationships among political, economic and cultural power elites. Instead, it focused on the illegal wiretapping conducted by NIS, the Korean CIA. The *Hankyoreh*, a publicly owned daily newspaper, paid more attention to the articles about connections among the Korean power elites and apparent corrupt deals involving those in power than did the *JoongAng Ilbo*, the private paper owned by the Lee family (Kim, 2007).

In addition, the Lee family used its media operations to connect to the Korean political elites. For example, in 1997, journalists from the *JoongAng Ilbo* wrote strategic reports about the presidential election for the ruling party to reflect Samsung's long-term businesses strategies over Korean economic policies (Yun, 1999). The Lee family also paid to create a positive image for the presidential candidate in the ruling party using Phoenix Communication. The Lee family further sent a JoongAng Ilbo man, Ko Heng-gil, ex-chief editor of the *JoongAng Ilbo*, to the presidential election camp of the ruling party as their agent (Lee, 2012). In 2009, 10 years later, Ko Heng-gil became chairperson of the media policy committee of the National Congress, playing a vital role in reintroducing cross-media ownership between the daily newspapers and broadcasting companies. Based on these revised media laws, the JoongAng Ilbo group acquired a comprehensive cable channel.

In sum, the Lee family tried to censor Korean journalism both directly and indirectly. This family was the most powerful advertiser and media owner, allowing the Lee family to exercise corporate censorship over the Korean information markets. The Lee family also created a web of social networking among Korean power elites and journalists and was able to exercise media influence over newsrooms.

5.2.2. The Lee family and entertainment markets

Overall, the Lee family within the Samsung, CJ and JoongAng Ilbo groups was the most powerful media investor, distributor and exhibitor in the entertainment markets. The Lee family paid more attention to entertainment businesses in the CJ and JoongAng Ilbo groups than the Samsung group. In spite of a slightly different pattern regarding the expanded media areas, these three chaebol groups owned by the Lee family commonly used mergers and acquisitions to increase their numbers of media holdings. As a result, the CJ group became the first-leading media company in the cable television and film markets. JoongAng Ilbo also used M&As to enter the film exhibition market, thereby becoming one of the top three exhibitors in 2012. The Lee family thus was also able to exercise corporate censorship over the Korean entertainment markets.

First, multiple media holdings owned by the Lee family directly and indirectly invested in media companies. Directly, they established media venture funds like CJ Entertainment Discovery 1, CJ Film 3•5•6 and Peta Entertainment 1. Indirectly, they got involved in production processes as members of media venture funds like K&J Entertainment, ISU Entertainment and Chicken Run Foreign Consortium. Media operations also loaned production costs to the popular film producers and major production companies. In addition, media operations owned by the Lee family included powerful MPPs (CJ Media and CJ E&M) and an MSO (CJ Hellovision) in cable television, as well as a powerful film distributor (CJ Entertainment) and film exhibitors (CJ CGV, Premus and Mega Box). These media holdings were able to manipulate cable television and film markets because they occupied the higher market shares in each media market.

For example, CJ Media with 16 cable channels was the most powerful program provider in Korean cable TV, occupying 20.8 percent of the total market shares in 2008. The Lee family also had a powerful place in the film exhibition market. As seen in Table 5.5, the CJ group increased from 15.33 percent in 2001 to 40.6 percent of the total exhibition market shares in 2010. This made the Lee family the most powerful gatekeeper in the Korean cable television and film markets.

To protect their enviable position in the media markets, the Lee family established exploitative structures in the media production, distribution and exhibition markets. Both the CJ and JoongAng Ilbo groups expanded their market power through M&As. In 2001, the CJ group took over 9.09 percent of the total shares in Myung Film, a major independent film production. In 2004, CJ acquired Cinema Service, which had been the first market leader in the film production and distribution markets, thereby becoming the most powerful film company in Korea. In 2006 and 2010, JoongAng Ilbo acquired entertainment media companies (Ilgan Sports and Mega Box respectively), thereby becoming one of the top three film exhibitors in 2012. These M&As by both chaebol groups facilitated the dependence of independent media producers on capital from major media investors like these two chaebol groups. Media producers with poor capital had to pass the commercial barriers to the market established by both financial institutions owned by chaebol groups and independent financial companies with foreign capital. As capital exerted its influence, media producers often had to revise their scripts in

Table 5.5 CJ's percentage market share in film exhibition

Year	2001	2003	2005	2007	2009	2010
Market share	15.33	22	28	30.6	37.7	40.6

Source: Author's elaboration of governmental data.

order to acquire capital for production costs. "Capital screening" inevitably forced media producers to manufacture less controversial commercial media contents, thereby establishing a hierarchical relationship between media investors and media producers.

Moreover, both the CJ and JoongAng Ilbo groups played central roles in collapsing the independent film theaters. The CJ group with foreign capital introduced the concept of the multiplex theater to the Korean exhibition market in 1998. The Orion and Lotte groups imitated CJ's market strategy. As a result, screens of multiplex theaters occupied 97 percent of total film market shares in 2010. Most independent theaters collapsed or became the subcontractors of the three chaebol groups in the form of commissioned managements. In this market situation, the JoongAng Ilbo group acquired Mega Box, owned by the Orion group, at the end of 2010. Thus, the Lee family through CJ and JoongAng Ilbo owned the market power to determine what would be distributed at the Korean film markets by 2012.

Similarly, the CJ group was the most powerful content provider in the paid broadcasting markets. CJ's market power was based on cable television, the most powerful media structures in the paid broadcasting markets. The CJ group was the most powerful multiple program provider in cable television. It focused on broadcasting the commercial genres (e.g., film, animation and sports) rather than non-commercial media products (e.g., documentary and education). At the same time, the CJ group rebroadcast cable media content to other paid broadcasting markets because the Korean broadcasting regulations recommended that the multiple program providers in cable television re-transmit media contents to digital satellite television in order to guarantee access to non-cable users.

Under this hierarchical market structure, the CJ group intensively organized more commercial programs (e.g., film, animation, recorded music, fashion and sports) than cultural programs (e.g., documentary and education) (Yang, 2008). Commercial media products were either produced by Korean companies related to CJ's media-invested businesses or imported mainly from Hollywood studios. Non-commercial media artifacts were produced by the independent media producers and rarely received investment capital from CJ group. CJ thus marginalized non-commercial media artifacts in the paid broadcasting markets due to the interlocked structures between cable television and other paid broadcasting channels.

Further, the CJ group stopped sending the popular programs (e.g., films, popular songs, animations and fashions) to Skylife, the brand name of digital satellite television, in 2003. This blackout was repeated in 2007. CJ argued that the re-transmission of Skylife rarely helps CJ's profits, but increases the costs of purchasing media content (Seo, 2007). Moreover, CJ group arbitrarily changed the popular cable channels from basic service to premium in 2006. This led to increased subscription fees for cable users without notification. In the same year, CJ rapidly raised the subscription fees of the cable users living in apartment complexes of big cities (Kim, Hong & Cho 2006). These examples show that the

CJ group became the market controller in paid broadcasting. Consequently, the CJ group was able to manipulate structures of the Korean entertainment markets, limiting the right to media access and restricting free competition with other media companies in these markets.

In sum, the Lee family directly and indirectly got involved in media production, distribution and exhibition. They pushed the independent media companies out of business or swallowed them in mergers and acquisitions. Further, they disseminated commercial media content to the media channels and manipulated prices on the Korean entertainment markets.

Conclusion

I have examined the nature of Korean media monopoly in terms of the relationship between market structures and media ownership. My goal was to show how media owners exercise corporate censorship over the media markets. Under neoliberal media reforms, chaebol groups, in conjunction with foreign capital and/or American cultural conglomerates, became the media market controllers. They occupied higher market shares than the independent media companies in advertising, cable television, daily papers and film markets. As a result, the Korean media markets were structured by chaebol groups and foreign capital. This led to 1) centralized chaebol control of the means of media production, distribution and exhibition; 2) collapse of the independent media companies; and 3) limitations on consumers' free and fair access to information and entertainment.

Within these circumstances, the Lee family used the Samsung, CJ and JoongAng Ilbo groups to expand their media businesses within and across media industries. They thereby established media empires with multiple media holdings. These media operations recorded higher market shares than media operations owned by other chaebol groups. They were also powerful media investors, distributors and exhibitors in the Korean entertainment markets. The Lee family was also the most powerful advertiser in the Korean information markets. With control over entertainment and information access in all Korean media markets, the Lees were media lords in Korea involved in media production, distribution, exhibition and advertisement. Depending on economic and media power structures, the Lee family exercised corporate censorship over Korean society to protect its private interests while earning record profits.

References

Ahn, K.S. (2010, March 12). The Hankyoreh refused the advertisement of thinking Samsung. *MediaToday*. Korean.
Atkins, R. (2006). Money talks: The economic foundations of censorship. In R. Atkins & S. Mintcheva (Eds.), *Censoring culture: Contemporary threats to free expression* (pp. 3–9). New York: The New Press.
Bagdikian, H.B. (2000). *The media monopoly* (6th Ed.). Boston, MA: Beacon Press.
Bagdikian, H.B. (2004). *New media monopoly*. Boston, MA: Beacon Press.

Cho, H.H. (2002, July 11). The collapse of paper distributing office due to unfair actions by Cho-Joong-Dong. *Mediatoday*. Korean.

Cho, H.H. (2004, March 10). Unfair deals of the *JoongAng Ilbo. The Mediatoday*. Korean.

Cho, H.K. (2010, November 2). Samsung looks in the news intranet of MBC. *The Mediatoday*. Korean.

Choe, S.H. (2007, November 7). Corruption scandal spreads as Samsung. *The New York Times*.

Editing Room. (2012). Research about 2012 advertising market, *Current situation of advertising companies in Korea*, 252, 20–36. Korean.

Erri. (2008). *The journalism stands at the crossroads of survival*. Seoul, Korea: Erri. Korean.

Erri. (2010). *A report about how the first-tier chaebol groups control the Korea's journalism*. Seoul, Korea: Erri. Korean.

Fair Trade Commission (2008, June 2). A decision on main film exhibitors regarding abuse of market power. Seoul, Korea: FTC. Korean.

Fair Trade Commission (2008, February 21). A decision on CJ CGV (Premus) about abuse of film market power. Seoul, Korea: FTC. Korean.

Im, B. (2006, March 9). The effects of chaebol's multiplex theater over the Korean film market. *The Hankyoreh*.

Jansen, C. (1988). *Censorship: The knot that binds power and knowledge*. New York: Oxford University Press.

Kang, Y.K. (2007). The overheated competition to catch up films between network television and cable television companies. *Munhwa Ilbo*, November 14.

Kunz, W. (2007). *Culture conglomerates: Consolidation in the motion picture and television industries*. Lanham, MA: Rowman & Littlefield.

Kwak, B.J. (2012, September 17). The vertical integration of the Korean film markets. *The Hankyoreh*, 7. Korean.

Keane, J. (1991). *The media and democracy*. Cambridge, MA: Polity Press.

Kim, S.C. (2008). Editorial integrity under assault in Korea. In C. George (Ed.), *Free markets free media: Reflections on the political economy of the press in Asia* (pp. 72–86). Singapore: Asian Media Information and Communication Center (AMIC).

Kim, S.H. (2008, November 19). Why *the Hankyoreh* disconnected to Samsung's advertisement. *The Journal of Korean Journalists*. www.journalist.or.kr/news/article.html?no=19012. Korean.

Kim, S.H. (2012, March 1). The media empire of CJ E&M. *The Hankuk Ilbo*, 19. Korean.

Kim, Y.H., Hong, Y.D. & Cho, K.W. (2006, March 31). Chaebol rapidly rose up the price of subscription fees. *The Hankyoreh*.

Lee, B.S. & Che, J.I. (2007). *The economic dependence of the Korean journalism on Chaebol groups: A study on the relationship between chaebol's reports and advertisement*. Seoul, Korea: The Press Foundation. Korean.

Lee, J.H. (2010, January 13). Why the Korean journalism shrinks in front of chaebol groups. *The Mediatoday*. Korean.

Lee, S.H. (2012). *X-file of Lee Sang Ho on the Lee family of pan-Samsung*. Seoul, Korea: Dong Asia. Korean.

Mazzocco, W.D. (1994). *Networks of power: Corporate TV's threat to democracy*. Boston, MA: South End.

Murdock, G. (1982). Large corporation and the control of the communications industries. In M. Gurevitch, J. Curran, & J. Woollacott (Eds.), *Culture, society and the media* (pp. 118–150). Beverly Hills, CA: Sage.

Murdock, G. (1990). Redrawing the map of the communications industries: concentration and ownership in the era of privatization. In M. Ferguson (Ed.), *Public communication: the new imperatives* (pp. 1–15). London, UK: Sage.

Power (2012, September 17). What is the future of Korean film? *The Korea Herald*.

Schiffrin, A. (2000). *The business of books: How international conglomerates took over publishing and changed the way we read*. New York: Verso.

Schiffrin, A. (2006). Market censorship. In R. Atkins & S. Mintcheva (Eds.), *Censoring culture: Contemporary threats to free expression* (pp. 67–79). New York: The New Press.

Schiller, H. (1991). Corporate sponsorship: Institutionalized censorship of the cultural realm. *Art Journal*, 50(3), Censorship I (Autumn), 56–59.

Seo, J.M. (2007, May 4). CJ abandon retransmission of programming to SkyLife. *The Hankyore*, 6. Korean.

Seo, J.Y. (2004). FTC launches investigation on newspapers' unfair sales practices. *The Korean Times*.

Soley, L. (2006). Private censorship, corporate power. In Atkins, R. (2006). In R. Atkins & S. Mintcheva (Eds.), *Censoring culture: Contemporary threats to free expression* (pp. 15–28). New York: The New Press.

Yang, M.S. (2008). *CJ invaded the rights of the public to access to the media*. Seoul, Korea: The Research Institution of the Public Interest. Korean.

Yang, M.S. & Kim, D.J. (2008). *To study the real condition of the Korean newspaper markets*. Seoul, Korea: The Commission of Newspaper Development. Korean.

6 Conclusion

I have explored the nature of family media monopoly in the era of Asian media marketization. I have selected three media conglomerates, the Samsung, CJ and JoongAng Ilbo groups, as a case study of Korean family-controlled conglomerates, called "chaebol," focusing on the relationship between structures of media markets and media ownership. While the characteristics of these three chaebol groups in the Korean media markets do not represent the nature of all Asian media conglomerates, I conclude that the Korean media giants with foreign capital have exerted structural control over the media markets. By controlling media holdings with high market shares, family capitalists exercise corporate censorship over a neoliberal Korea to protect their private interests. This is decisively the most significant finding to emerge from my analysis.

The neoliberal media model in Korea brought two big changes to the media landscape: 1) seismic shifts in total revenues, market sizes and the number of media companies and 2) growth of the Korean media that led to market polarization among a few major players and many minor ones in the information and entertainment markets. Within these oligopolistic structures, major players included the chaebol groups, transnational media corporations and existing mainstream papers. Chaebol groups held more market shares than the transnational media conglomerates and benefitted greatly from the centralized market structures resulting from Korean media reforms. However, domestic and foreign capital maintained two different tracks according to the situation of media markets. In both the advertising and cable television markets, chaebol groups and transnational media giants with foreign capital cooperated with each other, shared media ownership and established joint ventures. On the other hand, chaebol groups and Western media conglomerates rarely cooperated in the daily newspaper and film markets. Transnational media corporations hardly entered into the Korean daily papers in charge of creating public discourse, in spite of Korean papers being major advertisers. They also competed with chaebol groups in the Korean distribution market, but rarely entered the film exhibition market. Although chaebol groups, transnational media corporations and existing mainstream papers showed slight variations across the four media markets, I have consistently found that they were market controllers. Relying on the centralized market structures, they effectively exercised corporate censorship over the Korean information and entertainment markets.

Under these changed market situations, the Lee family in particular used economic and media power to establish media empires and control the structures of media markets. Methods used by the Lee family included: 1) advertisements; 2) lawsuits against journalists; 3) networking (or personal ties) between the Lee family and journalists; and 4) its media holdings. These visible and invisible tools structurally enabled the Lee family to exercise corporate censorship over the four media markets.

6.1. Media monopoly and family media monopoly

My findings regarding family conglomerates are similar to those of media scholars in the West. Smythe (1981) and Schiller (1989) acknowledged the roles of cultural conglomerates in capitalistic societies, as media giants would be in a position to censor the structures of media markets. Political economists have explored the connections between media markets and media ownership in relation to structural changes in the political, economic and cultural realms. They commonly found that media conglomerates were the gatekeepers who determined what to produce, distribute and exhibit in the media markets.

Specifically, the market-oriented ideology of the neoliberal media model allowed existing large media companies to transform into cultural conglomerates. This threatened fair competition among media companies in the media markets (Guback, 1986; Herman & McChesney, 1997; Herman, 1999; McChesney, 2000; Meehan, 2005; Kunz, 2007). My findings also confirm that the neoliberal media model allowed media markets to become the arena of competition for capital (Bagdikian, 2000, 2004; Croteau & Hoynes, 2001; McChesney, 2004, 2010). Further, this study has confirmed that the emergence of cultural conglomerates 1) facilitated interdependency among the major players in different media markets, 2) led to collapsing independent media companies and 3) marginalized the progressive media companies (Jansen, 1988; Herman, 1999; Bettig & Hall, 2003; Curran, 2003; Cohen, 2005). In other words, big-money market determinists were the gatekeepers of investment, production, distribution and exhibition.

The findings of this study – that family capitalists controlled structures of the four media markets through their media holdings with high market shares – are consistent with research outcomes found by critical media scholars. Media owners used family ties (e.g., blood and marriage ties) to establish media empires, control media corporate structures and connect to the power elites within corporate structures (Lent, 1966; Freiberg, 1981; Mazzocco, 1994; Bettig, 1996; Herman, 1999; McChesney, 2000; Wasko, 2001; Edge, 2007). Also, this study confirms that media owners utilized the structural changes initiated by the state to expand the media businesses within and across media markets (Mosco, 1979; Melody, 1985; Schiller, 1989; Streeter, 1996; Blevins, 2007). Finally, media owners were involved in manufacturing media content and exercising editorial privileges to shape public opinion when they were in crisis (Murdock, 1982; Schiffrin, 2000, 2006, 2010; Atkins & Mintcheva, 2006).

Theoretically speaking, these findings imply that media marketization structurally and institutionally allowed family capitalist media owners to determine all modes of cultural communication by controlling their media holdings with high market shares. With a few differences in patterns, this study found that Korean media giants exhibit characteristics similar to Western media conglomerates on two major points. First, Korean media conglomerates are market controllers that were established by the dynamics of structural changes in the country's economic and cultural foundations, changes that served the interests of a neoliberal state and its capitalists (Herman & McChesney, 1997; Meehan, 2005; Kunz, 2007). Second, the emergence of Korean media conglomerates facilitated interdependencies among media markets, thereby restricting free competition among media companies, collapsing independent media companies and limiting the right of media access (Schiffrin, 2000, 2006, 2010; Curran, 2003; Atkins & Mintcheva, 2006;; McChesney, 2010).

The consistency of my findings with the literature signifies that the political economy of communication can be applied to research on Asian media conglomerates. This answers one of this study's initial questions: whether the political economy of communication – rooted in Western monopoly capitalism – can be applied to studying state capitalist–rooted media in Asia. Although Korea has been in the transitional period from state capitalism to monopoly capitalism, the research outcomes of Western media scholars rooted in monopoly capitalism show similar findings. My research contributes to the body of literature by finding the similar patterns regarding power integration among political, economic and cultural realms and control of the media through markets. This shows that the use of the political economy of communication to analyze cultural conglomerates is not limited by a difference in the economic structures of monopoly capitalism and state capitalism.

It should be noted, however, that some aspects of Korean media conglomerates show differences from Western media conglomerates. First, this study does not demonstrate that the rise of cultural conglomerates resulted in decreasing the number of media companies in the media markets. Critical scholars in the U.S. such as Bagdikian (2000), Guback (1987) and Meehan (2005) have argued that active mergers and acquisitions (M&As) among major players inevitably decrease the number of media companies. Korea, however, as a newly emerged player in the international media markets, showed a pattern different from the U.S., a fully mature media country. In Korea, M&As and an increase in the number of media companies happened simultaneously. Under oligopolistic market structures, the number of media companies showed an increase in three markets (advertising, daily newspaper and film), but not in cable television. Also, in spite of active M&As in advertising, cable television and film markets, active M&As rarely occurred in the daily newspaper market. A possible explanation for this may be that Korea was a newly developed media country in the world of communication systems. Because of their high potential to be more developed, new companies consistently entered the Korean media market. Furthermore, in order to increase market shares in the Korean information and entertainment markets, Korean media conglomerates focused their M&As on media companies occupying high levels of market shares rather than newly established media companies.

The second difference is that family ties play a more central role in controlling Korean media empires than economic media ownership alone. On the basis of family ties, media owners have expanded their media businesses, connected to power elites and cooperated with foreign capital and Western media conglomerates. Conclusively, cultural value is a considerable player in the analysis of media ownership in Korean media conglomerates.

A third point of difference is that Korean media giants are media producers, distributors, exhibitors, advertisers and investors in corporate media systems. This has allowed Korean media giants to exercise more media power over the Asian societies than Western media conglomerates. This is related to a fourth point of difference concerning the close relationship between Korean media conglomerates and the neoliberal authoritarian state. Korean media giants composed of family capitalists were major partners of neoliberal authoritarian states in developing the media as a national industry. The fifth point of difference is that Korean media conglomerates show more interest than the West in producing, distributing and exhibiting new media content, as opposed to recirculating, repackaging, recycling and redeploying old media products. Although the Korean media giants have been able to control the structures of the media markets, they seemed to prefer new media content produced by independent media companies or imported media content to recycling existing media content. The final difference is that the emergence of Korean media conglomerates rarely affected a change in the number of media companies in the information and entertainment markets.

6.2. Limitations and future research

My study analyzed the structure of Korean media conglomerates with a focus on the interactions between media markets and media ownership. Although my project described part of the nature of Asian media conglomerates, it has hardly examined exactly how concentrated family media ownership has affected the media content produced, distributed and exhibited by the media holdings owned by these media giants. This matter needs further research using different methods. Critical discourse analysis could be a useful tool for exploring the relationship between media ownership and media texts (Freiberg, 1981; Chomsky & Herman, 1988; Golding & Murdock, 2000; Hobbs, 2010). Interviews of media producers and journalists could examine how media conglomerates directly and indirectly affect the process of creating public discourse and cultural products (Lent, 1966; Cristopherson, 2008; Tapsell, 2012).

In addition, I have focused on Korean media conglomerates, leaving unexplored research regarding the nature of other Asian media conglomerates rooted in different political, economic and historical backgrounds. This should be examined by future critical media scholars. Critical studies can be conducted to compare and contrast media giants from Asia, Latin America, the European Union and North America.

In sum, I have analyzed media ownership of the Samsung, CJ and JoongAng Ilbo groups. Media operations owned by the three chaebol groups have run media businesses in global media markets generally and Asian countries particularly. They have been major media players, producing, distributing and exhibiting media content in the Asian media markets. These three chaebol groups have all experienced the Korean Wave, the phenomenon of the popularity of Korean media commodities across East and Southeast Asia. In the future, I would be particularly interested in research that examines the relationship between the three media conglomerates and the Korean Wave.

References

Atkins, R. & Mintcheva, S. (Eds.). (2006). *Censoring culture: Contemporary threats to free expression*. New York: The New Press.

Bagdikian, H.B. (2000). *The media monopoly* (6th Ed.). Boston, MA: Beacon Press.

Bagdikian, H.B. (2004). *New media monopoly*. Boston, MA: Beacon Press.

Bettig, R.V. (1996). *Copyrighting culture: The political economy of intellectual property*. Boulder, CO: Westview Press.

Bettig, R.V. & Hall, L. (2003). *Big media, big money: Cultural texts and political economics*. Lanham, MA: Rowman & Littlefield.

Blevins, J. (2007). *The political economy of U.S. broadcast ownership regulation and free speech after the Telecommunications Act of 1996*. http://democraticcommunications.org/communique/issues/Fall2007/Blevins%20Article.pdf

Chomsky, N. & Herman, E. (1988). *Manufacturing consent: The political economy of the mass media*. New York: Pantheon Books.

Cohen, E.D. (Ed.). (2005). *News incorporated: Corporate media ownership and its threat to democracy*. New York: Prometheus Books.

Cristopherson, S. (2008). The effects of media concentration on the film and television workforce. In J. Wasko & P. McDonald (Eds.), *The contemporary Hollywood film industry* (pp. 155–166). Malden, MA: Blackwell.

Croteau, D. & Hoynes, W. (2001). *The business of media: Corporate media and the public interest*. London, UK: Pine Forge Press.

Curran, J. (2003). Press history. In J. Curran & Seaton, J. (Eds.), *Power without responsibility: The press and broadcasting in Britain* (6th Ed., pp. 1–106). London: Routledge.

Edge, M. (2007). *Asper Nation: Canada's most dangerous media company*. Vancouver, Canada: New Star Books.

Freiberg, J.W. (1981). *The French press: Class, state and ideology*. New York: Praeger.

Golding, P. & Murdock, G. (2000). Culture, communications and political economy. In J. Curran & M. Curevitch (Eds.), *Mass media and society* (3rd Ed., pp. 70–92). London: Arnold.

Guback, T. (1986). Ownership and control in the motion picture industry. *Journal of Film and Video*, 38(1), 7–20.

Guback, T. (1987). The evolution of the motion picture theater business in the 1980s. *The Journal of Communication*, 37(2), 60–77.

Herman, E. (1999). *The myth of the liberal media*. New York: Peter Lang.

Herman, E. & McChesney, R.W. (1997). *The global media: The new missionaries of corporate capitalism*. London: Cassell.

Hobbs, M. (2010). Neo-conned: The Murdoch press and the Iraq War. *International Journal of Media and Cultural Politics*, 6(2), 187–207.

Jansen, C. (1988). *Censorship: The knot that binds power and knowledge*. New York: Oxford University Press.

Kunz, W. (2007). *Culture conglomerates: Consolidation in the motion picture and television industries*. Lanham, MA: Rowman & Littlefield.

Lent, J.A. (1966). *Newhouse, newspapers, nuisances: Highlights in the growth of a communication empire*. New York: Exposition Press.

McChesney, R. (2000). *Rich media, poor democracy: Communication politics in dubious times*. New York: The New Press.

McChesney, R. (2004). *The problem of the media: U.S. communication politics in the 21th century*. New York: Monthly review press.

McChesney, R. (2010). *The death and life of American journalism: The media revolution that will begin the world again*. New York: The Nation Books.

Mazzocco, W.D. (1994). *Networks of power: Corporate TV's threat to democracy*. Boston, MA: South End.

Meehan, E. (2005). *Why TV is not our faults*. Lanham, MA: Rowman & Littlefield.

Melody, W. (1985). The information society: Implications for economic institutions and market theory. *Journal of Economic Issues*, xix(2), 523–539.

Mosco, V. (1979). *Broadcasting in the United States: Innovative challenge and organizational control*. Norwood, NJ: Ablex.

Murdock, G. (1982). Large corporation and the control of the communications industries. In M. Gurevitch, J. Curran, & J. Woollacott (Eds.), *Culture, society and the media* (pp. 118–150). Beverly Hills, CA: Sage.

Schiffrin, A. (2000). *The business of books: How international conglomerates took over publishing and changed the way we read*. New York: Verso.

Schiffrin, A. (2006). Market censorship. In R. Atkins & S. Mintcheva (Eds.), *Censoring culture: Contemporary threats to free expression* (pp. 67–79). New York: The New Press.

Schiffrin, A. (2010). *Words & Money*. New York: Verso.

Schiller, H. (1989). *Culture, Inc: The corporate takeover of public expression*. New York: Oxford University Press.

Smythe, D. (1981). *Dependency road: Communications, capitalism, consciousness and Canada*. Norwood, NJ: Ablex.

Streeter, T. (1996). *Selling the air: A critique of the policy of commercial broadcasting in the United States*, Chicago, IL: University of Chicago Press.

Tapsell, R. (2012). Old tricks in a new era: Self-censorship in Indonesian journalism. *Asian Studies Reviews*, 36, 227–245.

Wasko, J. (2001). *Understanding Disney: The manufacture of fantasy*. Oxford, UK: Polity.

Index

Note: Page numbers with *f* indicate figures; those with *t* indicate tables.

For Product Safety Concerns and Information please contact our
EU representative GPSR@taylorandfrancis.com Taylor & Francis
Verlag GmbH, Kaufingerstraße 24, 80331 München, Germany